INTEREST RATE & CURRENCY SWAPS

The Markets, Products and Applications

- Ravi E. Dattatreya
- Raj E. S. Venkatesh
- Vijaya E. Venkatesh

PROBUS PUBLISHING COMPANY
Chicago, Illinois
Cambridge, England

ISBN 1-55738-468-1

Printed in the United States of America

BB

1 2 3 4 5 6 7 8 9 0

To Srivatsa

Ravi E. Dattatreya

To Vinay

Raj E. S. Venkatesh

To Vinita

Vijaya E. Venkatesh

Table of Contents

List of Exhibits and Tables

Preface

The last dozen or so years have been very satisfying from the point of view of the corporate risk manager as far as the availability of tools is concerned. We saw the ripening of the Treasury and the Eurodollar futures markets. Fixed income options started trading in the early Eighties and have achieved their own level. However, the most exciting area has been that of interest rate and currency swaps. Paradoxically, this market is at once mature and still-developing. Its maturity is evidenced by the ease with which it was able to absorb the fall of some major players (e.g., Drexel) and the size and liquidity that it offers demanding customers. At the same time, new structures and uses in new markets (e.g., investments) are being developed almost every day, showing the potential for further enormous growth.

To the risk manager and the portfolio manager alike, the properties of swaps are of paramount interest: the ease of execution, the availability of large sizes, the flexibility of structuring, and, most of all, the ability to manage the risk in new ways not previously obtainable.

In *Interest Rate and Currency Swaps,* our goal is to introduce this influential market to the reader starting from the basics. The emphasis has been on understanding how the swap tool can be applied to various, real-life situations. As such, many of the examples used are simplified versions of actual transactions from our own files. We have also spent a signficiant part of the book on swap pricing. We believe that it is essential for every swap user to gain a good understanding of pricing, if not the ability to model and price an actual swap. In order to help the reader gain insight, we have provided a wealth of detail, including formulas in spreadsheet form. We encourage the reader to strengthen this insight by actually building a pricing model.

Any book on swaps is bound to quickly become dated given that the market is still growing at a rapid pace not only in terms of size but also in terms of the complexity and breadth of structures. (To address this issue, a companion book, *Advanced Interest Rate and Currency Swaps,* is under preparation, in which the reader will find detailed discussion of derivatives of swaps such as caps, collars, floors, swaptions as well as the new "exotic" options.)

Acknowledgments

We wish to thank Akira Kondoh, Kenji Kita and John Copenhaver of Sumitomo Bank Capital Markets, Inc., New York, and Atsuo Konishi of SBCM (UK) Ltd., London, for providing assistance and for their encouragement throughout this long project. We acknowledge the help of the following people for reading earlier drafts of the book: Joyce Frost, Joe Hanosek, Tarek Imran, Azam Mistri, Bruce Quackenbush, Tim Quinn, John Roesset, Lisa Schattinger and Michael Stewart. Special thanks are due to Joe Brennan and John Fox for their extensive and helpful comments and to Jose Luis Veiho Belon for his contribution to the discussion on swap pricing. Finally, we thank Joan Rosa and Pramod Srivatsa (the latter of Cooper Union, New York) for converting rough data and crude sketches into beautiful tables, exhibits and diagrams for the entire book. Pramod also built all the pricing models presented in Chapter 6.

Acknowledgements

1

Introduction to Interest-Rate Swaps

An interest rate swap is a contractual agreement between two parties to exchange a series of payments for a stated period of time. The nomenclature arises from the fact that typically the payments in a swap are similar to interest payments on a borrowing. When combined with an asset or a liability, a swap can change the risk characteristics of that asset or liability, by changing the net cash flow. For example, a fixed-rate liability can be converted to a floating-rate liability using an interest-rate swap.

Since its beginnings in the late 1970s, the interest-rate swap has grown into an indispensable product and has proved to be a major advancement in the evolution of the world financial market. The annual size of the swap business is in excess of $3 trillion of notional amount, as shown in Exhibit 1–1. Any market with such a large size can be expected to exert significant influence on other markets. In fact, the influence of the swap market is such that the swap curve is considered next only to the Treasury yield curve in importance.

The swap market has increased the interconnection between financial resources globally. It has changed, in a fundamental way, the manner in which institutions analyze funding decisions. This is a natural result of the fact that

EXHIBIT 1–1A Growth of the Interest-Rate Swap Market

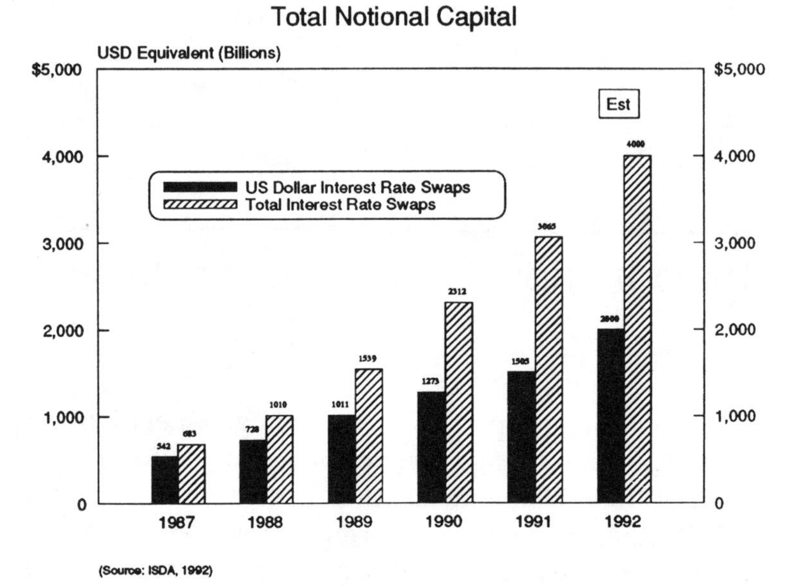

EXHIBIT 1–1B Growth of the Cross-Currency Swap Market

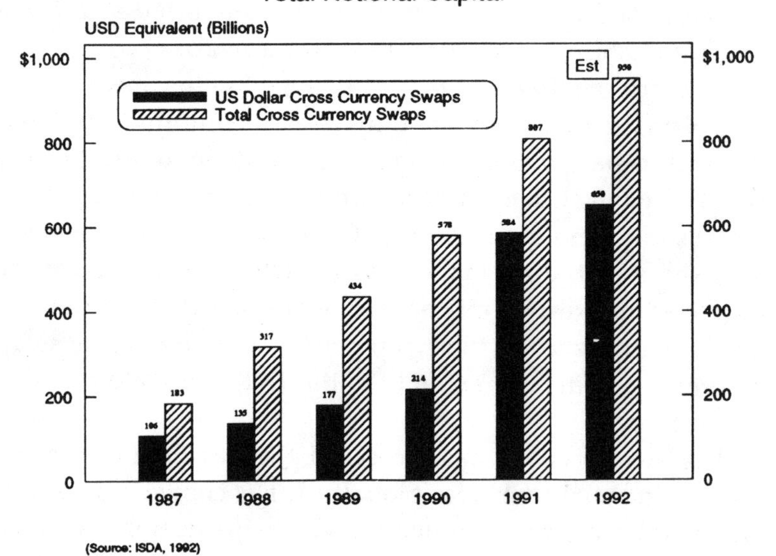

swaps provide new and efficient ways to manage assets and liabilities.

The use of swaps is broad; it is no longer a specialized gadget limited to a selected few. Swaps are used to reduce the cost of capital, manage risks and exploit economies of scale. It is now an accepted financing technique of financiers worldwide to the extent that it has become a routine requirement to consider swap financing along with traditional alternatives.

Swaps are also used to arbitrage the different capital markets of the world. Borrowers and lenders access new markets using the swap technology by creating synthetic instruments. Several innovations have been developed such as swap structures with optionlike features, and swap derivatives such as caps and floors. Exhibit 1–2 shows the size of the swap-derivative market. New users, notably insurance companies, and new uses emerge daily in parallel with the increased use of swaps. The popularity of the swap has also brought several advantages to the users

EXHIBIT 1–2 The Size of the Swap Derivatives Market: Swaps in the World's Financial Market

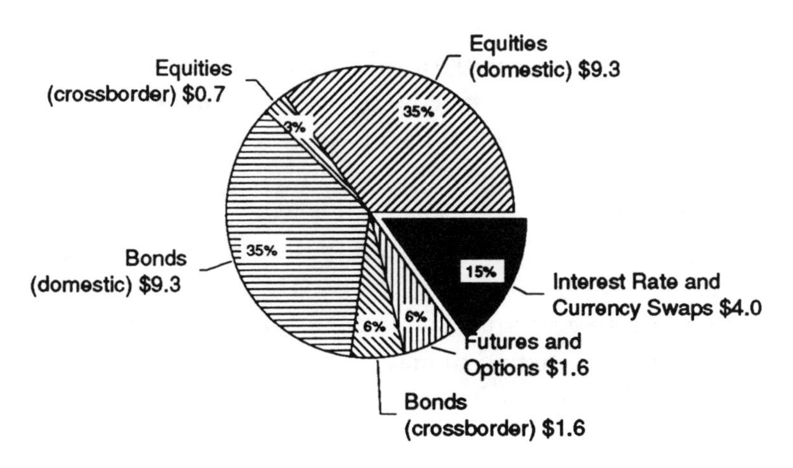

(Source: Morgan Trust Company, 1992)

such as increased liquidity and standard documentation. The swap business is cooperatively promoted by the International Swap Dealers Association, Inc. (ISDA) which has nearly one hundred and fifty members.

The capital markets have recently been characterized by unprecedented volatility. Institutional expectations naturally change in response to shifting market conditions. The swap provides an effective way for institutions to act on these changed expectations: they can lock in any gains, or minimize higher potential losses. Available alternatives are either too expensive or have balance-sheet implications, e.g., early retirement of debt. While hedging with the usual derivatives such as futures and options requires frequent monitoring and rebalancing, swap hedging requires no such constant attention and activity for long periods of time. The swap simply has no equal as a financing and risk- management tool.

Many banks run matched books, i.e., they offset or hedge one swap against another identical swap. Dealers who make markets in swaps use a portfolio approach applying advanced techniques for hedging purposes. The portfolio approach provides maximum flexibility in providing swap products to clients. The general availability of these valuation methodologies and the high level of confidence placed in them by the swap dealers has in no small way fueled the growth of the swap market.

The phenomenal success of the swap market justifies the prevailing sentiment that it is perhaps the single most important financing development in recent years. The success itself arises from the fact that the swap fills a need no other existing product can efficiently satisfy. It is qualitatively different from other innovations. The swap is not a specific response to a unique market condition. It is an outgrowth of a long unsatisfied demand.

The breadth and depth of the swap market, its enormous size, its liquidity and flexibility and its significant influence on the world's capital markets mean that it is essential for every participant in these markets to obtain a thorough understanding of swaps.

The World Bank/IBM Currency Swap

A celebrated swap transaction was executed between IBM and the World Bank in August, 1981. This transaction is considered to have heralded the beginnings of the swap market. It is worth examining the circumstances which led to this transaction.

In 1979, IBM borrowed in two European currencies, Swiss francs and Deutsche marks, as part of its capital markets funding program. By 1981, the dollar was well on its long march towards strength. The weakening of the European currencies in effect created a gain for IBM since the value of its Swiss franc and Deutsche mark liabilities had fallen much below the issue price. IBM wished to convert the liabilities to U.S. dollars by buying them back and reissuing in dollars or by other means.[1]

At the same time, the World Bank was concerned that its borrowings, especially in the then comparatively less developed European currencies, might have an adverse impact on the market by soaking up all credit available in those markets.

This situation created an opportunity for IBM and the World Bank to enter into a transaction for mutual benefit. The Bank issued $290 million of eurobonds in U.S. dollars,

---

1 Buying back bonds at less than issue price is normally the less attractive alternative because of the potential tax liability due to retirement of debt at a discount. Also, in Europe, bonds, usually sold in bearer form, are often difficult to find for repurchase.

and swapped this liability into Swiss francs and Deutsche marks directly with IBM. Under the transaction, structured as what can be called a parallel loan (discussed below), IBM paid a stream of U.S.$ cash flows and received a stream of Swiss franc and Deutsche mark cash flows. The cash flows received by IBM effectively converted its obligations into U.S. dollars. On the other hand, the Bank converted its U.S. dollar obligations into francs and marks.

The swap market essentially began[2] with this transaction, which for the first time, demonstrated that it is possible to manage (or trade) the liability side of the balance sheet. A corporation was no longer a prisoner of past borrowing decisions. It was possible to get out of or modify the nature of existing liabilities.

Evolution of the Swap Market

Prior to 1980, all borrowers funded *directly* in appropriate markets. In many cases, the funding matched the financial needs of the borrower exactly in terms of factors such as maturity, currency and whether the interest rate was fixed or floating. In other cases, the borrower accepted the risk or inconvenience due to any mismatch between what was required and what was obtained, either because the borrower had no other choice or because there was a tradeoff between mismatch and lower funding cost.

Then, borrowers discovered that, depending upon their credit rating, name-recognition and other factors, they had comparative advantage[3] in different markets. For example, a

2 Coincidentally, IBM, one of the counterparties of the first swap, introduced the IBM PC on August 12, 1981. The universal availability of the computational power via the PC has in no small way contributed to the growth of the swap market.

3 The concept of comparative advantage is discussed in more detail in later sections.

highly rated institution could obtain funds more cheaply than a lower rated institution in both the fixed-rate and the floating-rate markets. However, the difference in the rates at which the two institutions could borrow was greater in the fixed-rate market. In other words, the borrowing spread for the two institutions was greater for fixed-rate funding than for floating-rate funding.[4] In order to extract benefits from this advantage, they entered into *parallel loans,* illustrated below.

Situation *(Comparative Advantage).* X is an AAA-rated institution whose borrowing cost is 9 percent in the fixed-rate market and LIBOR – 25 b.p. in the floating-rate market. X seeks floating-rate funds. Y is an A-rated institution whose borrowing rates are 10 percent fixed and LIBOR + 25 floating. Y seeks fixed-rate funds for 5 years. Y's borrowing rate is 100 b.p. higher for fixed-rate borrowing. It is only 50 b.p. higher for floating-rate borrowing. Thus, Y has a comparative advantage over X in the floating-rate markets.[5]

X and Y can take advantage of the situation as follows. X borrows $100 million for five years in the Euromarket at a fixed interest rate of 9 percent. Y borrows $100 million of floating-rate funds from its bank at its rate of LIBOR + 25. Then, X and Y make parallel or back-to-back loans to each other. X lends $100 million to Y at the fixed rate of 9.50 percent. Y lends $100 million to X at the floating rate of LIBOR (flat). The net effect of these transactions is that X has floating-rate funding at LIBOR – 50 (LIBOR paid to Y plus 9 percent on its fixed-rate borrowing less 9.50 percent received from Y) and Y has fixed-rate borrowing at 9.75 percent (9.50 percent paid to X plus

---

4 One reason for this differential is that the lower rated borrower normally has good access to the short-term floating-rate market such as bank loans but limited access to the long-term capital markets.

5 Or, in other words, Y has a lower comparative disadvantage relative to X in the floating-rate markets.

LIBOR + 25 paid on its floating-rate loan less LIBOR received from X). Both X and Y have saved 25 basis points relative to their conventional borrowing costs.

EXHIBIT 1–3 Parallel Loans: Interest-Rate and Currency Swaps

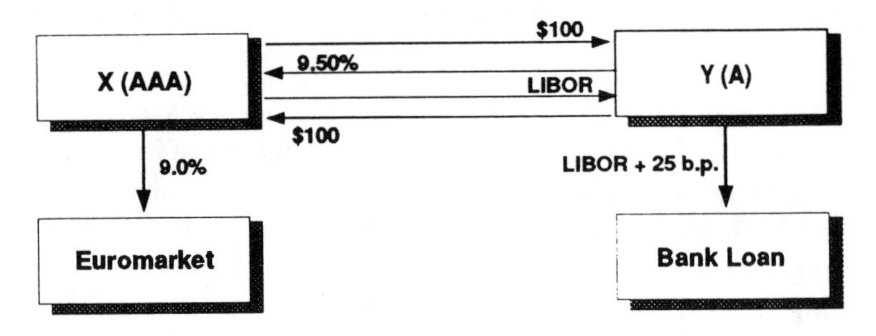

The parallel-loan transaction achieves the goal of both parties in obtaining the type of funding (fixed or floating) each desires at rates lower than available using conventional methods. However, the parallel loan structure has the drawback that it balloons the balance sheet of both X and Y. In addition, the structure exposes each of the two parties to the other's credit risk in a significant way.

As this type of transaction evolved, the exchange of principals at the beginning and at maturity was eliminated. The exchange of principals nets out[6] anyway, and therefore its elimination results in no economic charge. In other words, only the main effect of the transaction, the

---

6 It is possible for the two cash flows exchanged to be in different currencies. In such a case, the principals do not offset each other evenly, and therefore their exchange is retained. This transaction is called a currency swap, and is discussed in detail later.

EXHIBIT 1–4 Exchanging Interest Payments

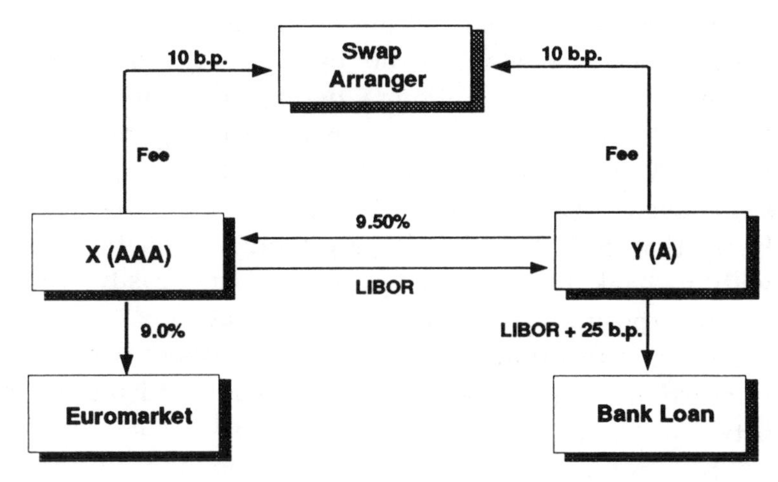

swap or the exchange of interest payments between the two parties, was retained. Thus the parallel loan concept was simplified into an interest-rate swap structure. Exhibit 1–4, which depicts this structure, is also more complete in that it includes the fee (10 basis points each from X and Y) earned by the arranger of the transaction. The savings, net of the fee, are now 15 basis points for both X and Y.

This swap structure has two major advantages over the parallel loan structure. Credit risk is significantly reduced, since each party owes to the other only the interest payments. Exposure is further reduced by using *netting* of payments. Under netting, on each payment date, the party required to make the larger payment simply makes a net payment equal to the difference between the two payments. The other party makes no payment. Note that in spite of the netting and offsetting arrangements, there still remains a marginal credit risk. The other advantage of the swap over a parallel loan is that the transaction was off-balance-sheet.

The next evolution of the swap was to remove another remaining inconvenience. X and Y are most probably unknown to each other and do not have an established financial relationship. In addition, X perhaps does not want to take on the credit risk, however small, resulting from exposure to Y. This problem can be solved by interposing a swap dealer, e.g., a bank, between X and Y. It is highly likely that both X and Y have established relationships with the bank. In any case, X and Y can more easily evaluate the exposure to the bank than to each other.

Note that this transaction actually consists of two swap transactions, one between X and the bank and the other between the bank and Y. As far as the bank is concerned, the two swaps offset each other, and thus the bank is not exposed to interest-rate risk. Of course, the bank is exposed to the credit risk of *both* X and Y. Credit intermediation, after all, is one of the primary functions of a bank. Note also that the bank earns a spread of 20 basis points,

EXHIBIT 1–5 Interposing a Swap Dealer

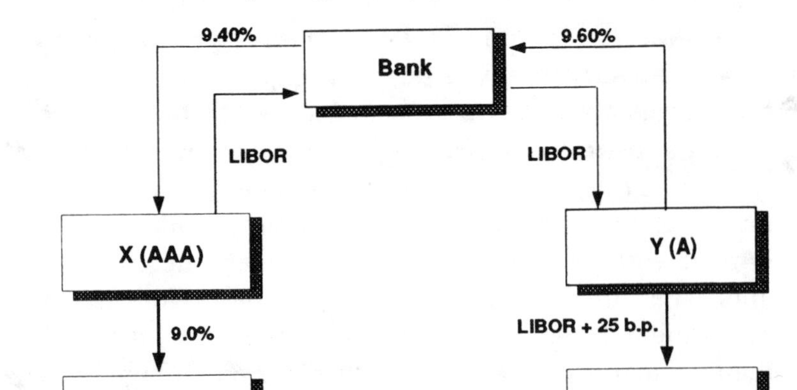

reflected by the difference in the fixed rate received and paid (9.60 percent less 9.40 percent).[7]

The swap market began growing rapidly with these advancements in place. The bank (i.e., the swap arranger) still had to simultaneously find two willing counterparties on each of the two sides of the swap. This ability was limited to the extent that institutions had differences in timing and funding amount. This problem was finally solved when banks began to warehouse swaps. That is, they began to enter into swap transactions with one party without a corresponding offsetting transaction. The bank hedged any net exposure using liquid market instruments such as futures and Treasuries. If and when another transaction, completely or partially offsetting the first, was found, the hedge was appropriately reduced.

This essentially is the current status of the swap market. It is still advancing, with significant progress being made in the standardization of documents and in the quantitative modeling of swap pricing and hedging. Risk-management technology now enables swap providers to effectively manage collections of swaps and derivatives as a homogeneous portfolio of cash flows. The application of modern financial theory to pricing and hedging has both increased the flexibility of the swap structures offered and the liquidity of the market itself.

A Simple Interest-Rate Swap Transaction

To understand how a swap works, let us look at a situation which can use a simple, so-called "plain vanilla" swap. Recall

---

7 The current level of volume, liquidity and competitiveness in the swap market is such that the bid-offered spread has narrowed significantly. A typical spread in the 5-year maturity is about 5 basis points.

EXHIBIT 1–6 The Floating Asset/Fixed Liability Gap

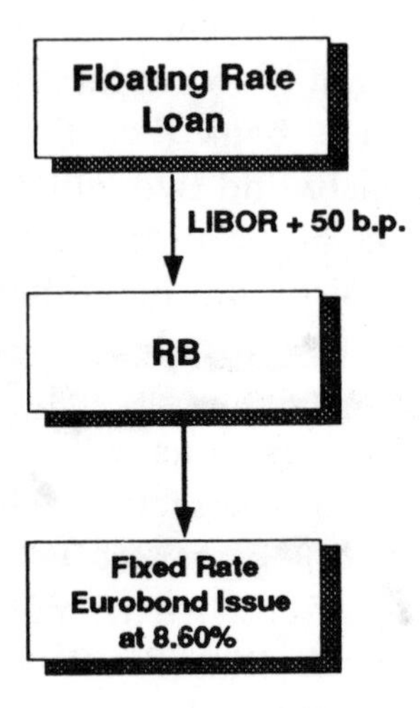

that a swap is an agreement between two parties, each called a *counterparty.*

> ***Situation*** *(A Simple Swap).* RB is a regional bank. RB has just issued $100 million of a fixed-rate Eurobond of 5 year maturity at a spread of 40 basis points over the 5 year Treasury. The Treasury yield is at 8.20 percent and therefore the coupon on the bond is 8.60 percent. RB is using the proceeds from the bond issue to fund a $100 million floating-rate loan. The loan is of 5 year maturity and has a rate of three-month LIBOR plus 50 basis points.

In this case, RB has a floating-rate asset, the loan, but a fixed-rate liability, the bond. This situation is known as an asset/liability *gap.* The gap is much more than an intellectual curiosity. It can have significant financial implications on RB in the following way: If rates fall, the cash flow from the loan will decrease but the cash flow due on the liability remains constant, resulting in a loss of the spread earned. Similarly, if the rates rise, the spread increases due to the higher level of cash flow from the asset. The spread that RB earns is thus subject to interest-rate risk.

Situation *(A Simple Swap, continued).* SMM is a swap market maker. SMM serves its clients by offering to enter into swap transactions of various kinds. SMM can help RB bridge the asset/liability gap and lock in the spread by providing an interest-rate swap. Assuming that the swap spreads are at 65 basis points, RB can contract with SMM to pay, for a period of 5 years, three-month LIBOR on a notional principal amount of $100 million in return for fixed annual cash receipts from SMM of 8.85 percent (8.20 percent Treasury rate plus the 65 basis point swap spread) on the same notional amount. RB pays LIBOR to SMM out of the cash flow received from the loan, retaining the 50 basis point spread. The 8.60 percent interest payments due on the bond issue is covered by the 8.85 percent swap payments from SMM. Even here, RB retains the 25 basis point spread. Thus, RB earns a total of 75 basis points (50 basis point spread over LIBOR from the loan, 25 basis point spread over the bond coupon from the swap) from the combined transaction.

More importantly, this spread is locked in. The earned spread is immune to interest-rate changes. As the interest receipts from the loan change, the payments due on the swap change in lockstep, effectively insulating RB from rate volatility.

The swap transaction between RB and SMM is usually illustrated diagrammatically as in Exhibit 1–7 with each party in a box and cash flows represented by arrows. If more details are necessary or if the cash flows are more complex, a swap can be represented by means of a cash flow profile, as in Exhibit 1–8. Here, payment flows are represented by arrows pointing upward and cash receipts are represented by arrows pointing downward. A cash flow can be fully described by means of a cash flow table, as in Table 1–1. In practice, a combination of a diagram for summary representation and a cash flow table for full details is used.

EXHIBIT 1–7 A Simple Swap Transaction to Bridge the Asset/Liability Gap

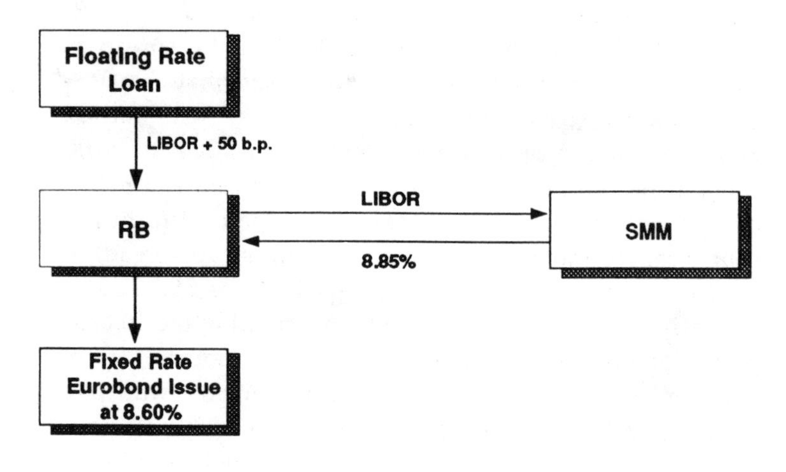

TABLE 1–1 Cash Flow Table for a Swap

Year	RB Pays	RB Receives
0.0		
0.25	L1	
0.50	L2	
0.75	L3	
1.0	L4	8.85%
1.25	L5	
1.50	L6	
1.75	L7	
2.0	L8	8.85%
2.25	...	

Review of the Simple Swap Transaction

Several important characteristics of a swap can be illustrated using the simple transaction above.

1. In an interest-rate swap transaction, only payments resembling or corresponding to the interest payments on a notional (loan) amount are exchanged, the principal amount itself is not. This fact has important implications on the amount of credit risk in a swap transaction.
2. One party pays a floating rate, the other party pays a fixed-rate. This is typical of most interest-rate swap transactions even though both parties could pay floating or fixed.[8] Typical U.S. dollar floating-rate indexes used are LIBOR, commercial paper, fed funds rate, prime rate and T-Bill rate. Most (about 75 percent) of the swaps in dollars are based on LIBOR.

EXHIBIT 1–8 Cash Flow Profile of Swap: Annual Fixed Rate Receipts

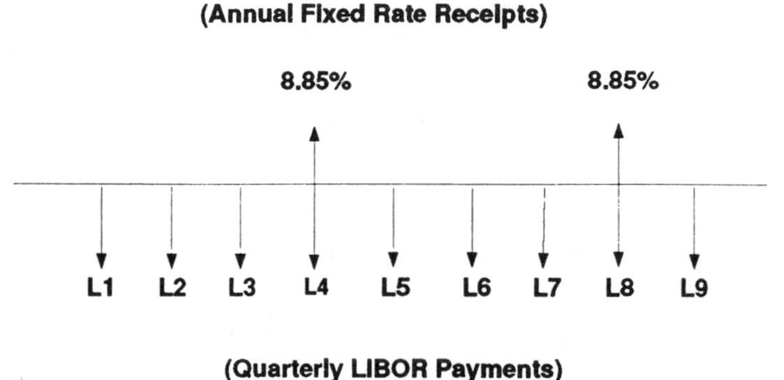

---

8 If both parties pay fixed or floating, the payments would differ in one of more attributes such as frequency or timing of payment, floating-rate index used and compounding method.

3. The swap has a specific notional amount and maturity. The floating side has a specified index, e.g., three-month LIBOR.
4. The swap rate, i.e., the fixed rate, is quoted as a spread over the appropriate maturity current coupon Treasury. The payments on the floating side are usually made flat, i.e., at the selected index rate without any spread.

Terminology

Interest Rate Swap. Refers to the contractual agreement to exchange specified cash flows between the two parties.

Counterparties. The two principal parties involved in a swap transaction.

Floating-Rate Payer. This is the party that pays floating rate in a swap. This party also receives fixed-rate cash flows and is said to be long the swap.

Fixed-Rate Payer. This is the party that pays fixed rate in a swap transaction. This party also receives floating-rate flows and is said to be short the swap.

Notional Principal Amount. This is the amount that is used to determine the actual cash flows paid or received by applying the corresponding interest rates for the appropriate calendar periods.

Coupon. The swap coupon refers to the fixed rate of interest in a swap. This is also known as swap price, swap rate and swap strike.

Term. This refers to the period commencing from the first day of coupon accrual and ending on the maturity date.

Trade Date. This is the date on which the counterparties enter into a swap transaction. The swap rate is also agreed upon on this date.

Settlement Date or Effective Date. This is the date on which the coupon starts accruing. This is the first day of the swap term, and is usually two business days after the *trade date.*

Reset Date. The date on which the floating rate is set. The rate set on this date is generally applicable for the subsequent period until next reset date.

Reset Frequency. Number of times reset dates occur in a year. Generally, reset frequency reflects the floating-rate index. This frequency is not necessarily the same as the number of payment dates in a year.

Maturity Date. Interest stops accruing on this date. Generally, there is an exchange of principal amount also on this date in the case of a currency swap. This date is also referred to as the *termination date.*

Intermediary. A third party that stands between two principal parties in a swap transaction.

At-Market or At-the-Money Swap. An interest-rate swap in which no upfront payment by either party is necessary, that is, the value of the swap is zero. The corresponding swap rate is the at-market or at-the-money swap rate.

Off-Market Swap.

(a) ***Above-market.*** The swap is above-market if the rate is greater than the at-the-money swap rate. The value of the swap is positive. In this case, the fixed payer will receive an adjustment, e.g., upfront premium.

(b) ***Below-market.*** In a below-market swap, the fixed rate is less than the at-the-money swap rate. The swap value is negative. In this swap, the fixed receiver will receive an adjustment or premium.

A Road Map

The flexibility of the swap contract can best be understood by studying various situations in which it can be effectively employed. Chapter 2 details several situations and problems that can be resolved by suitably structuring interest-rate swap transactions. Chapter 3 introduces currency swaps and illustrates their use with applications.

Swaps are used in most situations as hedges. In chapter 4 we discuss an asset/liability management approach to hedging. In addition to basic hedging concepts and a relatively new method for managing yield curve risk, we also cover here the philosophical question of the definition of a hedge. This inquiry is important because one's hedge is another's speculation.

In chapter 5, we present a procedure for evaluating a swap transaction. In addition, some pointers on where to look for value are provided. Chapter 6 extends the evaluation discussion and sets forth an outline for pricing a swap transaction. Numerical examples for pricing interest-rate and currency swaps are included here.

2

Applications and Structures

Examples of Swap Applications

There are countless ways of using interest-rate swaps to manage cash flows. The actual objectives sought by swap users are also numerous. Generally, swaps are used by institutions for the following major purposes:

- To hedge, or to modify for risk management purposes, a genuine existing (or future expected) asset or liability. This is the most straightforward case and is the most common use of swaps.
- To sculpt an existing cash flow to a desired structure. This application is similar to hedging.
- To capture value in the market, e.g., to decrease the effective interest cost on a borrowing or increase the realized yield on an investment. Value capture is usually achieved either by arbitraging different market segments or by taking advantage of market anomalies. The swap market also offers interesting risk-reward tradeoffs not easily available in the traditional debt markets. Borrowers and lenders who can tolerate these risks can achieve attractive financing or returns, respectively.

- To access, synthetically, markets otherwise not easily or efficiently accessible. Examples:

  (i) a U.S. corporation, not well known in Japan, can effectively borrow in yen by swapping its U.S. debt in U.S. dollars to into a yen liability
  (ii) a low-rated corporation with no access to long-term borrowing can swap its short-term floating-rate debt to fixed rate.[1]

- To improve the cosmetics of a transaction. In this application, optional characteristics are usually employed. For example, to reduce the initial interest rate on a borrowing, an issuer might take the risk of a higher future coupon on the issue.

One of the attractions of swaps in financing applications is based on the concept of comparative advantage. That is, two institutions can achieve mutual economic benefits by exchanging funds that are available to them at relatively cheaper costs. In many market conditions, it is observed in the fixed-income markets that the credit spread between higher- and lower-rated institutions for fixed-rate borrowings is wider than the corresponding spread for floating-rate borrowings. Obviously, the higher-rated borrower pays a lower rate in either market. Yet, the lower-rated borrower pays a lesser credit spread in the floating-rate market. In other words, the lower-rated borrower has a *relative* or *comparative* advantage over the higher-rated borrower in the floating-rate market. Conversely, the higher-

---

1 Note that the synthetic versions of the debt created are not exactly the same as the real thing. For example, even though the corporation can obtain fixed, long-term rates, it is still subject to funding risk from the short-term floating-rate debt.

EXHIBIT 2–1 Using a Swap to Exploit Comparative Advantage

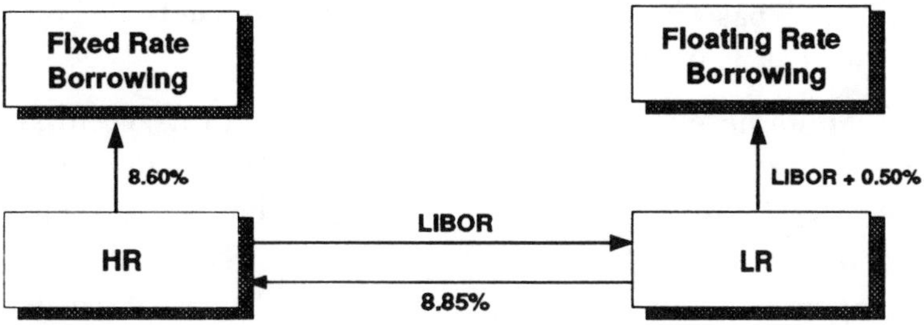

For HR:

Net Cost:	**LIBOR-0.25%**
Alternative:	**LIBOR**
Savings:	**0.25%**

For LR:

Net Cost:	**9.35%**
Alternative:	**9.60%**
Savings:	**0.25%**

rated borrower has the relative advantage in the fixed-rate market.

Now, if each borrower raises funds in the market in which it has the greater relative advantage, then the corresponding interest payments can be swapped to achieve cheaper funding rates for both. In order to illustrate this concept, consider the following situation:

> ***Situation** (Comparative Advantage).* HR, a high-rated borrower, can raise funds for five years at 8.60 percent fixed or in the short-term markets at LIBOR flat. LR, a low-rated institution, can borrow at 9.60 percent fixed for five years or at LIBOR + 0.50 percent short-term. That is, the credit spread in the fixed-rate market is 100 basis points whereas for floating-rate borrowings, it is just 50 basis points. Suppose HR borrows fixed at 8.60 percent and LR borrows floating at LIBOR + 0.50 percent. HR and LR can then enter into a fixed/floating swap where HR pays LIBOR and receives 8.85 percent. The net interest payments are LIBOR – 0.25 percent for HR and 9.35 percent fixed for LR. Thus, each borrower has achieved a saving on its own borrowing:

HR saves 25 basis points relative to a straight floating-rate borrowing (LIBOR – 0.25 percent vs. LIBOR flat); LR also saves 25 basis points compared to a straight fixed-rate borrowing (9.35 percent vs. 9.60 percent).

We note here that in many practical situations, comparative advantage may not always exist. When it does exist, the gross savings may not be enough to pay for expenses, e.g., the fee or the bid/asked spread required by the swap arranger or provider, or the net savings to each borrower may be too small to warrant the additional complexities of the transaction.

More importantly, the borrowing cost for LR is equal to 9.35 percent only if LR can roll over its floating-rate funding at LIBOR + 0.50 percent over the entire term of the transaction. In fact, one explanation for the existence of the comparative advantage is that the floating-rate lenders have the opportunity to examine the credit of LR several times and make appropriate adjustments to the spread over LIBOR. Therefore, the lender is willing to start with a comparatively lower LIBOR spread. The fixed-rate lender, however, has no such opportunity to reevaluate the credit risk. Therefore, the spread for LR in the fixed-rate, long-term market is relatively wider compared to the highly rated HR.

HR and LR could have used other derivative products such as exchange traded futures and options for converting their risk profiles between fixed- and floating-rate exposure. However, in addition to achieving cheaper funding, effective interest-rate risk management is also a common objective. Unlike the other derivative products, swaps can be used for interest-rate hedging over long periods of time without any need for frequent monitoring and rebalancing. Also, swaps do not have the inconvenience of daily margin cash flow. Swaps can achieve the conversion between fixed and floating rates highly predictably; transactions involving futures and options can have some inefficiency due to the divergence of the futures and cash markets.

The following additional examples should provide a flavor of the variety in swap usage.

> ***Situation*** *(Reduce Fixed-Rate Cost).* A Midwestern manufacturing company, MM, seeks fixed-rate funding for 5 years. It can borrow fixed for 5 years at 9.30 percent or floating at LIBOR + 1/8. Suppose that swap rates are at 8.85 percent. The company can borrow floating, and execute a swap transaction on which it would pay 8.85 percent and receive LIBOR. The net cost of funding using swaps is 8.975 percent (8.85 percent payment on the swap plus the 1/8 spread over LIBOR paid on the loan), a 32.5 basis point saving relative to the straight 9.30 percent financing.

> ***Situation*** *(Obtain Fixed-Rate Funds).* F500 is a Fortune 500 company that needs fixed-rate borrowing. It normally raises funds through a CP program. By using a swap transaction, F500 can achieve its goal of fixing its interest cost while continuing to raise funds in the traditional manner in the commercial paper market. It can enter into a 5-year

EXHIBIT 2–2 Using a Swap to Reduce Fixed Rate

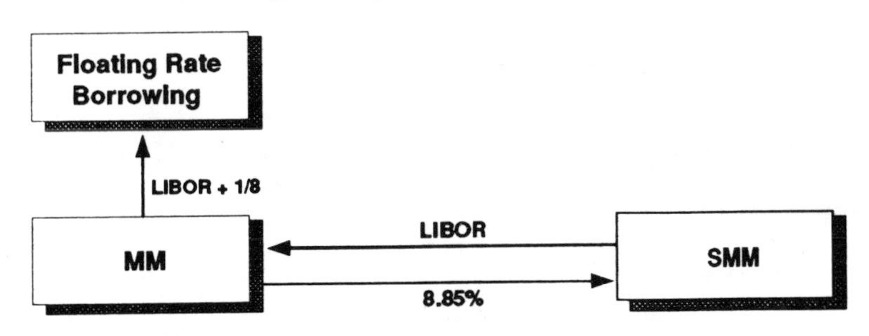

EXHIBIT 2–3 Obtaining Fixed-Rate Funding

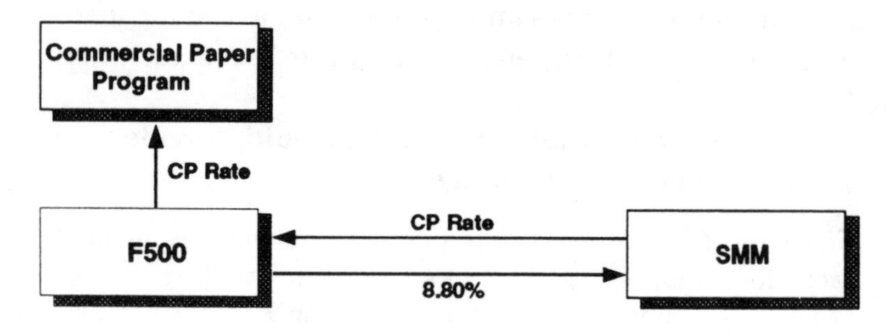

fixed/CP swap, paying 8.80 percent in return for monthly payments close to its CP funding cost. The cost of swap-related financing is 8.80 percent.

Situation *(Reduce Floating-Rate Cost).* A California retailer, CR, has traditionally borrowed at LIBOR + 1/8 from its banks. It discovers that 5-year funding can be obtained from a private source at 8.80 percent or 0.60 percent above Treasuries. Swap rates are at 8.85 percent. The retailer can borrow from the private source at fixed rate and enter into a swap paying LIBOR and receiving 8.85 percent. The combination of the bond and the swap results in a net funding cost of LIBOR – 0.05 percent (LIBOR payment on the swap plus the 8.80 percent coupon on the bond less the 8.85 percent receipt on the

EXHIBIT 2–4 Reducing Floating-Rate Cost

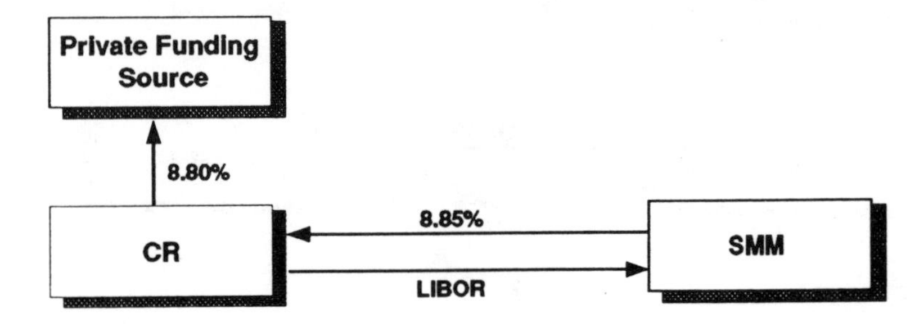

EXHIBIT 2–5 Guaranteeing Liquidity via Bond Issue

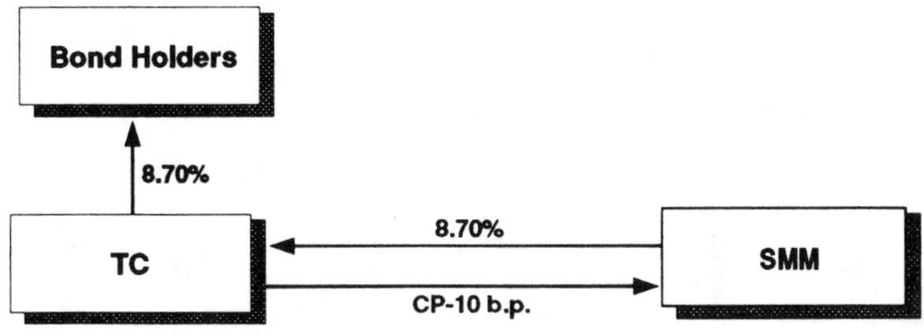

swap), at a savings of 17.5 basis points relative to traditional borrowing.

Situation *(Guarantee Liquidity).* A Boston technology company, TC, has an active CP program, but would like to reduce its dependency on the commercial paper market for liquidity reasons. Yet, it prefers to fund at CP rates from a risk management point of view. TC can borrow fixed for a 5-year term via a bond issue at 8.70 percent (.50 percent over Treasuries) and enter into a swap whereby it receives 8.70 percent and pays CP index[2] less 10 basis points. This rate is competitive with its own CP issue, and TC now has a liquidity cushion.

Situation *(Convert to Floating).* A European automotive company, AC, borrowed fixed dollars for 7 years at 11.25 percent 3 years ago. Now, with the 4-year U.S. Treasuries at 8.15 percent and swap spreads at 55 basis points, AC feels that, on the average, short rates will be considerably less than prevailing fixed rates (of 8.15 percent + 55 b.p. or 8.70

---

2 The Board of Governors of the Federal Reserve System publish for each day a composite commercial paper rate based on the rates paid by AA-rated financial institutions. A monthly average of these composite rates is commonly the CP index used in swap transactions.

EXHIBIT 2–6 Converting to Floating Rate

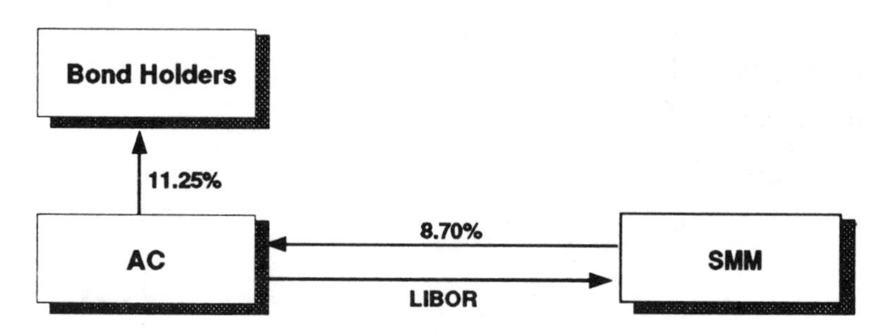

percent) for the remaining life of the debt. AC therefore swaps into floating, receiving 8.70 percent and paying LIBOR. With 6-month LIBOR at 8.06 percent, the net cost for the first 6 months is 10.61 percent (8.06 percent plus 11.25 percent on the bond issue less 8.70 percent received on the swap), a saving of 64 basis points (11.25 percent old coupon less 10.61 percent new initial coupon). AC has potential for further savings in the future if its forecast of lower levels of interest rates holds good.

EXHIBIT 2–7 Locking in a Low Fixed Rate

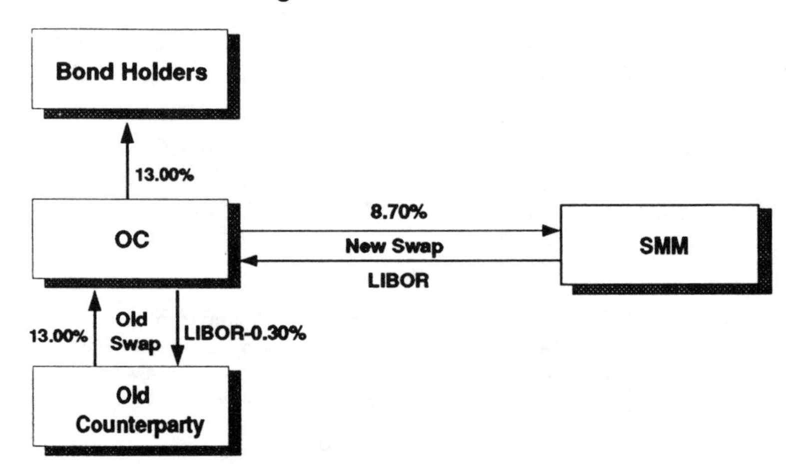

Situation *(Lock in Low Fixed Rate).* Four years ago an oil company, OC, executed an 8-year, 13 percent fixed-rate new issue swapped into floating at LIBOR – 0.30 percent. Today, the treasurer feels that the U.S. rates are at a low point. He wishes to execute another interest-rate swap to lock in today's rates for the remainder of the issue. He pays 8.70 percent for a new swap, receiving LIBOR. His net cost is 8.40 percent—8.70 percent payment on the new swap less LIBOR receipt on the new swap plus (LIBOR – 0.30 percent) net cost of previous financing—for the remaining life of the bond.

Situation *(Obtain Desired Structure).* A startup company, SC, has access to floating-rate funds from its traditional banker, TB. SC, however, would like fixed-rate funding. In addition, it would like to keep its interest costs low in the

EXHIBIT 2–8 Obtaining Desired Structure

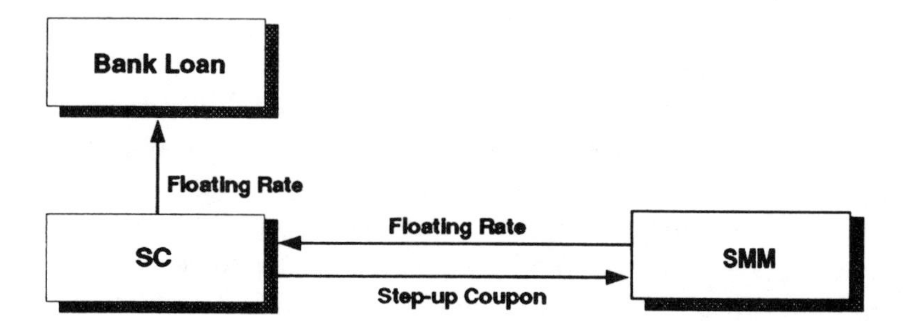

initial years and is willing to pay a compensating higher rate in the later years. In this case, SC can enter into what is known as a step-up coupon swap.[3] This swap starts with a low interest-rate coupon on the fixed side, and after a few years, the rate will step up. Note in this case that achieving the desired structure is perhaps more important to SC than squeezing the last basis point out of the market.

The swap participants in the situations discussed above all have different objectives. The swaps executed to meet these objectives are also different in overall structure. Yet, the attentive reader can observe that the needs of each party seem to mirror that of another, and can be fulfilled by combining them in swap transactions appropriately. MM and CR can enter into a 5-year fixed/LIBOR swap, where MM will pay fixed and CR will pay floating. JT and TC can execute a 5-year fixed/CP swap with TC paying the CP index and JT paying fixed. Finally, AC can enter into a 4-year fixed/LIBOR swap with OC, with OC paying fixed and AC paying floating.

However, in the real world, the selection of counterparties is not as obvious, nor is their ready availability as easy, as is implied by these illustrative cases. The swap required by SC is a good example. It is unlikely that SC would quickly find an appropriate counterparty wishing to pay floating and receive fixed on a step-up structure. In general, the situation is complicated by several factors such as:

a. the swapping needs of one party are not generally known to the other party
b. parties have very limited ability to evaluate and accept the credit risk of the counterparty

---

3 This structure is further discussed in the next section.

c. the payment date and maturity requirements of one party may not match the other's
d. some parties may not be able to meet the cash buyout requirements of their counterparties
e. the timing requirement of one party might differ from that of the counterparty
f. there might be differences in the funding sizes of the different parties

Many of these problems can be solved by the intervention of a swap dealer or swap market maker such as SMM. The dealer will be in contact with a number of swap users and will be aware of their specific needs. The dealer may perform a purely intermediary function, or hold one of the swaps in inventory until another closely matching swap is available. The dealer typically will use liquid market securities, such as Treasuries and futures contracts, to hedge a swap or a portfolio of swaps completely during the inventory period, and to adjust the hedge for any residual mismatches after an offsetting swap has been executed.

Swap Structures

One of the most striking features of a swap, which is such a liquid instrument, is the fact that it is a privately negotiated contract. As such, the terms and conditions of the swap contract can be customized to meet the needs at hand. As end users of swaps have aggressively used this flexibility, new swap structures with descriptive names have developed.

The currently prevalent cash flow valuation models, based on robust theoretical principles, have provided significant flexibility in the design of swap structures. However, when conceiving these structures there is the counterbalancing need for liquidity in the event that a swap transaction must be unwound. This need encourages swap structures to gravitate toward a select few formats. Market liquidity, aided by widely available sophisticated valuation models, also increases the ability of swap providers to hedge the swaps, resulting in a better price for the end user. In cases where liquidity is not a concern, both from the view of the end user and that of the provider, swaps can be engineered with almost limitless variety.

The Standard Interest-Rate Swap

The standard interest-rate swap consists of the exchange of a floating-rate payment stream for a fixed-rate payment stream. The agreement has a fixed maturity and the notional amount is held constant throughout the life of the swap.

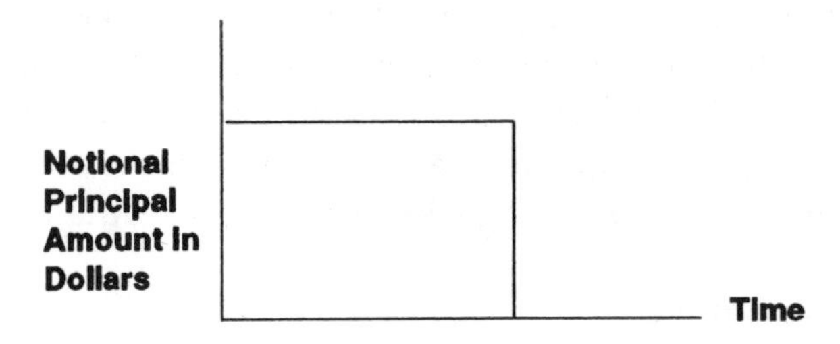

Situation (Achieving Funding Cost Target). ESD, an electrical systems developer, is seeking $30 million of funding for 10 years on a fixed-rate basis. It finds that its interest-rate cost of 8.10 percent for fixed-rate borrowing is slightly higher than its target rate of 7.90 percent. It can raise floating dollar funds in the Eurobond market at LIBOR flat.

ESD can achieve its fixed-rate funding target by raising $30 million floating-rate funds in the Euromarket and swapping into a fixed rate. Under the swap, ESD pays interest at the fixed rate of 7.89 percent and receives LIBOR.

EXHIBIT 2–9 Achieving Funding Cost Target

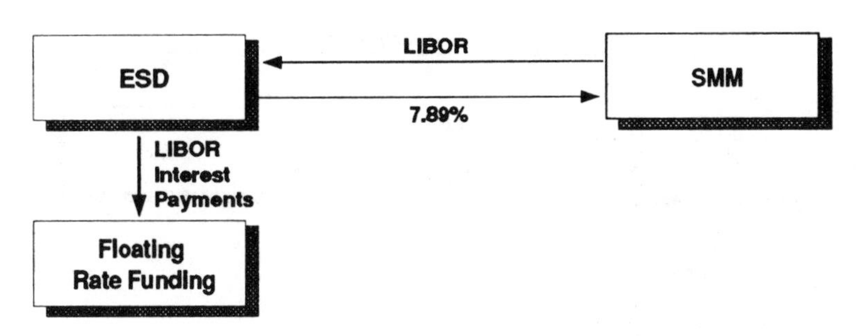

Effectively, ESD will have a 10-year funding at a fixed rate of 7.89 percent on $30 million.

Off-Market Swap

Interest-rate swaps are usually initiated such that their initial value is zero. That is, the present value of the cash flows to be paid equals the present value of the cash flows to be received. Any change in the market rates, or just the passage of time, can cause a deviation in the value of the swap. A swap with nonzero value is called an *off-market swap*. If a new swap is off-market, then a compensating upfront payment from one party to the other will be required to bring the net value to zero. The adjustment may also be made via a lower-than-market coupon.

Situation *(Hedging an Ex-Warrant Bond).* JLC is a Japanese leasing company which has just issued a fixed-rate, 4-year, dollar-denominated bond in the Euromarket with attached equity warrants. JLC would like hedge the bond issue alone, called the ex-warrant bond, by converting the bond cash flows into floating. The warrant exposure is left unhedged.

The coupon on the bond is most likely to be below market, given that the bond has attached warrants. Therefore,

EXHIBIT 2–10 Hedging an Ex-Warrant Bond

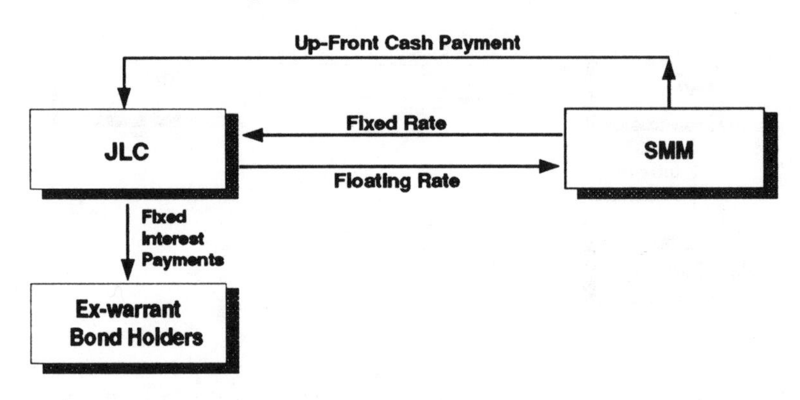

JLC enters into an off-market interest-rate swap. JLC receives cash up front from the swap provider, or, more likely, enjoys a lower-than-market floating coupon.

Off-market swaps are used mostly to unwind or reverse out of older interest-rate swaps when rates have moved since the inception of the swaps. They are also used in cases in which a given cash flow needs to be matched exactly (see asset swaps, below). They can also be used to create discount or premium assets or liabilities in conjunction with a change in rate basis (fixed or floating), as in the discussion of zero-coupon swaps below.

***Situation** (Reversing Out of an Old Swap).* DCC is a diversified chemical company that entered into a 10-year swap for $40 million, receiving fixed at 9 percent 2 years ago. The market has rallied, with prevailing 8-year swap rates at 7.20 percent. DCC now wishes to unwind the swap. DCC enters into an offsetting swap with another counterparty under which DCC pays 9 percent for 8 years (i.e., 1.80 percent above the market rate) and receives LIBOR. The new counterparty makes an upfront adjustment payment of

EXHIBIT 2–11 Reversing an Existing Interest-Rate Swap

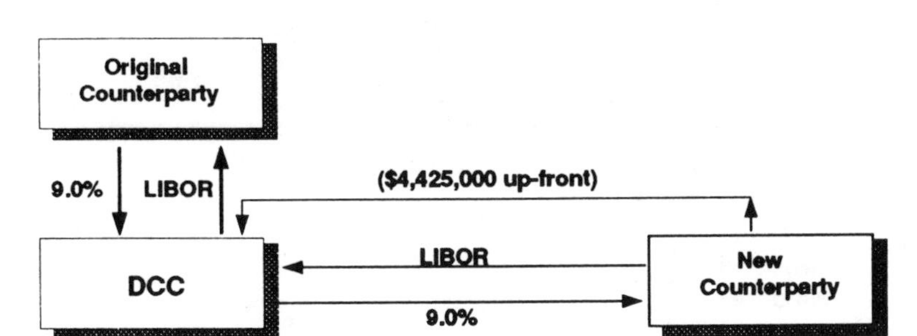

$4,250,000, reflecting the fact that the swap is off-market.[4] This payment is compensation to DCC for the above-market fixed-rate payments that it makes.

The natural way to have unwound the swap would have been simply to terminate or cancel the swap. The original counterparty would have paid to DCC a settlement amount reflecting the difference between the 9 percent existing rate and the 7.20 percent market rate. DCC chose to enter into a new, offsetting swap. This situation arises when the settlement payment offered by the original counterparty for termination is less than the adjustment payment offered by the new counterparty for the off-market swap. Note that in the former case DCC has no credit risk, but in the latter case, DCC is exposed to the credit risk of two counterparties.

---

4 The market adjustment value of $4,250,000 is determined by using a swap pricing model.

EXHIBIT 2–12 Creating a Zero-Coupon Liability

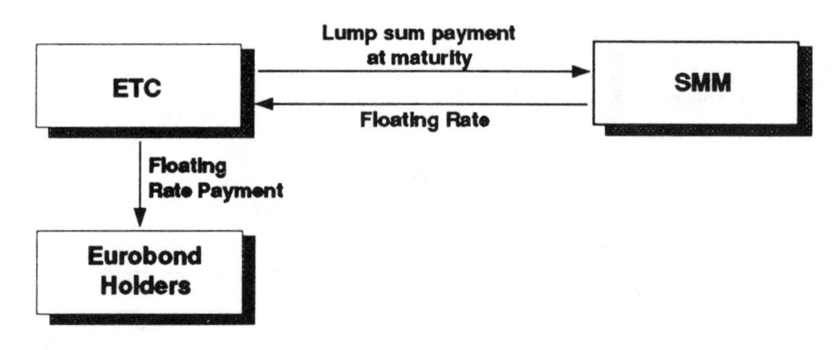

Zero-Coupon Swap

A *zero-coupon swap* is an extreme case of an off-market swap in which one of the counterparties makes a lump sum payment instead of periodic payments over time.

> ***Situation*** *(Creating a Zero-Coupon Liability).* ETC, a European trading company, has just issued a floating-rate, 5-year dollar-denominated bond in the Eurobond market. It is considering swapping the bond into a fixed-rate liability. However, it would like to conserve cash as much as possible for operational reasons, and would prefer a zero-coupon funding.

ETC can achieve its goal by means of a zero-coupon interest-rate swap. Under the swap, ETC will receive floating-rate dollar cash flows for 5 years. These cash flows will exactly service interest payments on the outstanding Eurobond. As part of the swap contract, ETC will make a lump sum payment at maturity. This payment is the effective zero-coupon liability for ETC.

Other variations of the zero-coupon swap are possible. The lump sum payment can occur at any time, upfront, at maturity, or during the life of the swap.

Swap-in-Arrears

Swap-in-Arrears (SIA) is an interesting innovation. Normally, the floating rate, say LIBOR, is set at the beginning of a period and the actual payment is made at the end of the reset period. In SIA swaps, the floating rate is set and the corresponding amount is paid at the *end* of the period. Swaps of this type have higher quoted fixed rates than simple swaps in a market environment where the yield curve is upward sloping. This is because the higher forward rates implied by the positively sloped yield curve take effect one period earlier than in the simple case, thus increasing the floating-rate cash flows.[5]

Basis Swap

A *basis swap* entails two floating-rate indexes. An example is when LIBOR interest payments are swapped against interest payments based on the commercial paper index on the same notional principal amount.

> ***Situation*** *(Asset-Liability Matching).* EFC, an eastern finance company, has an active Euro-commercial paper program. It has just purchased $25 million of a LIBOR-based dollar asset. The spread realized by EFC therefore is exposed to the spread variation between LIBOR and commercial paper. To eliminate the "basis gap" between the asset and the associated liability, it would like to convert the commercial paper liability into floating-rate dollars tied to LIBOR so as to match the floating-rate dollar asset.

---

5 Note here that the actual floating-rate cash flows in an SIA swap may be lesser or greater than the corresponding cash flows in a simple swap. However, for evaluation purposes, the swap market maker is willing to assume that the cash flows will be determined by the forward rates. Therefore, the fixed rate is set higher than in a simple swap.

EXHIBIT 2–13 Asset-Liability Matching

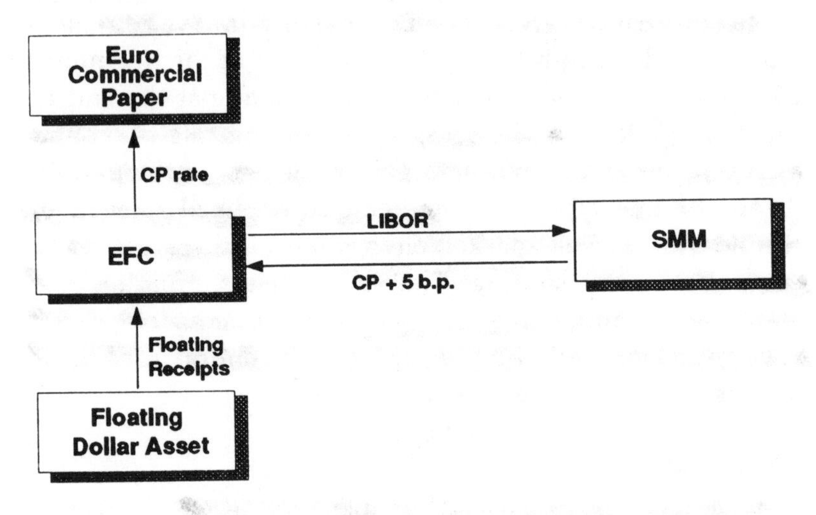

To effect this conversion, EFC enters into a basis swap, paying LIBOR and receiving the commercial paper rate plus a small spread (5 b.p.). Now, the spread earned on EFC's asset is more stable and predictable.

For certain indexes, the basis swap is a more common transaction than the fixed-for-floating swap. For example, the Fed Funds-for-LIBOR swap is more popular than the Fed Funds-for-fixed swap.

Conceptually, a basis swap locks in the spread existing at the time of the agreement between the two indexes. The CP-LIBOR swap is an interesting case. The spread between LIBOR and CP rates was quite wide (35 basis points) a few years ago and has since narrowed significantly, as can be seen in Exhibit 2–14. Some of the market factors that brought about this change are the increased issuance of CP, the lowering of the credit quality of CP issuers and the increased use of the CP market by banks. These factors have brought the average credit quality of CP issuers closer to that of banks. Thus, CP has moved closer to

EXHIBIT 2–14 Spread Between CP and LIBOR (Monthly, in Basis Points)

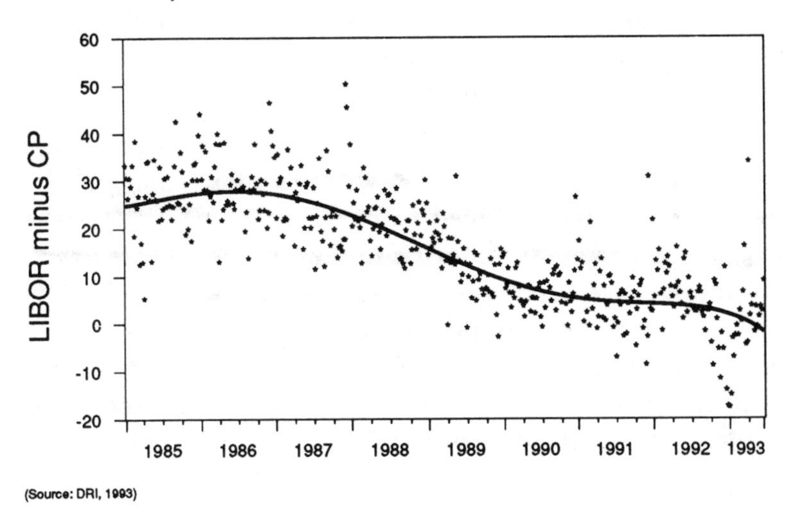

(Source: DRI, 1993)

LIBOR, which reflects the general credit of the banking sector.

Asset Swap—Synthetic Securities

Swaps are used not only for managing liabilities, but also for engineering the cash flows from assets into desired formats. For example, a floating-rate asset can be converted into a synthetic fixed-rate asset using an interest-rate swap.

EXHIBIT 2–15 Creating a Fixed-Rate Asset

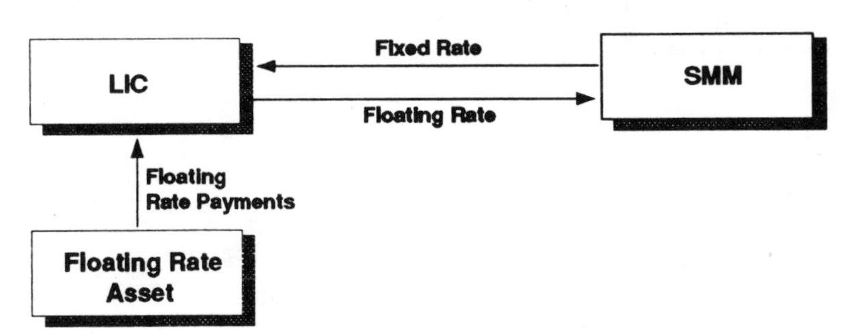

Situation *(Creating a Synthetic Fixed-Rate Asset).* LIC, a life-insurance company, has just acquired a floating-rate bond at an attractive yield. However, LIC's liabilities are typically long and fixed-rate. Therefore, LIC would like to convert the bond into a fixed-rate asset.

LIC can achieve its goal by entering into an asset swap. Under the swap contract, LIC will essentially pay all the floating cash flow received from the asset, except for the principal payment at maturity, to the swap counterparty. It will receive fixed-rate payments periodically. Note that the interest-rate swap may be an off-market swap in order to match the exact cash flows from the floating-rate bond. Also, the swap counterparty might require that the bond be pledged as collateral depending upon the credit rating of LIC.

Synthetic assets can provide attractive returns relative to conventional securities. However, it should be remem-

EXHIBIT 2–16 Hedging a Fixed-Rate Asset

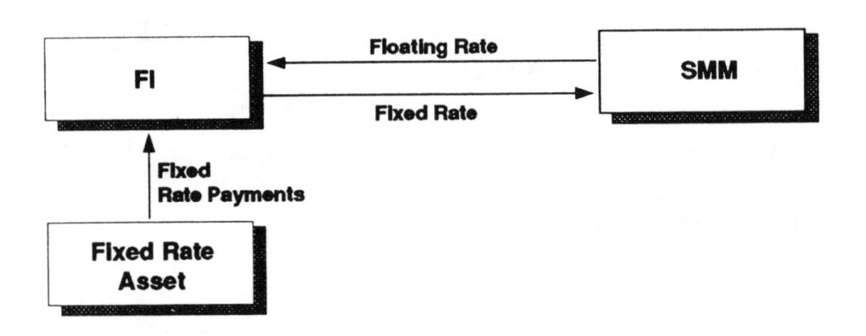

bered that synthetic assets in general have lower liquidity and are appropriate only in those cases where they are expected to be held to maturity.

Situation *(Hedging a Fixed-Rate Asset).* FI is a portfolio manager investing in fixed-income securities. He owns a fixed-rate bond that he considers a very attractive asset. However, he believes that interest rates will most likely rise, resulting in the fall of the price of the asset owned. He can sell the fixed-rate bond and purchase floating-rate or shorter-term securities. Alternatively, he can continue to hold the attractive asset, but at the same time hedge his interest-rate risk by entering into an asset swap. On the swap he will pay fixed and receive floating. The payments made on the swap are offset by the coupon received on the bond. The receipts on the swap effectively convert the fixed-rate bond into a floating-rate asset.

Another way to view this asset swap is that the change in the value of the bond due to a rise (or fall) in interest rates will be matched by an equal and opposite change in the value of the swap. Thus the swap effectively hedges the bond.

Forward Swap

A *forward swap* is one in which there is a significant delay between the date on which the swap is traded or committed to and the settlement or effective date of the swap.

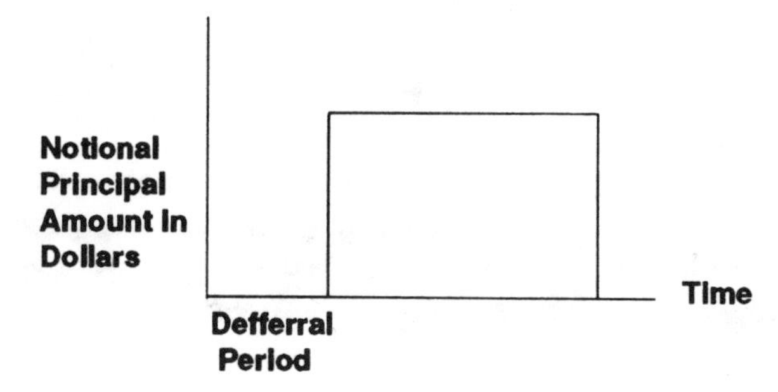

EXHIBIT 2–17 Hedging Future Bond Issue with a Forward Swap

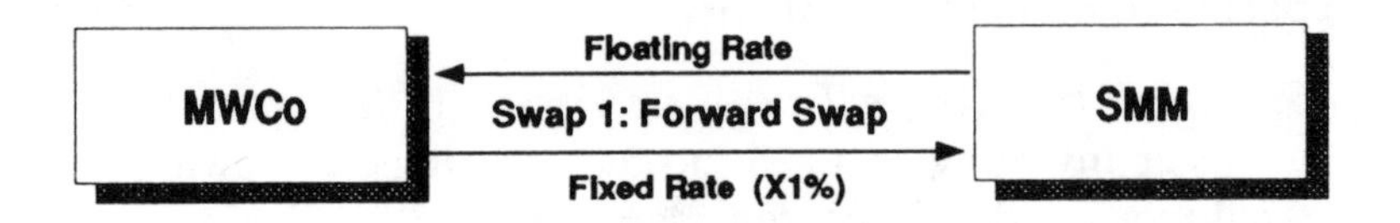

Forward Swap: **Trade Date: June**
Start Date: November

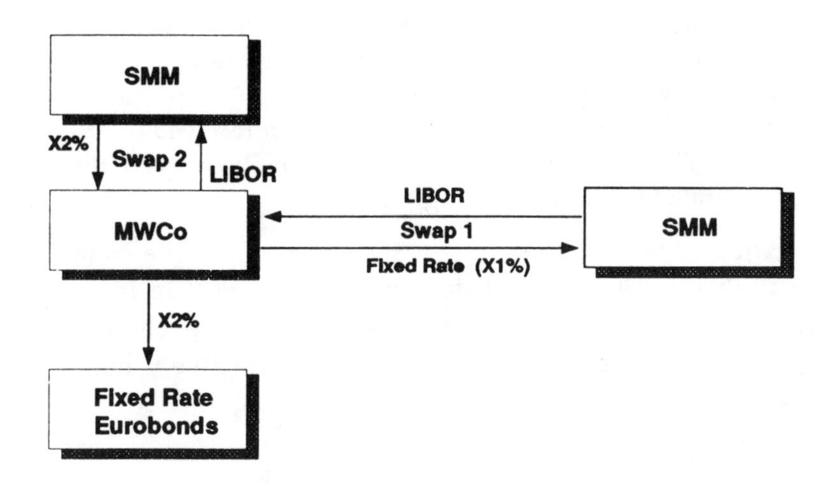

Situation (Hedging a Future Liability). MWCo is a midwestern manufacturing company. In June, MWCo plans to raise fixed-rate funds for a future project. Funds would not be necessary until November. MWCo has determined that the optimal strategy would be to issue fixed-rate bonds in Europe in November. The risk to the company is the possibility that interest rates might rise in the time period between now and the funding date in the future.

MWCo can hedge this risk by entering into a forward interest-rate swap immediately. The swap will settle or become effective in November, coinciding with the planned bond issue. Under the swap, MWCo will pay a fixed rate (equal to X1 percent, say) and receive floating-rate payments. Then, in November, at the time of the Eurobond issue, MWCo will enter into another swap under which it will receive a fixed rate (equal to the market rate of X2 percent, say) and pay floating. The coupon rate on the bond will also be X2 percent, reflecting the market levels.[6] The net cash flow from the forward swap, the coupon payments on the bond, and the second swap is simply the fixed payment on the forward swap. Thus, MWCo is hedged.

Forward swaps can be used similarly in conjunction with planned future asset acquisitions.

Variable Fixed-Rate Swaps

Sometimes, a swap on the fixed side has a series of fixed rates applied to nonoverlapping time intervals. Thus, even though all the payments are known, they are not equal. These swap are often called *step-up coupon* or *step-down coupon* swaps depending upon the structure. They are mainly used to manage cash flow needs and constraints effectively.

Situation *(Cash Flow Management).* EAMCo, an eastern appliance manufacturing company, would like to swap its floating-rate bank loan into fixed rate for 5 years. However, its cash flows cannot comfortably service the market fixed rate. Therefore, it enters into a fixed-rate swap with SMM under which SMM pays LIBOR in years 1–5. EAMCo pays

---

6 MWCo takes the risk that swap rates and its own bond rates might move by different amounts.

EXHIBIT 2–18 Cash Flow Management with Step-Up Coupon Swap

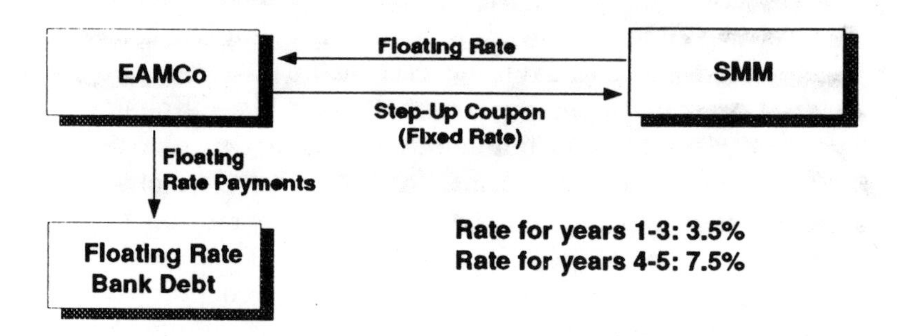

a low coupon rate of 3.5 percent for the first 3 years. To compensate SMM, it has to pay a significantly higher rate of 7.5 percent in the last 2 years. Hopefully, its cash flows will have improved by then.

Swaps with Variable Notional Amount

Usually, the notional or the principal amount of a swap is held constant throughout the life of the swap. However, situations might arise in which there is a need for varying the notional principal. The more common varieties of variable notional principal swaps are discussed below.

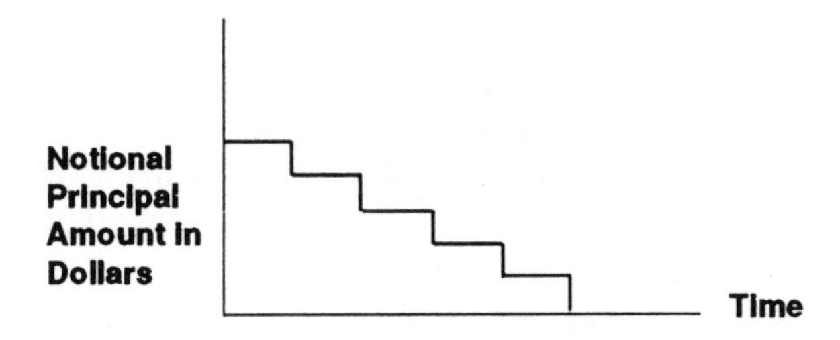

In *amortizing swaps,* the notional principal starts at a high level and gradually decreases. An amortizing swap is suitable when the asset or liability being hedged is itself amortizing. It is possible to analyze and price an amortizing swap as a combination of smaller swaps of different maturities.

An *accreting swap* is one in which the notional principal starts low and slowly increases over the life of the swap.

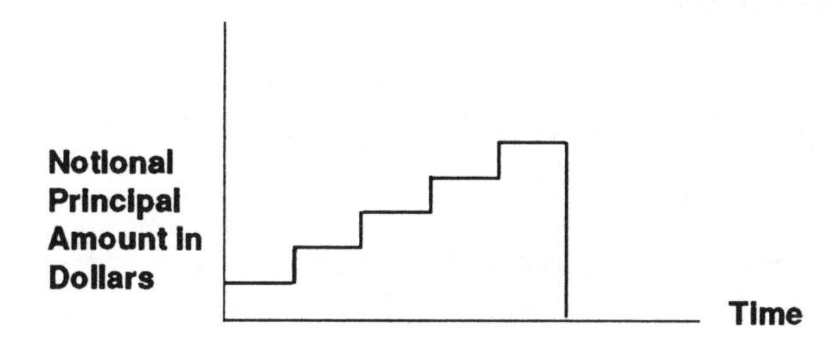

Situation *(Hedging a Construction Loan—I).* HEP is a construction company in the business of developing hydroelectric projects. It has secured a floating-rate loan for a new energy project. It intends to draw down on the loan as the construction progresses. Also, it wishes to convert the liability into fixed-rate now because it finds current interest rates to be attractive.

One alternative for HEP is to enter into a series of interest-rate swaps, receiving floating and paying fixed, as and when the loan is drawn down. In addition to the inconvenience of a potentially large number of small-sized transactions, this option also exposes HEP to changes in future interest rates. An acceptable alternative is to enter into an accreting interest-rate swap with the notional principal increasing in step with the planned drawdown of the loan. The swap would be priced based on current market condi-

EXHIBIT 2–19 Hedging with an Accreting Swap

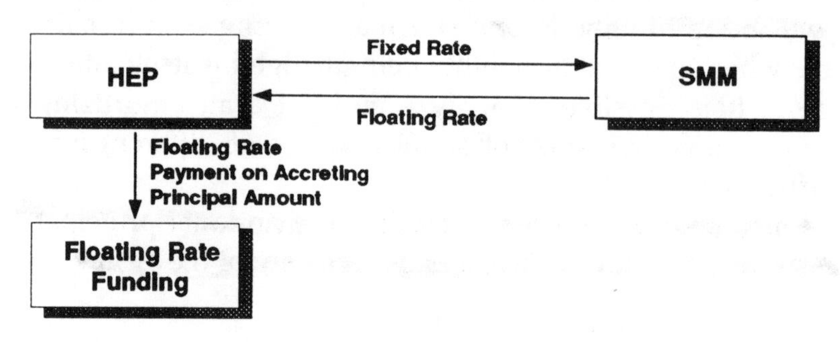

tions, thus providing HEP protection from future changes in interest rates.

Two observations are notable in the context of this example. First, HEP assumes the small risk that the actual drawdowns may not exactly match the planned drawdowns on which the swap is based. In most real-world situations, it is best to retain this type of small, unquantifiable risk rather than hedge it out to the last penny by introducing optionlike features in the interest-rate swap. The incremental cost of the optional features would probably not be justified in view of the small size of the risk. One reason for this is that any option incorporated into a swap is priced based on the potential movement of interest rates, whereas the drawdowns on the loan may not be so strongly correlated with interest-rate levels. Thus, buying optional features for the risk could be an overhedge. One simple principle to follow is to hedge *generic* risks in the market through derivatives, and retain *specific* risks. This way we apportion the task of hedging among different players optimally. In this example, HEP is far better equipped to handle the specific risk than any swap dealer. On the other hand, the swap dealer can easily hedge the market risk.

Secondly, notice that HEP could also achieve its goals by entering into a number of forward swaps, each corresponding to a planned drawdown. This illustrates the point that, conceptually, an accreting swap is simply a combination of forward swaps.

A *roller-coaster swap* combines the properties of accreting and amortizing swaps, with its notional principal increasing and decreasing at different times. Such a swap is used to engineer, in detail, cash flows to a specific need. They are relatively less common in practice.

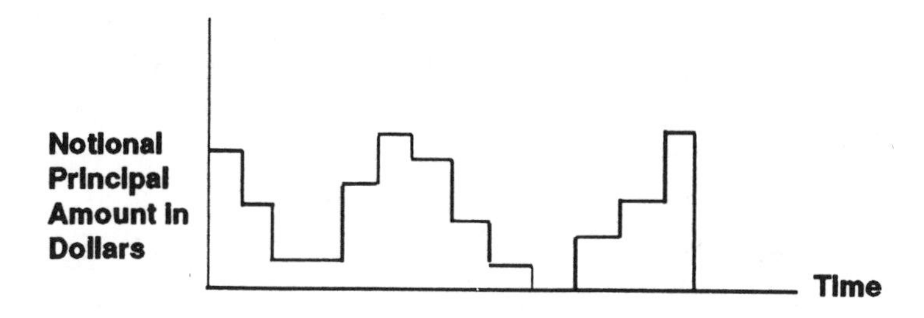

Situation *(Hedging a Construction Loan—II).* HEP is a construction company that develops hydroelectric projects. It has secured a floating-rate loan for a construction project. The terms of the loan require HEP to draw down the funds as the project progresses. The terms also require gradual repayment as soon as the project is completed and begins to produce income.

HEP can hedge the interest-rate risk inherent in this project and its funding by means of a roller-coaster interest-rate swap. The notional principal of the swap is set to increase in step with the projected drawdown schedule of the loan. Once the loan has been completely drawn down, the notional amount is set to decrease according to the projected cash flow to be received from the project.

As before, note that HEP retains the residual risk that the actual amounts drawn down and the actual cash flow from the project may not be exactly the same as the projected amounts as used in the swap. It is not unreasonable on the part of HEP to accept this risk.

Summary

These variations of the basic structure of interest-rate swaps that we have examined are just a representative sample. Since a swap is a privately negotiated contract between two parties, it has the ability to be sculpted to meet the needs of the situation. This flexibility is enhanced in cases where advanced and sophisticated valuation and hedging models are available to the swap provider. However, we should resist the temptation to complicate a transaction, unless otherwise warranted. Undue complexity always extracts its own price. Also, we recommend hedging generic risks rather than specific risks, unless the situation demands otherwise.

3

Currency Swaps

In the same way an interest-rate swap can effectively change the nature of a cash flow from fixed to floating, it is also possible to change the underlying currency itself via the swap mechanism. Such a transaction is called a *cross-currency swap*, or, simply, a *currency swap*. The major difference between a generic interest-rate swap and a generic currency swap is that the latter includes not only the exchange of interest-rate payments but also the initial and final exchange of principal amounts. The initial exchange occurs at the beginning of the swap; the final exchange occurs on the maturity date of the swap. In this sense, the currency swap closely resembles a back-to-back or parallel loan. Also, since the payments made by the two parties are in different currencies, the payments are not netted.

These differences mean that in a currency swap, the exposure of a counterparty to the other's credit risk is much larger than in the case of an interest-rate swap.

Depending upon whether the two sides of a currency swap pay a fixed or floating rate of interest, the transaction is classified as a fixed/fixed, fixed/floating, or floating/floating currency swap. As can be expected, the final exchange of principal imparts additional complexity to nonstandard structures and to terminations.

A Simple Currency-Swap Transaction

To understand how a currency swap works, consider a situation in which we can use a simple, "plain vanilla" swap.

> ***Situation*** *(A Simple Currency Swap).* USR is a well-known U.S. retailer. USR is funding a new project in Japan by means of a just issued $100 million of a 6.0 percent fixed-rate-dollar bond in the Euromarket of 5-year maturity. USR had modeled the Japanese project as a 5-year cash flow providing essentially floating-rate returns.

In this case, USR has a floating-rate yen asset, the Japanese project, but a fixed-rate U.S. dollar liability, the bond. This situation is an instance of an asset/liability *gap.* This gap is not purely of academic interest. It can have significant financial implications on USR. If the yen falls against the dollar, the cash flow from the project, measured in dollars, will decrease but the cash flow due on the liability remains constant, resulting in a loss of the spread earned. In addition, if floating yen rates fall, again, the cash flow to

EXHIBIT 3–1 The Yen Asset/Dollar Liability Gap

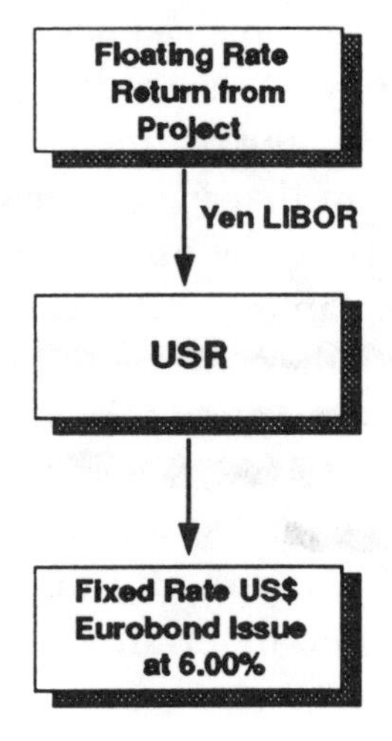

USR falls. The spread that USR earns is thus subject to both currency exchange-rate risk and interest-rate risk.

> ***Situation*** *(A Simple Currency Swap, continued).* USR can bridge the asset/liability gap and lock in the spread by using a currency-rate swap with SMM, a market maker in currency swaps. Assume that the currency swap rates are at 6.20 percent against yen LIBOR. Under the swap, USR will pay yen LIBOR and receive 6.20 percent in U.S. dollars. The notional amount will be $100 million on the dollar side and Y12.5 billion on the yen side. The yen notional amount is determined by using the exchange rate of 125 yen to the dollar on the dollar notional amount. In addition to the usual periodic exchanges of interest payments in yen and dollars, there will be two other exchanges. At the initiation of the swap, USR will pay $100 million, representing the proceeds from the bond issue, to SMM and receive Y12.5 billion from SMM. At the maturity of the swap, this exchange will reverse: SMM will pay to USR $100 million representing the principal payment due on the bonds at maturity. USR will pay to SMM Y12.5 billion. Thus, the swap and the bond together synthesize a 5-year floating yen liability for USR. USR pays yen LIBOR to SMM out of the cash flow received from the Japanese project. Of course, USR retains any spread over LIBOR that it earns. The 6.00 percent interest payments due on the bond issue are fully covered by the 6.20 percent swap payments from SMM. Even here, USR earns a spread of 20 basis points.

More importantly, the spread earned by USR is hedged and free from the risk that yen might become weaker against dollars or the risk that yen floating rates might fall.

The swap transaction between USR and SMM is usually illustrated diagrammatically as in Exhibit 3–2 with each party in a box and cash flows represented by arrows. Usually, the initial and final exchanges are also shown. However, even if the principal exchanges are not shown, they

EXHIBIT 3–2 A Simple Currency-Swap Transaction to Bridge the Asset/Liability Gap

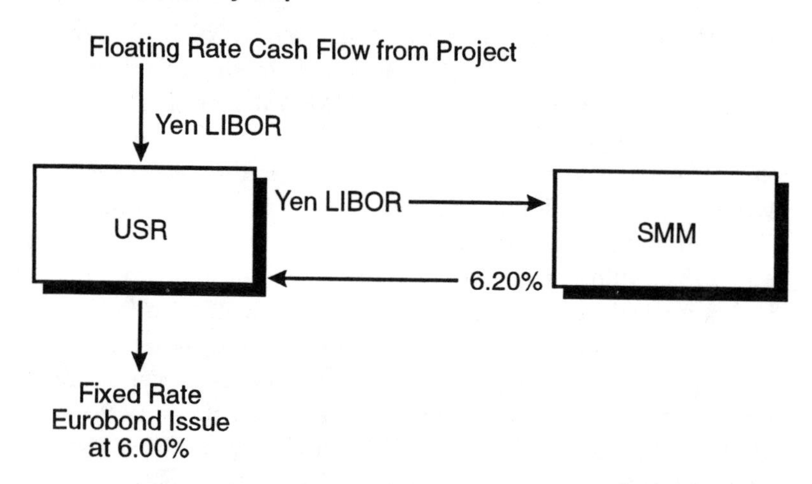

are implied. If more details are necessary or if the cash flows are more complex, a swap can be represented by means of either a cash flow profile or a cash flow table.

EXHIBIT 3–3 Cash Flow Profile of Swap

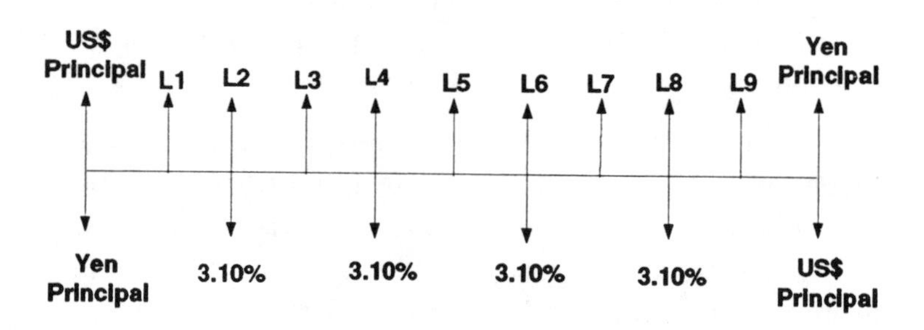

EXHIBIT 3–4 Cash Flow Table for a Currency Swap

Year	USR Pays (Yen)	USR Receives (USD$)
0.0		
0.25	L1	
0.50	L2	3.10%
0.75	L3	
1.0	L4	3.10%
1.25	L5	
1.50	L6	3.10%
1.75	L7	
2.0	L8	3.10%
2.25	...	...
	Principal Payments	
0.0	12.5bn Yen	$100mm
5.0	100mm US$	12.5bn Yen

Review of the Simple Swap Transaction

Several important characteristics of a swap can be illustrated using the simple transaction above.

1. In a currency, swap transaction, not only payments resembling or corresponding to the interest payments on a notional (loan) amount are exchanged, but the principal amounts are exchanged as well. The exchanges occur at the initiation of the swap and at the maturity of the swap. This fact has important implications on the greater amount of credit risk in a currency-swap transaction.

2. One party makes payments of a fixed- or floating-rate in one currency, the other party makes fixed- or floating-rate payments in another currency. This is typical of most currency-swap transactions.
3. The swap has a specific notional amount in each currency and maturity. Based on these two notional amounts, there is a corresponding implied exchange rate. Usually, in a fixed/fixed currency swap, the same exchange rate is applied to all payments. The floating side has a specified index, e.g., three-month LIBOR.

Structural Variations

All of the variations available in interest-rate swaps are present in currency swaps with the additional variable of the currency of the cash flows. In this section, we will examine some of the more common variants. The examples that have been employed to illustrate the structural variations mostly use the yen and the dollar as the currencies, but are equally applicable to all currencies. Many of the examples closely parallel those illustrating structural variations in interest-rate swaps. A comparative study would be insightful.

Standard Currency Swap

An interest-rate swap is an exchange of only the interest payments on a given notional amount. The principal amounts are not exchanged. In contrast, a currency swap consists of the exchange of interest payments as well as principal amounts. In an interest rate swap, we have the exchange of floating- and fixed-rate payments. In a currency swap, the addition of the currency element adds a new basic dimension. Thus, one is not restricted to swapping fixed against floating payments. For the yen/dollar combination, we thus have the following types of swaps:

(1) fixed yen vs. fixed dollar (2) fixed yen vs. floating dollar (3) floating yen vs. floating dollar, and finally, (4) floating yen vs. fixed dollar. Among these four variations, the fixed yen for floating dollar swap is currently the most common and most widely quoted. In other currencies, one of the other structures might be more popular. For example, among the four basic varieties of sterling swaps, the floating sterling vs. floating dollar swap is the most common.

Situation *(Funding below Cost Target).* JSC, a Japanese shipping corporation, is seeking Y3.5 billion of funding for 10 years on a fixed-rate basis. JSC can borrow domestically at 5.05 percent. This rate is slightly higher than its target rate of 5.00 percent. It can raise floating dollar funds in the Eurobond market at LIBOR flat.

Using the currency-swap market, JSC finds that it can finance below its fixed yen funding target by raising $28 million floating rate funds in the Euro market and swapping into fixed yen. The dollar value, $28 million, is determined by converting the yen amount of Y3.5 billion at the exchange rate of 125 yen to the dollar. Under the swap, JSC pays yen interest at the fixed rate of 4.92 percent on Y3.5

EXHIBIT 3–5 Funding below Cost Target

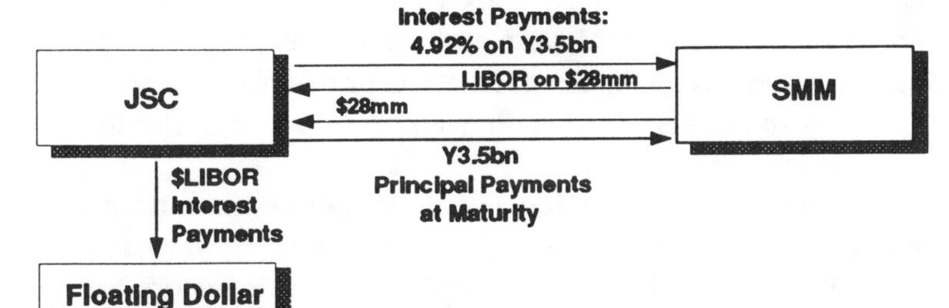

billion and receives dollar LIBOR on $28 million. At maturity, JSC will pay Y3.5 billion and receive $28 million. Effectively, JSC will have a 10-year funding at a fixed rate of 4.92 percent on Y3.5 billion.

Coupon-Only Swap

Currency swaps usually involve the exchange of principal amounts at maturity. Only by including this exchange can a borrowing (or asset) in one currency be converted effectively into a borrowing (or asset) in another currency. However, there are other situations where it is advantageous to eliminate the exchange of principal amounts and swap only the interest payments as in an interest-rate swap. This results in a *coupon-only swap.* This structure is sometimes also called an *annuity swap.*

Situation *(Hedging a Dual Currency Bond).* Uco, a U.S. multinational, is interested in raising cheap dollar funds for 5 years. Finding that investors in Europe pay a premium for instruments that offer opportunities to benefit from changes in the currency exchange rates, Uco is considering a dual currency bond. The bond is set up such that periodic interest payments are made annually in yen on a given notional amount, but the principal is paid in dollars.

Uco can swap the dual currency bond into a dollar liability by means of a coupon-only swap. Under the swap, as in Exhibit 3–2, Uco will pay dollars and receive yen to cover the interest payments on the bond. Since the principal on the bond is already in dollars, there is no need to include it under the swap agreement.

Uco, after hedging using the swap, achieves funding that is effectively in dollars; it is indifferent to the yen/dollar exchange rate. The premium paid by the investors for the dual currency bond translates into a lower net interest-rate cost for Uco. On the other hand, the investors have an opportunity to benefit significantly if the exchange rate be-

EXHIBIT 3–6 Hedging a Dual Currency Bond

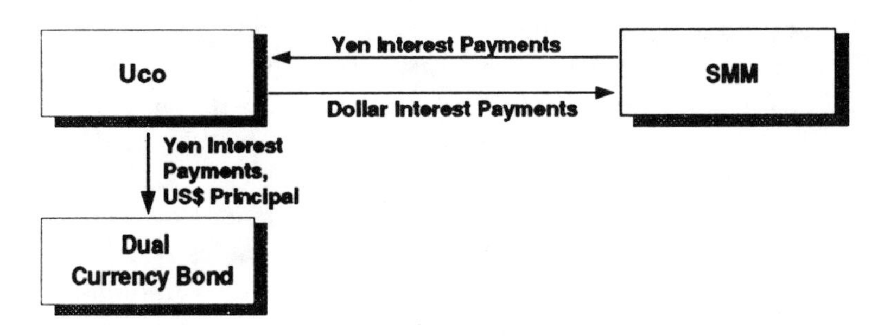

tween the dollar and the yen changes. Investors seeking dollars will benefit if the yen gets stronger via the yen coupon payments. Investors seeking yen will benefit if the dollar gets stronger against the yen as the dollar principal payment will be worth more in yen.

Off-Market Swap

Currency swaps are usually initiated such that their initial value is zero. That is, the present value of the cash flows to be paid equals the present value of the cash flows to be received. Any change in the market rates, i.e., interest rates in the two currencies as well as the exchange rate between the currencies, or just the passage of time, will cause the value of the swap to diverge from zero. A currency swap with nonzero value is called an *off-market swap.* If a new swap is off-market, then a compensating upfront payment from one party to the other will be required to bring the net value to zero. As an alternative to upfront cash payment, the value of a currency swap can also be adjusted to zero by using an off-market coupon on one side of the swap or by using an off-market exchange rate.

Situation *(Hedging a Convertible Bond).* JEC is a Japanese electronics company which has just issued a 10-year dollar-denominated convertible bond in the Euromarket. JEC has estimated that the bond will be outstanding for about 4 years, after which conversion is highly likely. JEC would like to convert just the fixed cash flows corresponding to the convertible bond into floating yen. JEC will leave the equity exposure due to the convertibility feature of the bond unhedged.

The coupon on the bond is most likely to be below market, given that the bond at the time of issue had conversion rights. Therefore, JEC enters into an off-market yen-dollar currency swap. JEC receives cash up front from the swap provider. As an alternative to receiving cash, JEC can also enter into a swap in which it pays a lower-than-market coupon.

Off-market swaps are used mostly to unwind or reverse out of older currency swaps where the interest rates or currency exchange rates have moved since the inception of the swaps. They are also used in cases (see "Asset Swaps," below) where a given cash flow needs to be matched exactly. They can also be used to create discount or premium assets or liabilities in conjunction with a change in currency, as in the discussion of zero-coupon swaps below.

EXHIBIT 3–7 Hedging a Convertible Bond

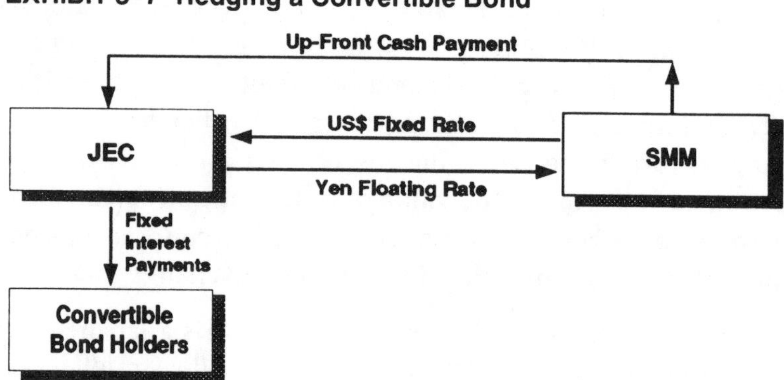

Zero-Coupon Swap

A *zero-coupon swap* is an extreme case of an off-market swap in which one of the counterparties makes a lump sum payment instead of periodic payments over time.

Situation *(Conserving Cash with a Synthetic Zero-Coupon Liability)*. JTC, a Japanese trading company, has recently issued a fixed-rate, 5-year dollar-denominated bond in the Eurobond market. It is considering swapping the bond into a fixed-rate yen liability. However, current considerations dictate that conservation of cash as much as possible for operational reasons is optimal. Therefore, JTC would prefer a zero-coupon funding. JTC has already explored a direct zero-coupon issue in the bond markets. However, the investor appetite for such a bond is very limited and retiring the just-issued coupon bond is expensive and difficult.

JTC can convert its current-coupon bond into a synthetic zero, coupon liability by means of a zero-coupon currency swap. Under the swap, JTC will receive fixed-rate dollar cash flows for 5 years and the dollar principal payment at maturity. These cash flows will exactly service the outstanding Eurobond. As part of the swap contract, JTC will

EXHIBIT 3–8 Conserving Cash with a Zero-Coupon Liability

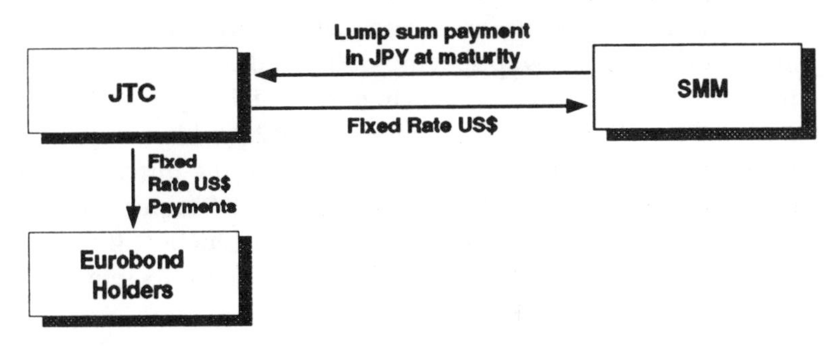

make a lump sum payment in yen at maturity. This payment is the effective fixed-rate zero-coupon liability for JTC.

Other variations of the zero-coupon swap are possible. The lump sum payment can occur at any time, up front, at maturity, or during the life of the swap.

Basis Swap

A *basis swap* entails two floating-rate indexes, one in each currency. An example is when yen LIBOR interest payments are swapped against dollar LIBOR interest payments on the same notional principal amount. A basis swap can be a full currency swap, that is, including the exchange of principal amounts at maturity, or it can be a coupon-only swap. LIBOR-based cross-currency basis swaps are generally not LIBOR flat to LIBOR flat mainly because of supply and demand pressures.

Situation *(Reducing Basis Risk).* JFC, a Japanese finance company, has an active Euroyen commercial paper program. It has just made dollar loan of $20 million based on LIBOR. It would like to convert some of its commercial paper liability into floating-rate dollars tied to LIBOR, so as to reduce the basis risk between the commercial paper liability and the LIBOR floating-rate dollar asset.

To closely match its asset and liability cash flow, JFC enters into a basis swap, paying dollar LIBOR and receiving yen LIBOR. Using an exchange rate of 125 yen to the dollar, JFC will exchange $20 million for Y2.5 billion at maturity. Note that JFC retains the exposure to the difference between yen LIBOR and Euroyen commercial paper rate, because it can obtain a better price for the LIBOR/LIBOR swap than a CP/LIBOR swap-generating enough savings to outweigh the CP-LIBOR spread risk.

EXHIBIT 3–9 Reducing Basis Risk

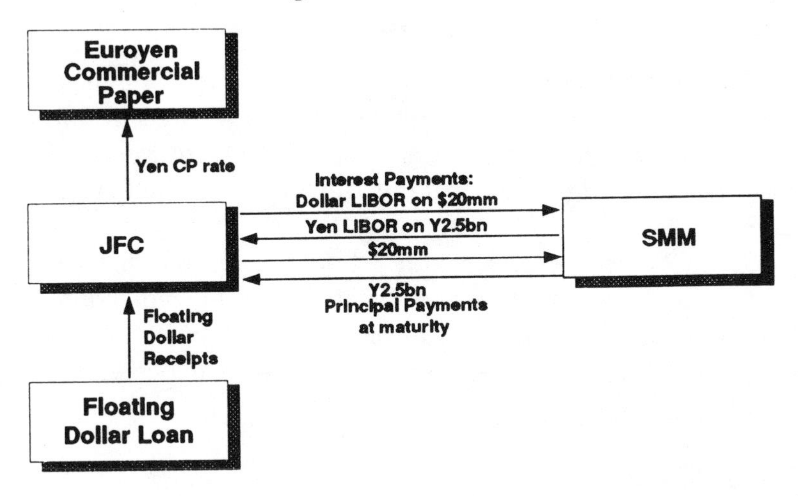

In some currencies, the basis swap is more common transaction than the fixed for fixed or even the fixed for floating swap. For example, the sterling LIBOR for dollar LIBOR swap is a very popular swap transaction.

The Asset Swap—Synthetic Securities

Swaps are used not only for managing liabilities, but also for engineering the cash flows from assets into desired formats. For example, a yen asset can be converted into a synthetic dollar asset using a currency swap.

> ***Situation*** *(Creating a Synthetic Dollar Asset).* JI, a Japanese investment firm, has just acquired a fixed-rate yen bond at an attractive yield. JI would like to convert the bond into a dollar LIBOR asset.
>
> JI can effect this conversion by entering into an asset swap. Under the swap contract, JI will essentially pay all the yen cash flows received from the asset, including the yen principal, to the swap counterparty. It will receive dol-

lar LIBOR payments periodically, and a dollar balloon payment (representing the principal) at maturity.

Note that the currency swap entered into may be an off-market swap so as to precisely match the cash flows from the yen bond. Also, the swap counterparty might require that the yen asset be pledged as collateral, depending upon the credit rating of JI.

Synthetic assets can provide attractive returns relative to conventional securities. However, it should be remembered that synthetic assets in general have lower liquidity and are appropriate only in those cases where they are expected to be held to maturity.

Forward Swap

A *forward swap* is one in which there is a significant delay between the date on which the swap is traded or committed to and the settlement or effective date of the swap.

Situation *(Hedging a Planned Bond Issue).* JC is a Japanese conglomerate that is planning to make a substantial capital commitment in the United States in the near future, three months from now. It has determined that the optimal strategy would be to issue fixed-rate yen bonds in the Euromarket and swap them into fixed-rate dollars. Clearly, the company is subject to two types of risk:

EXHIBIT 3–10 Creating a Synthetic U.S. Dollar Asset

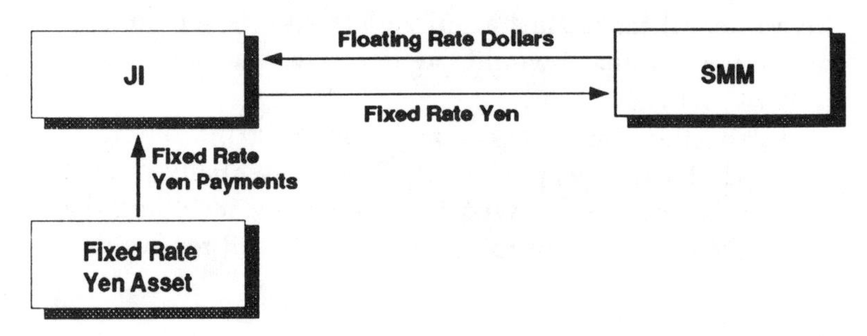

- the risk that the currency exchange rate might move in an adverse direction, i.e., strengthening dollar
- the risk that the fixed-yen interest rate might move up significantly

JC's problem is not as simple as it first appears, and cannot easily be solved with a straightforward forward currency swap. The situation is more complex because a simple forward currency swap will hedge just the currency risk but not the interest-rate risk.

JC needs a three-step approach.

Swap 1: First, JC can hedge its interest-rate risk in yen by entering into a forward starting fixed/floating yen interest-rate swap. The swap will settle or become effective three months from today, coinciding with the planned Eurobond issue. Under the swap, JC will pay a fixed rate (Y1 percent, say) and receive yen LIBOR. This forward swap effectively locks in the fixed cost of the future planned yen bond issue. Analytically, if yen interest rates are higher (lower), the increased (decreased) cost of the bond issue will be offset by the gain (loss) in this interest-rate swap.

Swap 2: Second, JC can hedge its currency exposure by entering into a forward starting currency swap. Under the swap, JC will pay fixed-rate dollars and receive fixed-rate yen at Y1 percent.

Swap 3: Finally, at the time of the bond issue, JC enters into a yen interest-rate swap, converting its fixed-yen obligation to floating. Under the swap, JC will receive a fixed-rate Y2 percent and pay yen LIBOR. On the bond issue, JC will pay a fixed rate of Y2 percent.[1] In the final situation, as

---

1 JC takes the basis risk between the bond rate and the swap rate, i.e., the risk that the interest rate on the bond issue and the swap rate might move by different amounts.

shown in Exhibit 3–11, all flows net out to the same fixed dollar cost as in Swap 2.

In practice, Swap 1 and Swap 2 are combined into one forward swap under which JC pays a fixed-dollar rate and receives yen LIBOR. It is interesting to note that a swap with a floating-yen leg is used to hedge a fixed-yen bond.

Forward swaps can be used similarly in conjunction with planned future asset acquisitions.

Swaps with Variable Notional Amount

Usually, the notional or the principal amount of a swap is held constant throughout the life of the swap. However, situations might arise where there is a need for varying the notional principal. The more common varieties of variable notional principal swaps are discussed below.

In *amortizing swaps,* the notional principal starts at a high level and gradually decreases. An amortizing swap is suitable when the asset or liability being hedged is itself amortizing. It is possible to analyze and price an amortizing swap as a combination of smaller swaps of different maturities. A *step-down swap* is similar to an amortizing swap. Its notional principal falls in one or more steps over time.

An *accreting swap* is one in which the notional principal starts low and slowly increases over the life of the swap.

Situation *(Hedging a Project Loan).* LAP is a Latin American Project that has secured a floating-rate yen loan from Japanese investors for a construction project. The revenues from the project are mainly in U.S. dollars. It intends to draw down on the loan as the construction progresses. Also, it wishes to execute a hedge to convert the liability into dollars now because it finds the current exchange rate to be attractive.

One alternative for LAP is to enter into a series of currency swaps, receiving yen and paying dollars, as and when the loan

EXHIBIT 3–11 Creating a Synthetic U.S. Dollar Liability

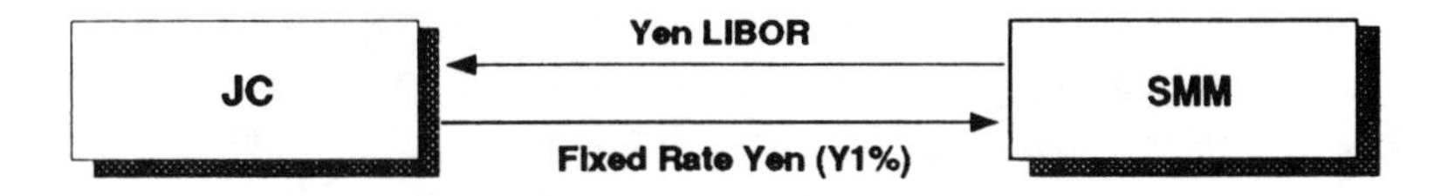

Forward Swap 1: Yen/Yen Interest Rate Swap

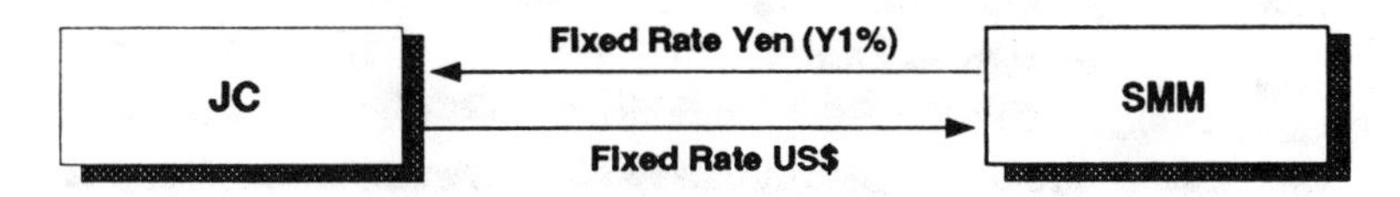

Forward Swap 2: Yen/US$ Currency Swap

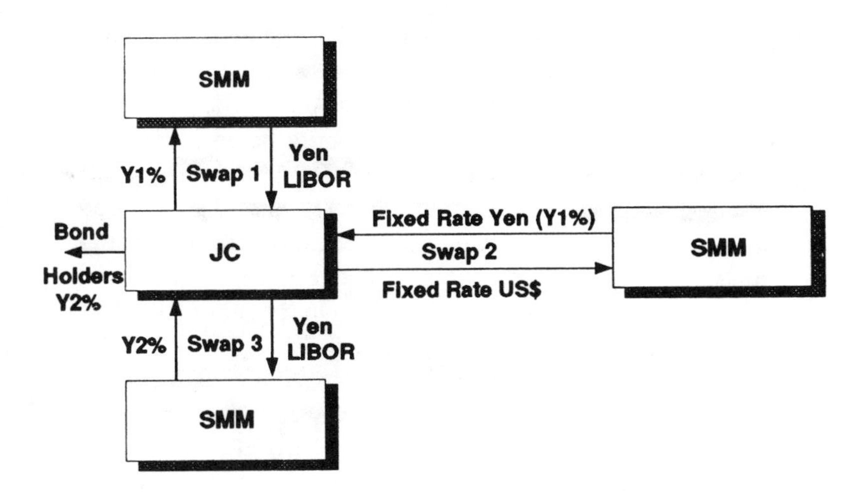

is drawn down. In addition to the inconvenience of a potentially large number of small-sized transactions, this option also exposes LAP to changes in future exchange rates. An acceptable alternative is to enter into an accreting currency swap with the notional principal increasing in step with the planned drawdown of the loan. The swap would be priced based on current market conditions, thus providing LAP protection from future changes in exchange rates.

Two observations are notable in the context of this example. First, LAP assumes the small risk that the actual drawdowns may not exactly match the planned drawdowns on which the swap is based. In most real-world situations, it is best to retain this type of small, unquantifiable risk rather than hedge it out to the last penny by introducing optionlike features in the currency swap. The incremental cost of the optional features would probably not be justified in view of the small size of the risk. One reason for this is that any option incorporated into a swap is priced based on the potential movement of interest and exchange rates whereas the drawdowns on the loan may not be so strongly correlated with market rate levels. Thus, buying optional features for the risk could be an overhedge. One simple principal to follow is to hedge *generic* risks in the market through derivatives, and retain *specific* risks. This way we apportion the task of hedging among different players optimally. In this example, LAP is far better equipped to handle the specific risk than any swap dealer. On the other hand, the swap dealer can easily hedge the market risk.

Secondly, notice that LAP could also achieve its goals by entering into a number of forward swaps,[2] each corresponding to a planned drawdown. This illustrates the

---

2 The main reason that this forward swap is much simpler than in the case of JC in the previous situation is that the yen loan is at a floating rate. A fixed-rate loan can also be hedged in a similar simple way as long as the loan rate is fixed at the outset.

point that, conceptually, an accreting swap is simply a combination of forward swaps.

A *roller-coaster* swap combines the properties of step-up and step-down swaps, with its notional principal increasing and decreasing at different times. Such a swap is used to engineer, in detail, cash flows to a specific need. They are relatively less common in practice.

Situation *(Hedging a Construction Loan).* JCC is a Japanese construction company. It has secured a yen loan for a construction project in the United States. The terms of the loan require JCC to draw down the funds as the project progresses. The terms also require gradual repayment as soon as the project is completed and begins to produce income. The expenses and income from the project are in U.S. dollars.

JCC can hedge the currency risk inherent in this project and its funding by means of a roller-coaster currency swap. The notional principal of the swap is set to increase in step with the projected drawdown schedule of the loan. Once the loan has been completely drawn down, the notional amount is set to decrease according to the projected cash flow to be received from the project.

As in the case of LAP above, note that JCC retains the residual risk that the actual drawdowns and the actual cash flow from the project may not be exactly the same as the projected amounts. We believe that it is prudent on the part of JCC to accept this risk.

Summary

We have examined several variations of the basic structure of currency swaps. This discussion is by no means exhaustive. We have touched upon just the major varieties. Since a swap is a privately negotiated contract between two parties, it can be sculpted to meet the needs of the situation. However, we recommend moderation in complicating a transaction, unless otherwise warranted. Undue complexity always extracts its price. Similarly, we recommend hedging generic risks rather than specific risks, unless the situation demands otherwise.

4

An Approach to Hedging

Hedging in an Asset/Liability Context

In most applications, interest-rate swaps are used for hedging. We can define hedging as the process by which we bridge the gap (i.e., eliminate or reduce the difference) between the needed cash flow and the cash flow that actually exists. The difference or the gap can be measured in terms of the actual cash flows, or in terms of certain summary measures of cash flows such as average life, maturity, etc., as discussed below. For example, a borrower corporation might have a gap between the floating-rate funds it has and the fixed-rate financing it needs. When the corporation executes an interest-rate swap under which it pays fixed and receives floating, it is entering into a hedging transaction.

Hedging is more clearly defined within an *asset/liability management (ALM)* framework in which we bridge the gap between the assets of a corporation and its liabilities.[1] ALM can best be discussed in the context of a financial institution, and it is worthwhile to digress a little to focus

1 ALM and hedging are so similar in concept that we use these two terms interchangeably in this chapter.

on this subset of swap users to understand the concept of hedging and ALM. The issues discussed and the conclusions drawn are applicable, though admittedly to a lesser degree, to other corporate users of financial instruments. An approach to corporate, i.e., nonfinancial institutional, use of swaps is presented in a later section of this chapter.

The main function of financial institutions is to intermediate between other parties. By taking the attendant intermediation risks, they provide a valuable service and, in return, earn a spread. Not long ago, intermediation mainly meant providing the liquidity demanded by the market, and, to some extent, provide insulation from credit risk. Today, a primary intermediation risk is related to interest rates. One of the chief reasons for this is the large magnitude and increased frequency of interest-rate moves.

Consider an example of the need for interest-rate intermediation. Suppose that the demand for short-term liabilities exceeds that for short-term assets. In this situation, a financial institution can play an important role by accepting the short liabilities and investing in long assets. However, in providing this service, the institution exposes itself to interest-rate risk because the values of the short-term liabilities and long-term assets change differently in response to interest-rate moves. Thus, being highly leveraged, financial institutions are exposed to significant interest-rate risk because of such intermediation. Massive losses are often a symptom of the failure to manage such risk properly. ALM is a systematic approach that attempts to provide a degree of protection to the institution from intermediation risk and makes such risk acceptable. As such, ALM provides the necessary framework to define, measure, monitor, modify, and manage interest-rate risk.

In a way, we can compare hedging or ALM to a form of insurance. It shields the institution from the necessary evil of intermediation risk. For example, in the absence of automobile insurance, we would probably find the risks of driving a car unacceptable. It is insurance that makes it possible for us to drive. The main function of ALM is similar: it is to enable the financial institution to be in business, that is, to assume intermediation risk. For example, it improves a bank's ability to make long-term loans that are in demand regardless of whether long-term funding for the loan is available, by providing acceptable techniques to hedge the resultant interest-rate risk. The more leveraged an institution, the more critical ALM is to that institution. This is because its net worth then is a small fraction of the size of its assets and even modest market moves can result in wide swings in the net worth. ALM is simply the process of preservation of net worth.

The function of ALM is not just protection from risk. The safety achieved through ALM also opens up opportunities for enhancing the net worth. ALM can make it possible for an institution to take on positions that would have been considered too large in the absence of the protection offered by ALM. ALM can also enable an institution to enter into new business areas as the demands of the marketplace change and grow. In many cases these businesses would have been beyond the reach of the institution without the comfort of the ALM insurance.

Every manager has two fundamental priorities. The first priority is to protect and preserve the existing business, provide damage control. The second priority is to enhance the returns, strengthen the business and enrich the institution. ALM, as discussed above, can be a vital ally to the manager in fulfilling these two priorities.

ALM is a more general concept than it appears at first blush. In fact, most financial activity can be analyzed from an ALM point of view. A transaction hedging a specific trading position is simply the process of creating a liability (or asset as the case may be) to match the price sensitivity of a portfolio. Pension investing attempts to match investments to implicit or explicit liabilities. Insurance companies routinely match investments to their liabilities such as guaranteed investment contracts (GICs). It is therefore essential for all participants in the financial markets to obtain a good understanding of the issues involved in hedging within an ALM framework.

Measures of Interest-Rate Risk

As a first step in developing a hedging framework, we have to define interest-rate risk and determine an acceptable way to measure it. This discussion naturally assumes the context of fixed-income securities. Many of the concepts have historically been developed in the investment area. They are equally applicable to the liability side and to interest-rate and currency derivatives as well.

Interest-Rate Risk.[2] We measure interest-rate risk by considering *price sensitivity,* that is, the change in the value of an asset (or liability) in response to change in interest rates. More precisely, price sensitivity is expressed as a percentage change in value for 1 percent (that is, 100 basis point) change in interest rates.

Different fixed-income instruments have different levels of interest-rate risk. Various risk measures are available, each with its own advantages and problems.

Maturity. The term to maturity is an indicator of interest-rate risk. Longer-maturity bonds usually move more in price than shorter-maturity bonds. However, this ordering

---

2 For a thorough discussion of interest-rate risk measures and convexity, see Ravi E. Dattatreya and Frank J. Fabozzi, *Active Total Return Management of Fixed-Income Portfolios* (Chicago: Probus, 1989).

does not always hold. Maturity takes into account only the timing of the final principal flow in a fixed-rate bond, and ignores other important information such as the size and timing of other cash flows. The actual interest-rate sensitivity depends upon these factors and therefore, maturity, though sometimes useful, is only an approximate indicator of risk. Maturity is also not a cardinal measure, that is, it does not quantify risk.

Average Life. When the principal on an instrument is not paid on the maturity date, but rather is paid down in partial amounts over time, then an average life is computed for such a security. This is simply the weighted average of the times at which the principal pays down. The weight used for a given time is the proportion of principal paid down at that time. In terms of risk measurement, the average life is just as useful and has the same limitations as maturity.

Duration. Frederick Macaulay discovered that it is possible to blend information contained in the size and timing of all cash flows into one number, called *duration,* that can be a more useful measure of risk. Duration is the weighted average time of all of the cash flows, the weights being the present values of the cash flows. For bonds with only one cash flow, e.g., zero-coupon bonds and money-market instruments, duration is equal to maturity. For others, duration will be shorter than maturity.

We can also think of duration of a security or a cash flow as the maturity of a zero-coupon bond of equal price sensitivity. This definition is a more general one in that it can be used with more complex securities such as options and with leveraged positions. For example, if the duration of an option is 150, it simply means that the price sensitivity of the option is equal to that of a zero-coupon bond of maturity equal to 150 years.

TABLE 4–1 Computing the Duration of a 5-Year 4% Bond Priced at Par

Semi-Annual Period	Time	CF	Pr. Val of CF	PR. Val of CF x time
1	0.50	2.00	1.96	0.98
2	1.00	2.00	1.92	1.92
3	1.50	2.00	1.88	2.83
4	2.00	2.00	1.85	3.70
5	2.50	2.00	1.81	4.53
6	3.00	2.00	1.78	5.33
7	3.50	2.00	1.74	6.09
8	4.00	2.00	1.71	6.83
9	4.50	2.00	1.67	7.53
10	5.00	102.00	83.68	418.38
		Totals:	**100.00**	**458.11**
		Duration:	**458.11/100 = 4.5811**	

It turns out that by slightly adjusting duration by dividing by a factor (1 + Y/2) where Y is the annual yield to maturity of the bond in decimal form, we get *modified duration* which is exactly equal to the price sensitivity of the bond as we have defined above. Since the adjustment factor is very close to 1, duration and modified duration can be used interchangeably in most situations. This is also justified because duration is an approximate measure anyway. By this reasoning, we diligently avoid the common temptation to dwell on the (inconsequential) difference between the two durations.

Dollar Duration. Duration represents the *percentage* change in value in response to a change in rates. By weighting duration by the value of a holding, that is, by multiplying the market value of a holding by its duration (expressed as a decimal percentage), we get dollar-weighted duration. Known as *dollar duration,* this number represents the actual dollar change in the market value of a holding in a bond in response to a percentage change in rates. When expressed as a dollar change per one basis point move in rates, dollar duration is sometimes called the *price value of a basis point,* or *PVBP.* Other than the factor of 100, there is no difference between dollar duration and PVBP.

The major advantage of using dollar duration is that it is additive. The concept, therefore, extends easily from individual securities to portfolios. The dollar duration of a portfolio is simply the (algebraic) sum of the dollar durations of the individual holdings.

Duration of an Interest-Rate Swap.[3] Unlike a bond, a swap has two-way cash flows. The additivity of dollar duration is helpful in determining the risk parameters of a swap. The dollar duration of a swap is simply the algebraic sum of the dollar durations of the two cash flows.

The dollar duration of each leg of a swap can be more easily determined by modifying the cash flow in the following way: if we add a principal cash inflow and another equal and opposite cash outflow, both at maturity, the situation gets simplified without changing the price or risk of the swap. The cash flow on the fixed side of the swap now resembles the cash flow from a fixed-rate bond. The cash

3 The duration of a swap is more completely discussed in chapter 6, "Pricing and Risk Characteristics."

flow on the floating side of the swap resembles that from a floating-rate note. The dollar duration of a floating-rate note just before the rate is set is very small. Thus, the dollar duration of an at-market swap is equal to the dollar duration of a par bond with equal maturity and coupon equal to the swap rate. When rates move, the dollar duration of the floating side essentially remains small. Therefore, the dollar duration of the swap can be assumed to be equal to that of the corresponding bond with equal coupon and maturity even when the swap is not at market.

It is less useful to define the duration of a swap. Since the present value of an at-market swap is zero, duration, which is the percentage change in value, is undefined.[4] In general, dollar duration is a much better parameter to use with derivatives than duration.

Convexity. Duration (or dollar duration) is not a constant. It changes as a result of changes in the market rates and because of the passage of time as well. This is known as *duration drift*. For simple fixed-coupon bonds, the dollar duration increases when the rates fall. That is, as the market rallies (falling rates), for each successive basis-point drop, the bond price increases at an increasing rate. Similarly, if rates increase and the market declines, the rate of decline slows down as the rates rise. This property is called *convexity*. It is a desirable property in an asset since the price sensitivity changes in a way beneficial to the holder of the asset.

There are certain securities with optionlike features such as callable corporate bonds and mortgage-backed securities that show a contrary behavior: their duration can fall

---

4 Note that duration of an off-market swap is well defined. Also, in a portfolio context, when a swap is combined with an asset or a liability, the duration concept becomes useful.

in rallying markets and increase in falling markets. This property, called *negative convexity,* is not a desirable property in an asset as the price sensitivity moves in a way not beneficial to the holder. Negative convexity is desirable in a liability.

In most situations, convexity is a second-order effect. That is, its influence on the price behavior of a bond is small compared to that of duration. However, for large moves in market rates, for highly leveraged positions, and where optionlike features are involved, convexity can be important.

Simple Hedging Concepts

Once we have defined interest-rate risk and determined the risk in assets and liabilities, the second step is to ensure that the net worth, that is, the difference between the assets and liabilities, has no (or the desired) interest-rate risk. Since dollar duration is additive, the risk or the dollar duration of the net worth will be the difference between the dollar duration of the assets and that of the liabilities:

Net Worth = Asset Value – Liability Value
Dollar Duration of Net Worth =
Dollar Duration of Asset – Dollar Duration of Liability

If the dollar duration of the assets exceeds that of the liabilities, then the net worth has positive duration, that is, it will increase in falling rate environments and decrease when the rates rise. On the other hand, if the dollar duration of the assets is less than that of the liabilities, then the net worth has negative duration. In this case, it behaves like a short position in a bond, that is, its value increases as rates rise and decreases as rates fall.

The goal of hedging is to bring the dollar duration of the net worth as close to the desired level as possible. Usually, in order to insulate the net worth from interest-rate movements, we would want this dollar duration to be zero.[5] In other words, we would want the dollar durations of the assets and liabilities to be equal. In addition, we would want some stability in this equality, that is, we would want the convexity of the assets to be equal to (or greater than) that of the liabilities.

Since the dollar duration of a swap is equal to that of a similar bond, when a swap is used to hedge a bond, it is a general practice simply to match the notional amounts of the swap and the bond.

The additivity of the dollar duration is helpful in the hedging process. We can increase the net dollar duration by purchasing appropriate hedging vehicles or decrease it by selling them. There are also negative-duration assets, e.g., put options, that can be purchased to decrease dollar duration.

> ***Situation*** *(Using Dollar Duration for Hedging).* ELC is an equipment leasing company. Its assets are leases which generate mostly fixed cash flow and its liabilities are mostly fixed-rate bond issues and commercial paper swapped to fixed. In getting ready to borrow $5,000,000 of new money, ELC has done duration analysis on its portfolio of assets and liabilities and has determined that the dollar duration of its assets is $2,000,000. That is, for every 100 basis-point change in rates, the value of the assets will change approximately $2,000,000. The dollar duration of the liabilities is $2,500,000. Thus, there is an asset/liability gap. The dollar duration of the net worth is –$500,000

---

5 This position is known as *delta-neutral* in terminology related to the option markets. If we think of dollar duration as the delta, a duration-hedged position will be delta-neutral, i.e., has a dollar duration of zero.

($2,000,000 – $2,500,000). Since the dollar duration is negative, the net worth will increase if rates rise and decrease if rates fall. That is, ELC is net short.

In order to match the dollar durations of assets and liabilities, ELC has to purchase some long assets, or enter into an interest-rate swap in which it receives fixed, to add the additional duration that it needs. Suppose that a swap with a dollar duration of $105 for every $1,000 of notional amount is available. Also suppose that ELC raises $5,000,000 in floating-rate funds based on 6-month LIBOR.

This will create a liability of $5,000,000 with a duration of (approximately) 6 months (0.5 year) or a dollar duration of $25,000 ($5,000,000 times the decimal representation of duration, 0.005). Therefore, the dollar duration of the liabilities will increase to $2,525,000 ($2,500,000 + $25,000).

If ELC enters into a swap in the notional amount of $5,000,000, then, the swap will add a dollar duration of $525,000 ($5,000,000 of swap with $105 dollar duration per $1,000 of swap). Therefore the total dollar duration of the assets becomes $2,525,000 ($2,000,000 + $525,000). The dollar durations of the assets and liabilities are now equal.

This situation illustrates an important methodology for managing assets and liabilities. By using summary measures, it is possible to make hedging decisions on a portfoliowide basis rather than at the level of each single asset and liability. In general, the portfolio approach is more efficient as it eliminates wasteful offsetting hedges. At the same time, it allows the manager to optimally select the hedge instrument.

When we use duration to hedge, we are making a fundamental, though unstated, assumption that the yield levels of the different assets and liabilities and the hedging vehicle will move in parallel, that is, by equal amounts. We will see how to relax this assumption later. Also note that the requirement of zero dollar duration does not help determine the duration and the amount of the hedging instrument. Since dollar duration is the product of the duration and the amount, various combinations of the two can result in a duration-neutral hedge. In addition, duration hedges are vulnerable to duration drift.

Hedging Cost

The stated cost of a liability (or the stated return on an asset) changes when it is hedged. The posthedging cost (or return) will be in line with the reduced nature of the risk involved and will be similar to that obtainable on instruments of similar risk in the market.

Situation *(Illustrating Hedging Cost).* ACC is an automotive credit company. The market environment is that the 6-month LIBOR is at 8 percent, the 10-year Treasury is at 8.05 percent, and the 10-year swap spread is at 75 basis points. ACC is considering two alternative ways to raise funds:

(a) Short-term borrowing at LIBOR less 10 basis points. This borrowing will be rolled as long as needed.
(b) A 10-year bond issue with a coupon rate of 8.75 percent.

If the short-term borrowing option is chosen, ACC is considering hedging by swapping into fixed.[6] On the swap, ACC will pay Treasury + 75 b.p., or 8.80 percent, and receive LIBOR. Thus, the net initial coupon rate will be 5 basis points below the bond coupon, or 8.70 percent. (Swap receipt LIBOR, less 8.70 percent swap payment less LIBOR – 10 b.p. interest expense on the borrowing.) This is 80 basis points (8.70 percent minus 7.90 percent) above the coupon rate of 7.90 percent (LIBOR, 8 percent, less 10 b.p.) on the unhedged borrowing.

---

6 The question of whether a short-term borrowing can be hedged by swapping to fixed is discussed in a later section under "Duality in Hedging."

The difference between the stated cost before and after hedging is often considered to be the *cost of hedging*.[7] However, it is important to distinguish between true costs and stated costs.

First, the stated cost, e.g., the coupon rate or the yield to maturity on a bond, is rarely the actual cost paid by the borrower. The total cost realized depends upon other factors such as the financing rate applied to intermediate (i.e., coupon) cash flows and the call or redemption price of the bond. Thus, the actual cost is subject to various market risks.

Second, costs achieved under different risks are not directly comparable. For example, the (lower) stated cost on the (unhedged) short-term borrowing and the (relatively higher) cost from a long bond are not directly comparable. It is not correct to conclude that the short-term borrowing is a more attractive investment simply because its coupon rate is lower. Similarly, the cost of a hedged borrowing and that of an unhedged borrowing cannot be directly compared. This situation is somewhat similar to the case of an investor attracted to the relatively higher coupon rate on a low-rated or junk bond. It has a higher stated cost to compensate for the higher probability of default. Therefore, the investor should not conclude that a junk bond is an attractive investment simply because of its higher coupon. Similarly, in the example above, we should not directly compare the 7.90 percent rate on the short-term borrowing and the 8.70 percent effective coupon after hedging.

After hedging, it is reasonable that the net coupon (or cost) will be of the same order of magnitude as other instruments in the market with similar risk characteristics. If

---

7 Note that this cost is known only for the first 6 months.

this were not the case, arbitrage by astute and aggressive market participants will bring the spread into line. Depending on the market environment, e.g., when the yield curve is negatively sloped, a hedge transaction might actually *decrease* the effective coupon. Again, we should not conclude that this decrease is a hedging *profit*.

Third, the spread before hedging is not locked in.

> ***Situation*** *(Illustrating Hedging Cost—Continued).* Suppose that ACC can acquire a fixed-rate asset with the proceeds of the short-term borrowing and that the asset has a yield of 9.80 percent. This does not mean a spread of 190 (9.80 percent – 7.90 percent) basis points over the life of the bond since it could be larger or smaller subject to the level of LIBOR in each financing period.

On the other hand, after hedging the short-term borrowing by swapping it into fixed, the spread is locked in. After hedging, the spread is 110 basis points (9.80 percent from the asset less 8.70 percent swapped cost) over the entire life of the bond.

Again, the loss of 80 basis points of spread (190 b.p. spread before hedging less 110 b.p. after) is not to be considered the cost of hedging, as the two spreads, one locked in, one not, are not directly comparable. The same analysis also implies that we should not compare the 8.75 percent fixed-rate long bond to the alternative short-term rate of 8 percent. It is, however, appropriate to compare the bond issuance alternative, (b) in the example above, which costs 8.75 percent, to the hedged borrowing which costs 8.70 percent. The hedged alternative is more attractive by 5 basis points.

Hedging, therefore, makes possible fair comparison between alternative borrowing and investment strategies. It uncovers the true costs and true spreads. This is the proper way to view hedging rather than as a transaction that creates a cost.

The *true* cost of hedging is in the *mispricing* of hedging vehicles. If we pay too high a price when purchasing a hedge or sell it too cheaply while lifting the hedge, then the excess price paid or the part not realized on the sale will result in an increase in interest expense, creating a genuine cost. For this reason, hedging should be approached with the same care and prudence as in investing when determining the relative values of the securities.

The discussion above of the cost of hedging reveals a very fundamental truth: the singular function of hedging is the preservation and enhancement of the net worth of an institution; duration matching and other activities associated with hedging are just tools and procedures to serve this primary purpose. It is best to view hedging within a total cost (or total return) framework. Then, hedging will begin to look very much like traditional portfolio management with the additional flexibility of using various hedging instruments and issuing liabilities.

Yield Curve Risk[8]

When corporations use the swap market for hedging, more often than not, the swap is designed to match precisely the gap between the existing cash flow and the desired cash flow. However, there do exist situations in which either the tailor-made swap may not be available due to maturity or credit restrictions, or it is considered not efficient. Or, the corporation might be using a hedging approach considering the portfolio as a whole. In these

---

8 For the discussion of yield curve risk, we will use the U.S. dollar market. The arguments and the development are applicable to other currencies as well.

cases, the corporation may decide to use the summary measures such as duration to arrive at an acceptable, though not an exact, hedging swap. This type of hedging is very common on the investor side in portfolio management, and is used by swap dealers as well.

As usually stated, duration of cash flows such as that from a fixed-income asset (or liability) is the price sensitivity relative to interest rates in certain maturities. Therefore, when we use duration for hedging purposes, we are implicitly assuming that the interest-rate levels of the various maturities move in parallel, that is, in equal amounts. In fact, however, different credit, coupon, or maturity sectors of the market move differently in terms of the appropriate rate. This difference is known as the *basis risk* among the sectors. Basis risk with respect to different maturity sectors is also known as *yield curve risk.* In fact, we can view the interest rate applicable to (i.e., the yield on) a security as the sum of the market rate, represented by the Treasury rates, and the spread or basis between the Treasury and the security. In certain cases, rates other than on Treasuries are used as a representation of the market. An example is LIBOR used as a standard in dealing with short-term rates and floating-rate instruments.

In general, basis risk is difficult to measure and hedge. Most hedging vehicles address the market risk,[9] that is, changes in the Treasury (or LIBOR) rates, not basis risk. It is possible to take the view that only market risk is hedgeable and treat basis risk as a prudent business risk that an

---

9 This makes sense because a hedging instrument, in order to ensure its wide usage, should represent the broad market rather than a specific security or too narrow a sector. Otherwise, it would suffer a severe lack of liquidity and the cost of hedging would be unacceptably high.

institution has to take. This is the only approach in dealing with certain types of basis risk, e.g., credit risk.[10]

It is important to understand basis risk, yield curve risk in particular, because perfect hedges are not always available or not always optimal from a price point of view. A second motivation to explore this risk further is that swap providers use liquid market instruments to hedge their swap positions and are open to yield curve risk. An understanding of the methodology by which swap providers hedge this risk is essential to gaining a good understanding of swap pricing.

Yield curve risk is also important from the corporate risk manager's point of view in another way. Usually, one of the goals of risk management has been to develop a judicious mix of fixed- and floating-rate funding. This is the way that the risk manager measures and manages yield curve risk. Floating-rate obligations, independent of their maturities, fall in the short-term sector of the curve. Fixed-rate obligations are grouped on the long-term sector of the curve. However, it is no longer sufficient to have a black-and-white view of liabilities and divide them into fixed and floating or short-term and long-term. Each maturity sector has developed its own characteristic behavior and it is now necessary to look at more finely divided buckets when analyzing liability portfolios. In addition, a liability with associated derivatives such as options and caps can change its nature of funding purely due to the passage of time or due to change in interest-rate levels. An excellent example is the callable bond that is commonly issued by corporations. When rates are much lower relative to the

10 Recently, however, there have been some interesting developments in the area of credit derivatives that can be used to hedge, to some extent, credit risk.

coupon, the bond behaves like a short-maturity bond. When rates are much higher relative to the coupon, the bond behaves like a long-maturity bond. At rate levels closer to the coupon, the bond has variable behavior somewhere between short-maturity and long-maturity.

Situation *(Variable Behavior of a Liability).* EC is an energy company. It issued a 10-year bond and swapped it into floating LIBOR. To provide for insurance against rising short-rates, EC also bought a 10-year cap at 8 percent.

EC's bond issue, along with the swap, is a floating-rate obligation. However, the cap can change the nature of the obligation depending upon interest-rate levels. If rates are high and, in particular, LIBOR is much above 8 percent, then the floating obligation of EC is for all practical purposes a fixed bond with a coupon of 8 percent. On the other hand, if rate levels are low (LIBOR much below 8 percent), then the effect of the cap is less and the obligation is a floater. For intermediate levels, the combination of the bond, the swap and the cap has behavior that is neither like a pure floating-rate bond nor a pure fixed-rate bond.

Thus, we need a more colorful way to describe the nature of liabilities (and assets) than the common binary or black-and-white method of characterizing them into fixed and floating. Fortunately, an acceptable method can be developed by fully understanding yield curve risk.

It is possible to address yield curve risk in many acceptable ways.

One method is to divide the assets and liabilities into smaller maturity baskets, and analyze each basket separately. If each basket covers a sufficiently small maturity range, then we can assume that the yield curve risk is acceptably small within that range. We would then use hedging tools suitable for that maturity range to match dollar durations. If each sector is thus matched, then the assets and liabilities are matched as a whole because of the additivity property of dollar duration. To the extent that the yields of all assets and liabilities as well as the hedging instruments used within a sector move in step, this approach is satisfactory.

There is a problem, however. It turns out that an asset of a given maturity might react to changes in rates in another maturity. Consider, for example, a 10-year bond with a coupon of 10 percent. The cash flows from this bond occur every six months throughout its life. Since the value of a bond is simply the sum of the present values of the individual cash flows, it stands to reason that the value of the 10-year bond is influenced by rate changes not just in the 10-year maturity but also in all shorter maturities representing the cash flows.

In this context, it is appropriate to clarify what we mean by a rate. In fixed-income analysis, we use two type of interest rates: full-coupon rates and spot or zero-coupon rates. Full-coupon rates are analogous to the yield to maturity on bonds trading at or close to par, e.g., the yield on an on-the-run (current coupon) Treasury. The spot rate for a given maturity, on the other hand, is the yield on a zero-coupon bond with that maturity. When dealing with individual cash flows, it is appropriate to use spot rates; when dealing with bonds trading near par, full-coupon rates can be used.

Since a bond is just a collection of cash flows, its yield is a complex blend of the individual spot rates corresponding to the coupon and principal flows. Given the spot rate curve, we can easily determine the coupon yield curve. Conversely, a given spot rate is a complex blend of all coupon rates. Given the coupon rate curve, we can determine the spot rate curve. In summary, a given spot rate depends upon all intermediate coupon rates; a given coupon rate depends upon all intermediate spot rates.

The value of a 10-year par bond, then, responds to all intermediate spot rates, but depends only on the 10-year coupon rate. Thus, to hedge a 10-year par bond, all that we need is another 10-year bond, e.g., the current 10-year Treasury. If we wish to use zero-coupon bonds for hedging, then smaller amounts of all intermediate maturity zero-coupon bonds will be required for hedging. Similarly, a cash flow occurring in the tenth year can be efficiently hedged by a 10-year zero-coupon bond. On the other hand, if we wish to use current-coupon Treasuries for hedging, then, in addition to the 10-year Treasury, we will also need shorter maturity Treasuries.

If the bond we are hedging is not priced at par, then it behaves like the combination of a 10-year full-coupon bond and a 10-year zero-coupon bond. For example, a $100 million holding of a 9 percent bond selling at 90 can be viewed as the sum of $90 million of a 10 percent par bond and $10 million of a zero-coupon bond.[11] Thus the sensitivity of the 10-year discount bond is the sum of that of each of its components. The hedge for a bond not near par, therefore, is a blend of the hedge for a zero- and that for a full-coupon bond.

In summary, then, an asset (or a liability) of a given maturity might respond to spot or coupon rate changes in other, shorter maturities. Therefore, we need to do more than simply group the assets and liabilities in maturity sectors.

---

11 In both cases, there is an annual cash flow of $9 million and a payment at maturity of $100 million.

One way to handle this problem is to first break down each asset and liability into its cash flow components. Then the individual cash flows can be grouped into maturity buckets. Now, the price sensitivity of each bucket is more clearly defined, at least with respect to spot rates corresponding to each bucket.

The cash flow approach provides very valuable insight into the relative natures of the assets and the liabilities. However, it represents risk in terms of spot rate, that is, in terms of zero-coupon bonds, which are rarely used for hedging. A more sophisticated approach is the *risk point method,* discussed below.

Hedging Yield Curve Risk—The Risk Point Method

Since risk is a measure of change in value, it stands to reason that risk management and security valuation ought to be closely related. Therefore, it is advantageous to use a procedure that integrates these two aspects in a hedging context. The risk point method attempts such an integration. It also has practical advantage in that it measures risk relative to available hedging instruments.

At the outset, the method acknowledges that in most situations a single hedge instrument is not adequate. We have seen in the earlier sections that the value of a security can change in response to market changes in many sectors along the yield curve. Thus, it is more efficient to use a collection of hedge instruments. The choice of hedge instruments depends upon the goal of the analysis. If a high-precision hedge is desired for trading purposes, then a broader range of tradeable, liquid securities should be used. If the aim is just risk measurement and monitoring, then, perhaps just a few bellwether securities, such as the on-the-run Treasuries, might be sufficient. Also, since we are combining valuation and hedging, the hedge instruments chosen will represent the market broadly, and their prices[12] (or yields) will provide enough parameters for valuation purposes.

We can think of the *risk point* of a portfolio relative to a given hedge instrument as *relative dollar duration*. It represents the change in the value of the portfolio due to a unit change in the price or yield of the hedge. The unit chosen depends upon the hedge used. For example, if a Treasury bond or note is the hedge, then the unit is usually one basis point. If a Eurodollar futures contract is the hedge, then a price change of one tick is used as the unit.

If we divide the risk point by the dollar duration of the hedge, it gives us the dollar amount of the hedge instrument to be used as a hedge. This hedge amount will protect the portfolio against risk from change in the value of the hedge.

Unlike dollar duration which measures the *total* interest-rate risk, the risk point measures only one component of the total risk.[13] This component represents the risk due to a change in rates in a given maturity sector. Thus, to determine a complete hedge, we need a full set of risk points, relative to a set of hedge instruments. From this set of risk points we can determine the portfolio of hedge instruments that will hedge a given portfolio.

The essential part of the risk point method is a model that values the assets and liabilities relative to the hedge instruments chosen. In order to be able to deal with a vari-

---

12 Other market data such as volatility will be needed to value options.

13 If only one hedge instrument is used in the computation of risk points rather than a comprehensive collection, then the risk point collapses to a form of the traditional dollar duration measure. Thus, the risk point measure for a security or a portfolio relative to a given hedge instrument depends upon what other hedge instruments are being used in the valuation.

ety of assets and liabilities, the set of hedges chosen must also be broad. The risk point method consists of three main steps:

- **Hedge Instruments**. We first select the hedge vehicles that we are willing to use. For a U.S. dollar asset or liability portfolio, a starting point would be the set of on-the-run Treasuries. For swap hedging, is it usual to include plain vanilla swaps and Eurodollar futures in this set. For dealing with short-term assets and liabilities, LIBOR based hedges such as Eurodollar futures are common.
- **Valuation Model**. We then apply a model that values the assets and liabilities *relative* to the prices of the hedge vehicles.

  An example of a valuation model of this type is as follows. Using the Treasury yields to maturity, a full-coupon yield curve is first generated by filling in the intermediate yield levels either by linear interpolation or by means of a smooth curve. Given this curve, it is possible to determine the spot curve by means of an iterative process.[14] Using LIBOR rates and/or Eurodollar futures and other rates, yield curves and corresponding spot curves are created for different credit classes as required. Once the spot rate curve is known, the value of any security is simply the sum of the present values of its cash flows, discounted at the appropriate spot rate. The spot rate curve is often more conveniently represented as a discount function which shows the price, that is, discounted value, of $1 at different maturities.

---

14 For a description of this procedure, see Ravi E. Dattatreya and Frank J. Fabozzi, *Active Total Return Management of Fixed-Income Portfolios*, (Chicago: Probus, 1989). See also the chapter on swap pricing.

Determination of Risk Points. To determine the risk point corresponding to a given hedge instrument, the following steps are taken: First, the yield on the hedge instrument is changed slightly, say, 1 basis point. Then the spot rates are recomputed using this new price for the particular hedge instrument, keeping the prices (and yields) for all other hedges the same as before. The value of the asset, liability, or portfolio is now recomputed. The change in the value of the asset due to the change in the price of the hedge upon normalization (i.e., expressed on the basis of a 100-basis-point change in yield) gives us the risk point relative to that hedge instrument. This procedure is repeated for all hedge instruments in the set of hedges chosen. The risk point relative to a hedge tells us the amount of the hedge to be bought (or sold) to hedge the portfolio against changes in the price of that hedge.[15]

The last step can be clarified by means of an example:

Example. Suppose that the 10-year current Treasury bond is one of the hedge instruments. First the portfolio is valued with the prevailing price of the hedges including the 10-year bond. Then the yield of the 10-year bond is changed by a small amount, say, one basis point. The portfolio is revalued. Suppose that the value of the portfolio changes by $210. That is, for a one basis-point change in the yield of the 10-year, the portfolio changes in value by $210. For a 100-basis-point change, the corresponding change in value is $21,000. This is the risk point of the portfolio relative to the 10-year Treasury.

---

15 It is also possible to express the risk point as a **hedge equivalent,** i.e., the actual amount of the hedge required. The vector of risk points, then, would simply be the hedging portfolio. Representation of the risk point as a relative dollar duration has the advantage that alternative hedge instruments can be easily substituted.

Suppose the dollar duration of the 10-year bond is 7 or $70 per $1,000 par holding. Then, the par amount of 10-year Treasury needed to hedge the portfolio is $300,000 ($1,000 times the ratio $21,000/$70). That is, $300,000 par value of the 10-year has the same dollar price sensitivity as the portfolio for changes in the 10-year yield levels. Note that even after this hedging, there might be residual risks relative to changes in rates at other maturities.

Clearly, the hedge for the portfolio is to go short $300,000 of the 10-year bond. Risk points, and therefore the hedge levels, for all other hedge instruments are determined in a similar way. The total risk of the portfolio is stated as a list of numbers representing the risk points for each hedge instrument.

Extensions

The application of the risk point method is not limited to swaps and securities with simple, known, and fixed cash flows. It is in fact a general approach and can be used to hedge virtually all instruments. As long as a security can be valued relative to a set of hedge instruments, the method is applicable. For example, suppose that we are considering an option on a 10-year zero-coupon bond. Then, we can easily determine the risk point for the option by first determining the change in the price of the zero relative to the current 10-year Treasury. Secondly, we determine the corresponding change in the price of the option due to the change in the zero price. This directly gives us the risk point of the option relative to the current 10-year Treasury.[16]

---

16 The risk point for the option relative to the 10-year Treasury is the product of (1) the risk point of the option relative to the zero and (2) the risk point of the zero relative to the 10-year. Mathematically, we can restate this relationship as follows: d(option)/d(10-year UST) = [d(option)/d(zero)] x [d(zero)/d(10-year UST)].

The concept can also be extended to include risks other than interest-rate risk. For example, suppose that we would like to hedge the option on the 10-year zero-coupon bond against changes in volatility. We would choose a hedge instrument that responds to volatility, such as an option on the current 10-year Treasury. To determine the risk point, we compute the change in the value of the hedge as well as the option on the zero per unit change in the volatility. The ratio of the two represents the risk point of the option relative to the hedge with respect to volatility. This number, the *volatility risk point,* is the number of units of the hedge instrument required to hedge the option on the zero to protect against changes in volatility.

Simulation

Monte Carlo simulation can also be helpful in the hedging process. However, simulation is used more often as a tool to evaluate a hedge than to determine what it ought to be. The issues involved in simulation are therefore covered in the next chapter on approaches to evaluating a transaction.

Exchange-Rate Risk—Multicurrency Hedging

Recently, funding and investing activities have attained a global nature and most of the large financial institutions have some form or other of currency risk. In many instances, an institution might actually seek exposure to currency risk, perhaps as a means of diversification or perhaps as a market play or to hedge or manage existing exposures. Given the large swings in exchange rates, currency risk can often dwarf interest-rate risk.

When dealing with different currencies, there are two types of risks to consider:

Exchange-Rate Risk. If assets and liabilities are denominated in different currencies, the ability to meet the liability with the cash flow from the assets and the spread earned depends on the prevailing exchange rate among the currencies involved.

Foreign Interest-Rate Risk. In addition to the exchange-rate risk, the assets and liabilities are also exposed to the interest rate in the denominating currency.

In certain cases, an institution might seek a specific exposure level to either of these two risks. Tools are available to handle each risk.

There are several ways to address currency risk.

In *hierarchical* or *vertical hedging,* the interest-rate risk is managed in each currency separately using the concepts developed above. Then the currency risk is hedged to the desired level at the macro level.

In *matched* or *horizontal hedging,* each asset is individually matched with a hedging liability such that the net cash flows from each micro hedge is in the domestic currency. This results in a single-currency interest-rate risk at the macro level (portfolio level) which is managed using the concepts developed above.

The type of multicurrency hedging used, whether vertical or horizontal, depends upon the types and the efficiency of hedging tools available as well as the ability to closely match individual assets and liabilities. Horizontal hedging is efficient when such matches are available. Vertical hedging is suitable when practical interest-rate hedging tools are readily accessible in the foreign currency.

Duality in Hedging

There is an interesting difference in the way lenders and borrowers view hedging. This is best illustrated by means of an example.

> ***Situation*** *(Investor Point of View)*. FII is a fixed-income investor who lends money to corporations by purchasing their bonds. FII has just purchased a 10-year fixed-rate bond priced at par. The *coupon* on the bond is fixed; it does not respond to market rate moves. Therefore, as interest rates change, the *value* of this bond will change in response. Therefore, the FII concludes that it is not hedged, considering only the value of this asset and not the potential liabilities that the asset is intended to fund.
>
> If FII were to swap the fixed-rate bond into floating, then the resulting synthetic floating-rate bond will closely hold its price near par. Then, FII would conclude that the floating-rate bond is a hedged bond. The *coupon* on the synthetic floater changes in step with changes in the market rates so that the *value* of the bond is almost constant.

Thus, the flexible coupon of a floating-rate note effectively absorbs the shocks that result from the hills and valleys in the movement of rates over time. This phenomenon gives the value of the security a level, smooth ride. On the other hand:

> ***Situation*** *(Issuer Point of View)*. FRB is a corporation that is a fixed-rate borrower. It has just issued a fixed-rate 10-year bond. Since the coupon on the bond is fixed, the interest cost for FRB is fixed, independent of any changes in market rates. FRB feels that it is perfectly hedged.
>
> If it were to swap the bond into floating, the coupon rate on the resulting synthetic floater liability will change with market rates, exposing FRB to risk. In that case, FRB assumes, it would not be hedged.

This example shows how the same fixed-coupon bond is viewed as a risky investment by FII and as a safe borrowing by FRB. Viewed in isolation, this situation is paradoxical, but resolves itself easily once we recall that a hedge modifies an existing position into a desired position. FRB desired a fixed-rate liability and he has a fixed-rate liability.

Therefore, he needs no other hedge; he is already hedged. To FII, on the other hand, the stability of the market value of the investment is important. Therefore, he needs a swap to convert the fixed-rate investment into floating to achieve a hedge.

Note, however, that outside of ALM considerations, the investor point of view is technically more correct. FRB, even though it has a fixed coupon, is exposed to the fact that the present value of the interest payments varies with changes in market rates. If rates fall, the present value increases because the fixed coupons will then be discounted at lower rates. If rates increase, the present value falls due to the increase in the discount rate. Secondly, the total cost of a liability (or the total return on an asset) depends upon the future course of interest rates in terms of the financing cost of (or the reinvestment rate on) interim cash flows (e.g., coupons).

In the case of a floating-rate obligation, on the other hand, if market rates rise, the coupon rate increases by just the right amount such that the change in present value due to the rise in discount rate is matched by the increase in the size of the coupon. A similar effect holds if the market rates fall. Thus, the present value of the floating-rate obligation remains relatively constant.

Another way to analyze the situation is to realize that a fixed-rate borrower suffers opportunity cost if market rates fall. If rates rise, he has an opportunity gain. Most often, this loss or gain is hidden due to the current book or tax accounting traditions. These practices seem to be on the verge of changing. Recently, the FASB issued a ruling (FASB 107) which requires disclosure of the market value of certain financial instruments under GAAP accounting. If this trend continues, eventually, corporations may be required to mark to market all financial instruments, both assets and liabilities. We believe this is a positive trend as it will provide strong incentive for corporations to think in terms of asset/liability management in order to reduce the volatility in their books. In cases where a corporation's assets are largely nonfinancial, there will be a tendency toward floating-rate financing, again to ensure stability of the market value of liabilities, and, in turn, reduce balance sheet volatility. However, even though the market value of the liabilities may be stable, the issuer will not necessarily be hedged from an ALM point of view, unless the cash flow from the nonfinancial assets closely follows floating market interest rates.

Even an Efficient Market Is Inefficient

It is not uncommon on the part of borrower corporations to have the view that the market is efficient and therefore it really does not matter whether any hedging activity takes place or not. That is, floating-rate funding is as good as fixed-rate funding because the floating rates will, on the average over the maturity of the borrowing, be not far from the fixed-rate that can be obtained in the market. The efficient market will ensure this eventual equality. The conclusion is that, in the long run, everything will even out.

There are several reasons why this argument may not always hold. We will present a few.

First, the markets are not always efficient. It is often possible to discover values by arbitraging in the markets. Even if we assume that the market is efficient at the global or macro level, it is possible to find inefficiencies at the local or micro level.

Secondly, each financial instrument has general properties (e.g., maturity, coupon rate) that it shares with many other instruments as well as certain special properties (e.g., liquidity, callability) specific to itself. Each of these properties makes the instrument more or less expensive depending upon whether the property is a positive or negative one. Now, when an investor buys a security, or an issuer sells one, the price depends upon the collection of different properties and whether or not the buyer or seller needs them. It is in this area that market participants can optimize to create value, or, not lose value.

Situation *(Avoiding Loss of Value).* AMC is an automotive company with a pension program that can be characterized as largely a defined benefit plan. Unhappy with its outside fixed-income money managers' performance, it has recently brought its pension money inside for internal management. In the past, the rates of return that its outside money managers achieved were much below the market. Based on this experience, AMC has concluded that it is not possible to beat the market. Therefore, AMC will simply invest in the "market." To achieve the broad and well-diversified distribution that this decision implies, AMC has been advised to allocate to each market segment an amount of money proportional to the size of the market segment.

Analysis. Two issues arise immediately that question both the reason for being unhappy with the outside money managers and the decision to invest in the market:

1. Is the market, represented perhaps by the available broad bond indices, the right standard by which the money managers of the pension fund should be measured?
2. Should not the pension fund analyze its potential liabilities[17] and invest in securities that are appropriate to

17 There are two major types of pension plans. In the case of defined-benefit pension plans the sponsor of the plan promises a specified cash flow independent of the nature and success of the investment program. The ALM approach is recommended in this type of a plan. In defined-contribution plans the entire investment risk is borne by the beneficiary.

match those liabilities under a suitable ALM framework rather than invest in the "market"?

Let us simplify the situation by setting aside these two issues. Let us assume that investing in the broad market in a well-diversified manner is in general a reasonable approach to money management. Let us assume, in addition, that not only is the market efficient on the average, but that each single security is correctly priced. Even under these simplifying assumptions, we find that we can find value and avoid loss of value by careful selection of securities.

Consider the fact that there are many tax-advantaged securities such as tax-exempt municipal bonds, fixed-coupon preferred stock, discount bonds, Treasury bonds (free of state tax), and taxable municipal bonds (free of federal tax). Clearly, these securities sell at a premium to reflect the tax advantages that they have. However, the pension fund, being a tax-exempt investor itself, achieves no positive gain by investing in these securities. Our conclusion, therefore, is that these market segments should be avoided by the pension fund. On the other hand, the fund should consider investment in tax-disadvantaged instruments such as zero-coupon bonds and discount bonds.

Other properties in securities should also be selectively considered. For example, the low yield of T-bills reflects not only their high credit quality, but also their high liquidity. If the pension fund does not need that level of liquidity, it should not invest in T-bills. High quality commercial paper is perhaps a good alternative. Similarly, premium bonds usually sell at higher yields because of the accounting requirement for certain investors to amortize the premium as a loss. If the fund does not have this limitation, it should seek value in the premium bond segment of the market.

Thirdly, and perhaps most importantly, there is the issue of short-term volatility. Even if we grant the postulate that everything evens out in the long run, the corporation might be exposed to cash flow or mark-to-market risks due to market movements in the short run. In certain cases, a firm might not have the luxury to wait till the long-run averages come to the rescue.

We conclude, therefore, that prudent management of risks is more appropriate for a corporation than a dependence on market forces.

Hedge Timing

One of the most difficult issues after the decision to hedge is the timing of the hedge. This is more of a factor of consideration for those borrowers and lenders who have the need and the flexibility to choose the timing of the hedge. For example, a borrower seeking U.S. dollar funds but borrowing in the German market in order to optimize funding cost will hedge the borrowing immediately by means of a currency swap. This borrower has very little flexibility in hedge timing unless it is willing to take on the risk that the German mark will appreciate against the dollar. Similarly, many bank lenders usually hedge any mismatch right away as they run a spread business. There are a vast majority of lenders that are ultimate investors (e.g., pension funds) who are seekers of the type of risk-reward tradeoff that the lending provides. These lenders do not usually hedge their investments.

The hedge timing question is also more common when the borrower has floating-rate funds and wants to fix the rate via a swap transaction. The issue is, always, should the hedge be executed now, or should the firm wait for a lower rate. This consideration leads the corporation to delay hedging. If rates do fall, there is the natural tendency to expect and wait for a further fall in rates. If rates rise, the corporation waits with the hope that rates will fall eventually. In some cases, when the rates rise, the corporation might panic and lock in the higher rate.[18]

In our opinion, this dilemma, known in mathematics as a *stopping-time problem*,[19] whether to hedge now or not, can be viewed in a simplified fashion, and can be analyzed under two cases:

Case 1: If a true hedge is desired, it should be executed immediately, independent of market conditions. This case can be compared to a similar dilemma for a gambler. The optimal solution to the stopping-time problem for a gambler is *now*. Given that the odds are against him, a gambler should stop speculating or wagering immediately in order to maximize his expected returns (by minimizing his future losses). So is the case with a corporation desiring to reduce risk via a hedge.[20] Immediate action, as soon as possible, is prudent.

Sometimes there is one exception to this rule: If the hedge would lock in a loss and the corporation is indiffer-

---

18 This phenomenon, where the corporation appears to "buy high and sell low" by not fixing when the rates are low, but fixing at a high rate after the rates rise, also occurs in another context. Usually, at relatively high rate levels, the yield curve tends to invert. That is, short-term rates are higher than longer-term rates. In this situation, a borrower corporation can "save" interest costs by swapping into fixed for a longer term, achieving a lower (fixed) rate than the short rate. Thus the corporation is locking in a rate in a high rate environment. Conversely, when rate levels are relatively low, the yield curve tends to be steeply positively sloped. In this environment, many corporations are reluctant to "pay up the curve" by fixing the rate on their floating-rate obligations.

19 Hedge timing is a stopping-time problem because the issue is when to stop procrastinating and execute the hedge.

20 Note that just as the odds are against the gambler attempting to maximize his returns, a corporation with the goal of minimizing risk also finds that the odds are against it. Therefore, the two cases are similar and have the same optimal stopping-time solution. The corporation is not maximizing returns, but minimizing volatility.

ent to the magnitude of the loss, then it is better to wait for rates to fall.

> ***Situation*** *(Waiting for a Better Hedging Time).* MLC is a midwestern leasing company. Its assets are fixed-rate leases, and normally it raises fixed-rate funds. This strategy matches its assets and liabilities and earns MLC a fixed spread. MLC currently has some amount of floating-rate funding via its commercial paper program. These funds are invested in fixed-rate leases. MLC intended to swap the funding to fixed, but rates have suddenly risen and the fixed rate that MLC can obtain will reduce the returns so much as to make that segment of the business a loser and could force it into bankruptcy.

MLC has decided to wait for a more opportune time for hedging. As far as MLC is concerned, the only thing worse than the risk of loss is *certain* loss.

Case 2: If the corporation is not really hedging as part of an asset/liability matching goal, but is seeking to achieve as low a fixed rate as possible, then it should determine where values are available in the market and lock in fixed rates opportunistically.

> ***Situation*** *(Opportunistic Hedging).* MCC is a midwestern chemical company. It is considering fixing the rate on its commercial paper program via an interest-rate swap under which it will pay fixed and receive floating. Interest rates are historically low. The yield curve is very steeply positively sloped. MCC has determined that the market expectations are for the rates to remain low for an extended time. Therefore, the steepness of the curve indicates that investors are demanding a high premium (i.e., high yield) for longer-term fixed-rate investments.
>
> MCC decides that the long rates, even though historically low, are too high relative to the short rates. Therefore, it enters into a swap in which it *receives* the fixed rate and pays floating. It intends to unwind the swap for a gain that can reduce

its interest costs at an opportune time. At that time, it might enter into a hedging swap as well.

It is clear from the situation above that Case 2 can be considered speculation. It would have been equally speculative for MCC to wait and do nothing. Indeed, most transactions not driven by ALM considerations are of a speculative kind. Even inaction, i.e., a decision not to hedge, is speculation. These transactions include fixed-rate borrowing as well. Unfortunately, industrial corporations can rarely create an acceptable ALM framework given that their assets are not financial in nature and the cash flows that the assets generate cannot be modeled adequately.[21] In these cases we recommend that the liability portfolio consist of a diversified mix of maturities of fixed- and floating-rate obligations. A multinational corporation should consider currency diversification as well. We present an approach to ALM for industrial corporations in a later section.

Diversification

Whenever we deviate from the strict asset/liability matching norm, diversification should be our guiding principle. This concept is widely applied to asset management, but is equally applicable to a liability portfolio. Diversification is appropriate in cases where the usual techniques of defining assets and liabilities are not adequate, e.g., industrial corporation with physical and real assets and financial liabilities.

---

21 We highly recommend that each firm conduct a study of how the value of the firm responds to interest- (and currency-) rate fluctuations.

EXHIBIT 4–1 The Double Swap

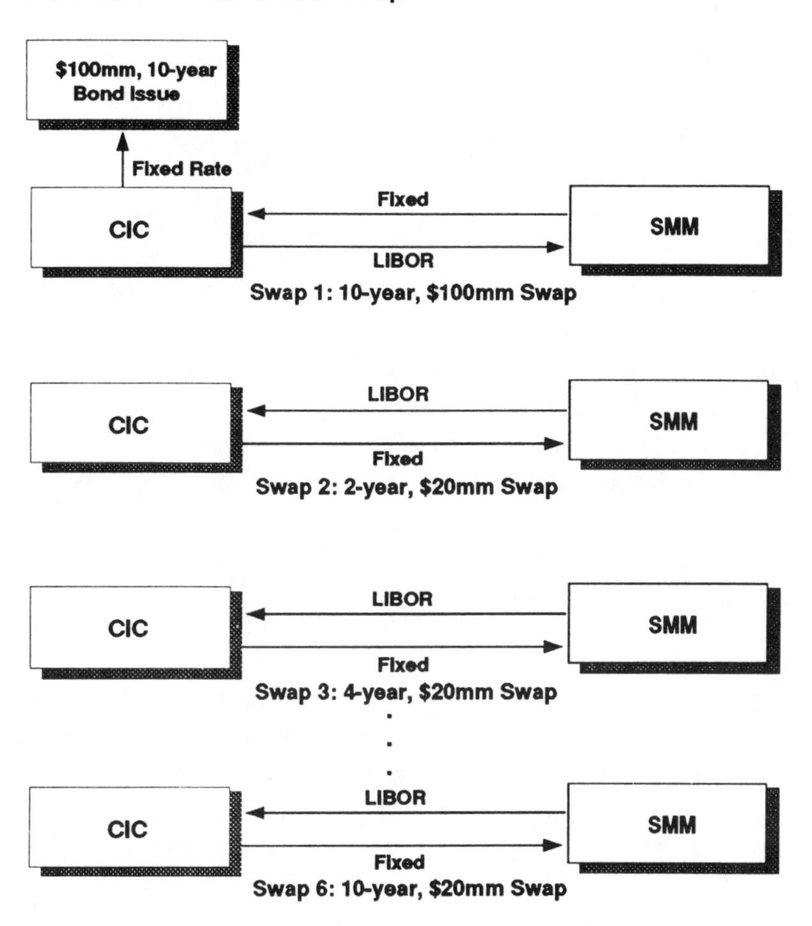

***Situation** (Diversification).* CIC is a Californian industrial corporation. It has just issued a $100 million, 10-year bond. The proceeds have been used to retire most of its (expensive) commercial paper and a maturing bond. CIC selected the 10-year maturity from pricing and size considerations. However, from a risk management point of view, it would prefer a balanced maturity ladder. That is, it would like the interest risk (and levels) to fall at different maturities along the yield curve.

CIC's goal of distributing the maturities for risk management purposes can easily be achieved by using swaps by applying a technique known as the *double swap* in which the fixed-coupon bond is first swapped into floating. Then, portions of the bond, say a fifth of the total each, are swapped back into fixed to the required maturities.

Analytically, this procedure looks like a series of seven swaps. In practice, it is executed as a smaller number, usually one or two, swaps by combining the cash flows from the different swaps appropriately.

Note that the double-swap technique is superior to issuing a series of bonds of different maturities in that the issuer has guaranteed funding for ten years in the former case. From an interest-rate exposure point of view, the two positions are equivalent.

Hidden Factors

Even in these cases where asset/liability modeling is difficult, e.g., industrial corporations, it is possible to analyze cash flow patterns using historical data. The goal is to determine, albeit loosely, the relationship between interest and currency exchange rates and cash flow. Such a modeling exercise can not only suggest appropriate ways to manage the liability portfolio, but also reveal hidden factors that can influence a corporation's business and profitability. These factors are hidden usually because they are part of a universe much larger than the corporation itself.

Situation *(Hidden Factor—I).* CPC is a U.S. consumer products company with the majority of its sales generated within the country. It has very little debt mainly consisting of its commercial paper program. CPC believes that its sales are correlated positively with interest rates to the extent that the economy itself is similarly related. Therefore, it has concluded that the floating-rate liability is appropriate. Since CPC has no expenses or revenues in other currencies, all of its liabilities and assets are in dollars. CPC has no currency exposure.

Yet, CPC has been experiencing wide swings in its profitability. To determine the cause of this volatility in earnings, it has modeled its revenues in relation to interest rates. The study seems to support the initial assertion that the revenues increase when rates rise. However, the data appears to show another factor dominating this relationship at certain times.

To uncover this unknown factor, CPC included various cross-currency exchange rates as independent variables in its analysis. To its surprise, CPC found that whenever the U.S. dollar was strong against the European and Japanese currencies, its revenues fell. This phenomenon perhaps reflects the fact that when the dollar is strong, imported alternatives to CPC's products become more cost-competitive, reducing sales.

Thus, CPC, a purely domestic corporation with the U.S. dollar as its functional currency, is exposed to currency risk. CPC now plans to include currency hedging in its risk management program.

The situation of CPC above illustrates how risks that are totally external to a corporation can affect its financial performance. The effect of such external risks becomes greater as the economies of countries become more interrelated and global.

Hidden risks can also take the form of opportunity cost. For example, a domestic corporation whose products become more price-competitive when the dollar weakens, may not be able to exploit fully the increased demand for its products with rapid increases in production. The currency relationships move too quickly perhaps.

There are other interesting effects closer to home.

Situation *(Hidden Factor—II)*. MAC is a midwestern appliance manufacturer. MAC has a well-developed asset/liability management system that includes the modeling of its cash flows and revenues relative to interest rates and currency exchange rates. Based on such analysis, MAC is funding mostly in floating rate. MAC is concerned because of the variability of its market share. Its market share falls especially when appliance sales are booming.

MAC has just completed an industrywide analysis and discovered an interesting point. All of its major competitors have a larger proportion of fixed-rate financing. Thus, when interest rates rise, indicating a strong economy and a corresponding increase in appliance sales, they have a relatively lower financing cost, prompting them to gain market share by offering better pricing. The loss of their market share when rates are low is less pronounced because of lower overall sales activity.

As a result of this analysis, MAC has now opportunistically fixed some of its debt and its balance sheet is now more balanced in comparison with its competition. The market share is expected to be more stable.[22]

Thus, ALM and hedge management should be modified by the astute manager in the context of the company's situation in the outside universe such as its own industry and the global markets.

Hedging, Arbitrage, and Speculation

Swap and other derivative transactions executed by a corporation are usually classified into three categories: hedging, arbitrage, and speculation. Each derivative transaction, taken in isolation, can result in losses and gains to

22 This situation is somewhat reminiscent of a standard business management case called *"prisoner's dilemma."*

the corporation depending upon the subsequent movement of market rates. It is possible to label every transaction speculative. In reality, however, speculation is a highly tainted attribute in the corporate world and liability managers seek to find contexts in order to be able to justify even speculative transactions as hedging or arbitrage driven. Traditional accounting rules foster this arbitrariness by providing hedging contexts for speculative transactions and not providing such context for genuine hedges. For example, transactions not treated as hedges are required to be marked to market and brought on the balance sheet.[23]

Even though the discussion above implies that the boundaries among the three types of transactions is obscure and thin, it is useful to define them. We can use the risk and reward framework of traditional financial theory for this purpose. Let us assume that risk can be represented by the variance (or standard deviation) of return and reward by the mean (or expected) return. Also, without loss of generality, assume that the market's fair pricing of risk and reward can be represented by a straight line called the *fair-market line*, as in Exhibit 4–2.

We represent the corporation's current position on the fair-market line corresponding to its mean and variance. Any new transaction executed will modify this mean and variance and move the corporation's position.

An *arbitrage* transaction raises the expected return for the corporation while maintaining the level of risk or reduces the risk while maintaining the level of return. An arbitrage, therefore, will move the position of the corporation on the risk-reward plane upward and to the left, as

23 This situation is improving due to recent advances in accounting, e.g., FASB 107 which is tending toward marked to market treatment for all financial instruments regardless of hedging or other context.

EXHIBIT 4–2 Fair Market Line

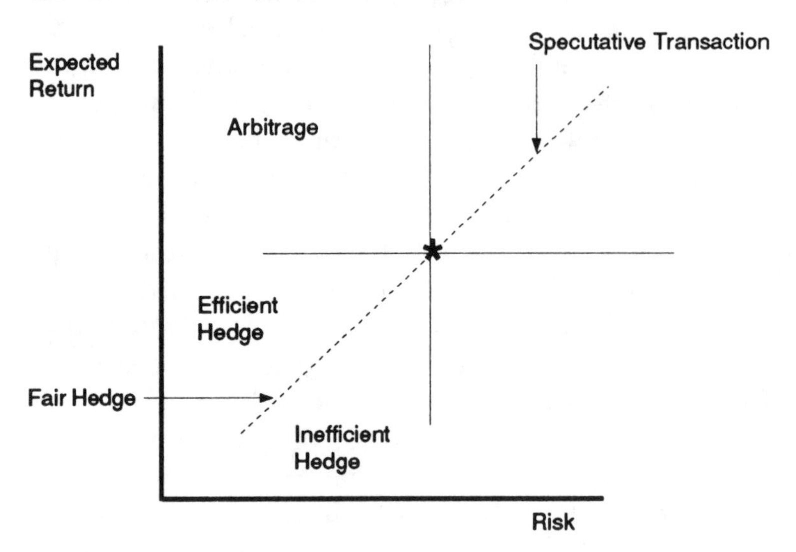

indicated by the shaded top-left quadrant in the exhibit. Arbitrages are a result of market imbalances and inefficiencies and result in the corporation achieving a better-than-fair price for the transaction.

A *hedging* transaction reduces both expected return and risk. A hedge, therefore, will move the corporation's position downward and to the left, into the bottom left quadrant in the exhibit. A hedge can further be classified: A hedge is *efficient* if the resulting position is on or above the fair-market line. It is *inefficient* if the resulting position is below the fair-market line. An efficient hedge can be viewed as a combination of an arbitrage and a fair hedge. A *fair* hedge moves the corporation's position to the left on the fair-market line.

A *speculative* transaction raises expected return as well as the level of risk. Such a transaction moves the position of the corporation upward and to the right on the fair-market line.

If the risk-reward position moves to the right but lies above the fair-market line, we consider a transaction leading to that result a *risk-arbitrage.* Such a transaction can be viewed as a combination of arbitrage and pure speculation.

This discussion provides a feel, but not a concrete mold into which transactions can be cast. The area below the fair-market line, in general, represent undesirable transactions. However, it should be noted that many types of financial instruments, e.g., options, do not fit neatly into the mean-variance model. Also, it is more useful to define risk as the *difference* between the initial position and the goal, that is, where the corporation is and where it wants to be. The goal itself can be determined by an asset/liability framework. To the extent that the initial position and the goal are not the same, not entering into an appropriate transaction can then be clearly seen to be speculative. Also, in cases where the goal is not a clearly defined point because the financial attributes of assets and liabilities are not clearly known, then diversification should be used as discussed earlier.

ALM for Industrial Corporations

The standard ALM[24] concepts, widely used by financial institutions, can be applied to an industrial corporation,

---

24 In a broad ALM context, we first have to decide between equity and debt. On the equity side, we have stock, various types of preferred stock, warrants and rights, etc. On the debt side we have borrowings in each of the different currencies, and in each currency the maturities of each borrowing. Then there are hybrids such as convertible bonds. In addition, we have to decide on the funding source (public debt, private placement, bank loan), seniority of the debt, etc. For our purposes, we will focus on debt and on only those issues that have an impact on the interest-rate risk characteristics of the debt. Most conclusions developed here can be easily extended to the management of the currency mix in a debt portfolio.

but in only a modified manner since its assets tend to be nonfinancial but its liabilities are usually represented by financial instruments. Consider the following situation:

> ***Situation*** *(Financing a Real Asset).* MIC is a multinational industrial company. It is seeking to finance a new plant. The plant has a useful life of about 10 years. MIC has therefore decided to finance the plant by means of a noncallable 10-year fixed-rate bond issue. This funding structure is also in line with its traditional financing practices.

Financing a plant with a life of 10 years with a 10-year borrowing makes obvious sense. By matching the life of the asset with that of the liability, MIC is minimizing future funding risk. Note also that any bond issue with a maturity longer than 10 years will equally protect MIC from funding risk, though at a slightly higher coupon level in a positively sloped yield curve environment.

The problem, if any, is with the fact that the bond is a fixed-rate issue.

> ***Situation*** *(Financing a Real Asset—Continued).* MIC's past experience has shown that the net income from the business generated by plants of the kind being built varies with the general level of interest rates. In particular, MIC has found that the net income moves roughly in step with the 1-year interest rates. At higher interest-rate levels, the net income is usually higher.

MIC's experience, then, is that the plant behaves approximately like a floating-rate financial asset. MIC can therefore achieve a much better asset/liability match by converting the bond into a floating-rate funding. This can easily be achieved by means of a swap transaction under which MIC will pay the 1-year LIBOR rate and receive a fixed rate.

EXHIBIT 4–3 Financing a Real Asset

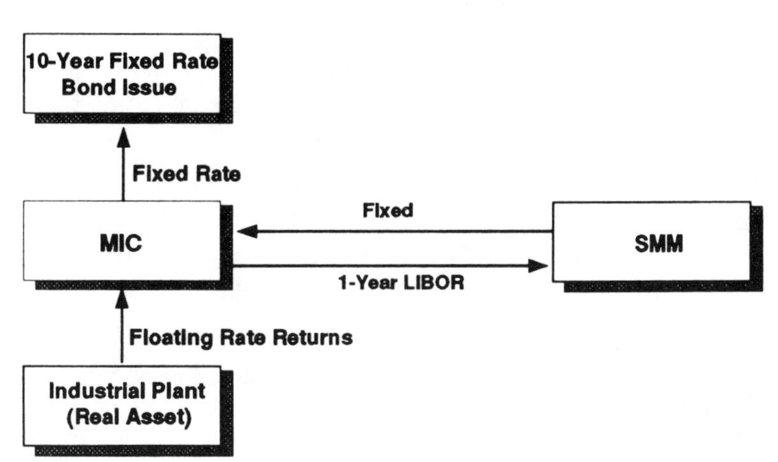

Thus, it is not enough just to match the maturity of a borrowing to the life of an asset. It is also necessary, where possible, to model the asset as if it were financial in nature and match its cash flow characteristics such as duration to that of the liability.

For certain sectors of the industrial community, e.g., durable goods, housing and construction, revenues can be expected to be inversely correlated with interest rates. At higher levels of interest rates, the output of these companies, which are usually goods that need to be financed, become less attractive to consumers and the sales level will drop. For certain other companies, e.g., utilities, falling rates tend to decrease revenues. This type of conventional wisdom holds in most cases. However, there can be certain exceptions. For example, the recent drop in interest rates to historically low levels was not accompanied by a corresponding explosion in the sales of homes, major appliances, and automobiles. Such exceptions indicate the necessity for a diversification philosophy in financing where possible.

Financial institutions have usually achieved hedging by means of process called matched funding, i.e., by matching the cash flows of the assets and the liabilities closely. Thus, in matched funding, the maturity as well as the duration of an asset is closely matched with that of its financing. Industrial corporations have also achieved some level matching by financing long-term investments in plants and equipment via long-term bond issues (as MIC did above). Short-term requirements such as for inventory are financed with short-term financing, e.g., commercial paper.

Whether an asset (e.g., plant) or a liability (e.g., bond issue) is long-term or short-term from an interest-rate risk point of view depends not on the expected life (of the plant) or the maturity (of the bond) but on how its value responds to changes in interest rates, i.e., on its duration. Computing the duration of a nonfinancial asset is by no means simple. Asset values cannot easily be determined as they may be influenced by numerous factors other than interest rates, e.g., changes in the competitive situation, technological advances, and environmental considerations. In addition, characteristics of assets cannot be easily, if at all, modified. Finally, assets are controlled by operations, not financial, management whereas ALM issues are largely a financial concern.

Fortunately, ALM hedging can be achieved purely by managing the liabilities. The characteristics of a borrowing can be changed even years after issuance by means of swap transactions. Any such adjustment should be driven by modeling the cash flows generated from the businesses supported by the assets. Admittedly, asset values and cash flows are a complex function of numerous market factors. Yet, by suitable analytical modeling, it is possible to extract those components of asset behavior that are dependent upon interest-rate levels. For some companies, these components will be a significant portion of total behavior; for others they may be too insignificant to be useful for ALM purposes.

We can classify the components or businesses of a corporation into three groups depending upon how a business segment responds to changes in interest rates:

Group 1: those that have no correlation with interest rates but vary randomly as other market factors change. Such businesses can best be handled by a diversified mix of liabilities. There might be need for frequent management of these liabilities as the nature of the response of these businesses to changes in interest-rate levels becomes more discernible.

Group 2: those that are not correlated with interest rates, but whose revenues are not random. The revenue from a business in this group is relatively stable independent of the level of rates. Such a business can be financed by a fixed-rate liability. Again, the liability can be a traditional fixed-rate borrowing or it can be a floating-rate liability converted into fixed by a swap.

Group 3: those that have a strong positive correlation with interest rates. In this case, the revenues from the business increase as the level of interest rates rises. A business in this group can be "match-funded" via a floating-rate liability so that the funding cost moves in tandem with the revenues. The liability can be a traditional floating-rate funding such as commercial paper or a floating-rate note. It can also be a fixed-rate borrowing converted into floating via a swap transaction.

Group 4: those that have a strong negative correlation with interest rates. In this case revenues increase as rates fall. The traditional approach to financing businesses in this group is to use fixed-rate funding. However, even though superior to floating-rate financing, fixed-rate funding does not provide full matching. Since interest costs are fixed, any volatility in revenues will be passed through into net income. A more optimal solution is to use the swap market to synthetically create an inverse-floating-rate liability.

Situation *(Creating an Inverse-Floating-Rate Liability).* WHC is a western housing company. WHC believes that it is fully hedged since most of WHC's debt is fixed-rate. However, the housing industry is subject to volatility, and WHC has found that its operating results decline as rates increase.

WHC has recently issued a 10-year 8 percent coupon bond. It enters into a swap transaction in which it receives floating (LIBOR) and pays a fixed rate of 7.90 percent. Effectively, the

EXHIBIT 4–4 Creating an Inverse Floater Liability

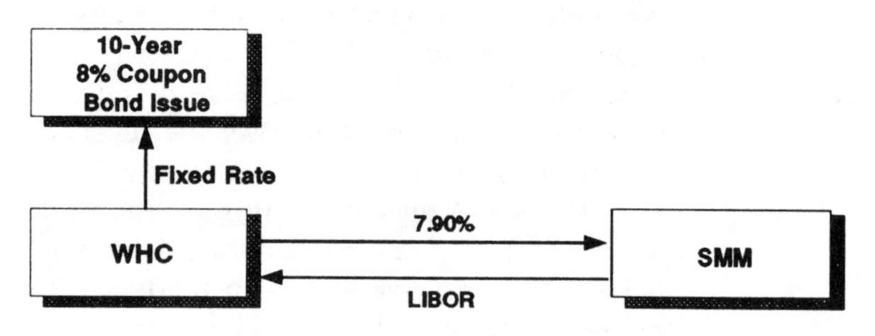

10-year borrowing becomes an inverse-floating-rate funding with the net coupon at (15.90 percent minus LIBOR). For every basis point that LIBOR goes up, the net coupon declines 1 basis point. This reduction in interest cost when rates rise provides WHC with welcome relief when its business is expected to decline.

Most large industrial corporations will have a mix of businesses in each of these groups. Business in groups 3 and 4 usually offset each other resulting in a net variation that is either positively or negatively correlated with interest rates. Therefore, we can view an optimal liability portfolio of an industrial company to comprise three parts:

- A core fixed-rate borrowing which funds those businesses which are affected little by interest-rate levels and whose revenue flows are relatively stable. The traditional long-term fixed-rate bond issue with a call option is an excellent choice in most instances for the core fixed-rate part of the liability portfolio.
- A core floating-rate or inverse-floating-rate borrowing which funds those businesses which are positively or negatively correlated with the level of interest rates. Whether the funding is floating or inverse floating depends upon how the interest-rate-dependent businesses net out. If the positively correlated businesses are dominant, then floating funding is needed; otherwise inverse floating funding is needed. Floating and inverse floating can most conveniently be obtained by using the swap market since the primary market for long-term floating bond issues is relatively small and inverse floating bond issues are quite uncommon.
- A managed part that funds remaining parts of the business that do not depend upon the level of interest rates.

The relative proportions of these three parts should be reviewed periodically both to determine if the cash flow modeling of the company is still valid as well as to determine if market conditions warrant alternative approaches.

Situation *(Temporary Alternative Funding).* IMF is an industrial manufacturing concern. IMF issued a long-term fixed-rate bond to fund its core business which it has determined to be largely stable and independent of interest-rate levels. However, the recent downturn in the economy has resulted in a significant decline in revenues. In spite of the historically low levels of interest rates, IMF's interest costs have remained high, since the borrowing is fixed-rate. Fortunately, the bond is callable and the first call date will occur soon. IMF is considering calling the bond and refinancing it.

IMF analyzed the situation as follows:

- Long-term fixed rates are very attractive. Yet, they are much higher than the short-term rate which are at historically low levels. Thus floating rate funding is clearly more attractive at least in the near term.
- Floating-rate funding does not necessarily mean that IMF is deviating from its ALM philosophy since the cash flow model, on which IMF's ALM depends, has temporarily become invalid due to the economic environment.
- Finally, IMF can always swap a floating-rate funding to fixed if the environment were to return to normal. The risk of a higher interest-rate level at that time is tolerable since most likely IMF's revenues will return to normal as well.

In light of this analysis, IMF issued a long-term fixed-rate bond and swapped a substantial portion of it into floating rate.

In the context of a new borrowing, we normally tend to think of two possible choices: fixed rate or floating rate. However, using the power of the swap market, we can create an unlimited variety of characteristics in a borrowing. We have already seen the inverse floater above. Others include super floaters whose coupon goes up more than the increase in interest rates. Various optional characteristics such as caps and floors on each interest payment should be considered as well.

***Situation** (Super Floater Funding).* SWC is a southwestern company whose revenues are unusually sensitive to interest rates. SWC does not have a lot of debt, but its business declines substantially if rates fall. It currently uses floating-rate funding, but the lowering of interest cost does not offset the decline in sales when rates fall.

SWC enters into a swap contract under which it receives a fixed rate of 6.5 percent and pays floating-rate LIBOR. The effective interest cost then becomes (2 times LIBOR less 6.5 percent). Thus, if LIBOR declines by 1 basis point, the interest cost declines by 2 basis points.

SWC also gets the advantage of an abnormally steep yield curve by receiving fixed on the swap. Its initial interest cost drops from a low rate of 3.5 percent (current 6-month LIBOR) to the still-lower 0.5 percent (2 x 3.5 minus 6.5 percent). SWC now has super-floating-rate funding. Its exposure to changing

EXHIBIT 4–5 Creating a Super Floater Liability

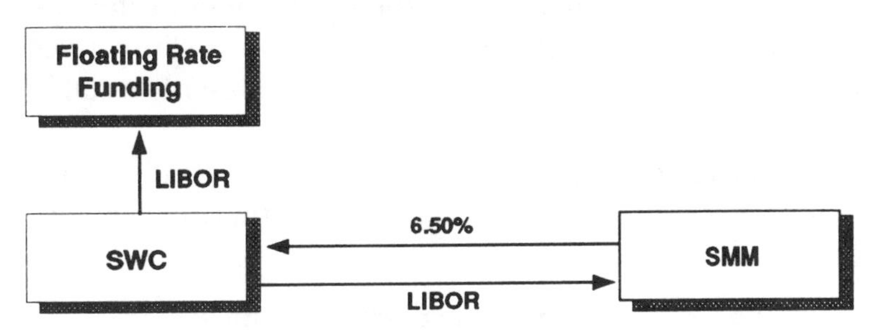

short rates is twice as much as that of normal floating-rate borrowing.

Implementation

Suitable modeling of a company's business is a necessary first step in implementing ALM. The model should be complex enough to include all determinants of the business, but should be simple enough to be tractable and provide summary results that can be used as decision parameters and can be acted upon.

Various statistical techniques such as correlation analysis, multivariate regression analysis, and factor analysis can be used for modeling purposes. Initial modeling steps will indicate parameters such as exchange rates or inflation indices that might be important and other parameters that are not and can easily be dropped. Once an acceptable model has been developed, an ideal or benchmark liability portfolio can be generated that is as responsive to market forces as the businesses. This portfolio should also satisfy the liquidity and other concerns of the company as well. This benchmark portfolio can not only be used to simulate future market environments but also be validated by historical data analysis. The benchmark portfolio will be more efficient if it is built with more than the simpleminded approach of fixed and floating financing. We would include many of the possibilities now available with derivatives such as capped and floored floaters, callable and putable fixed-rate funding, etc.

A satisfactory liability portfolio, especially an ideal or a benchmark portfolio, should have three important attributes:

- it should provide for short-term cash needs
- it should be consistent with the long-term ALM goals

- it should provide the liability manager the ability to move quickly in order to respond to market changes and to reduce costs by capturing values in the market.

In order to meet these three needs, we propose a three-pronged portfolio approach.[25] We conceptually divide the debt of a company into three parts to satisfy the three requirements:

1. ***The Liquidity Portfolio.*** This portfolio is designed to meet the day-to-day short-term cash needs of the company and usually comprises short-term financing such as commercial paper and bank revolving loans. The size of this portfolio can vary widely as the cash needs vary or as short-term needs become long-term. The borrowings in this portfolio mature periodically and the liability manager has the option not to roll over certain amounts depending upon cash needs.
2. ***The Strategic Portfolio.*** This represents the bulk of the borrowings and therefore is also called the core portfolio. This portfolio consists of floating, fixed, and other types of borrowings and reflects the long-term goals of the company as determined by suitable ALM modeling. Essential market judgments are represented here. For example, if this portfolio has a greater proportion of fixed-rate funding than is indicated by ALM modeling, then a bearish expectation (rising rates) is implied. A strategic portfolio that is

---

25 These concepts closely parallel the development of an investment portfolio. See, Ravi E. Dattatreya and Frank Fabozzi, *Active Total Return Management of Fixed Income Portfolios*, Probus Publishing, Chicago, 1989.

floating-heavy relative to ALM recommendations is bullish (expectation of falling rates). If the goal is to be neutral, then this portfolio should be as close to the ALM ideal as possible. Note here that whether a portfolio is risky or not is determined relative to the ALM model, not in an absolute sense. Thus, we would consider an all-fixed-rate portfolio very risky if the assets have a short duration, i.e., behave as though they were floating-rate.

The strategic portfolio will require periodic course correction or rebalancing to realign its attributes within the ALM framework as market changes impact the properties of both assets and liabilities. New maturing and callable liabilities provide useful opportunities to make long-term adjustments to attributes of this portfolio.

3. ***The Tactical Portfolio.*** This portfolio is usually smaller than the strategic portfolio and is designed to provide the manager with enough agility to react quickly to changing market conditions. It can be used to realign the strategic portfolio on a temporary basis. For example, if a decision has been made to lengthen the duration of the portfolio, the manager can take action quickly in the tactical portfolio by means of derivative transactions. The duration portfolio can be transferred (at least conceptually) to the strategic portfolio as opportunities arise.

   The tactical portfolio is also where the liability manager attempts to fund those components of the business that are not dependent upon interest-rate levels. A prudent mix of debt securities with frequent monitoring is the only way to handle this issue.

   Another important function of the tactical portfolio is to capture exceptional values in the market. For this reason, it is best to have few restrictions on this portfolio as to the class of transactions that can be used. Thus the tactical portfolio is not necessarily similar to the strategic portfolio in goals or content.

Finally, the tactical portfolio, given its relative freedom and smaller size, can be used as a scout to investigate new techniques and sources of funding. Once enough experience has been gained in a new sector or strategy, it can be considered for inclusion in the core portfolio.

This way of dividing the liability portfolio is only one of several acceptable ways of managing debt. The basic concepts are common to most such approaches.

Situation *(Using the Tactical Portfolio for Realignment).* IIC is an international industrial corporation whose strategic portfolio is largely floating-rate debt. Recent ALM modeling has indicated the need for more fixed-rate exposure. However, the market conditions are not optimal for a long-term fixed-rate bond issue.

EXHIBIT 4–6 Using a Place Holder Swap in the Tactical Portfolio

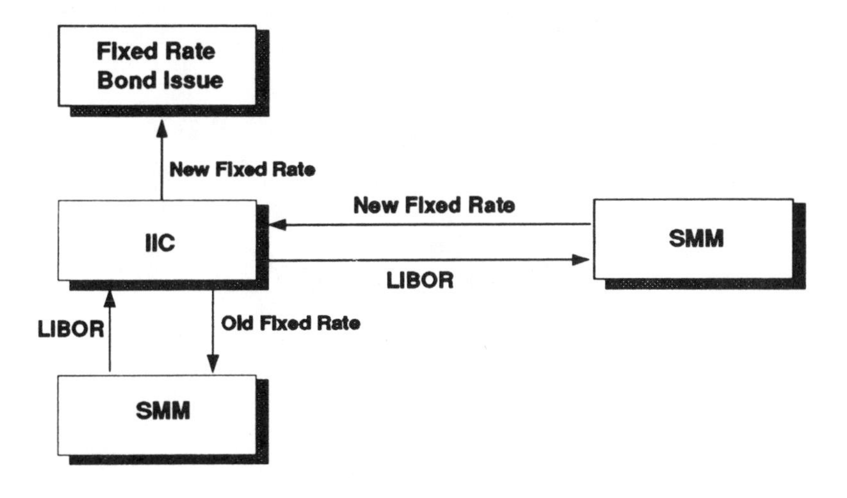

IIC can use a *placeholder swap* in preparation for realigning its portfolio. IIC enters into a swap transaction (in the tactical portfolio) under which it pays fixed rate and receives floating. At a later time, when the market conditions are friendlier, it plans to issue a long-term fixed-rate bond. At that time, the swap will be offset by a reverse swap under which IIC will receive fixed and pay floating. The floating-rate legs of the two swaps will net out leaving IIC with the two fixed-rate legs. Any excess or deficit in the fixed rate received in the second swap relative to the fixed rate paid on the hedging swap will be offset by a corresponding increase or decrease in the bond coupon due to change in the level of interest rates. Thus, IIC has essentially locked in long-term interest rates.

5

Analyzing a Transaction

Evaluating a Transaction

If a swap transaction, or any transaction for that matter, is being contemplated by a corporation, prudent risk management procedure requires that the transaction be analyzed from different points of view. The conclusion from each analysis then contributes input to the decision-making process. Since, without exception, every transaction has positive and negative attributes, these inputs are necessary to determine if the transaction is appropriate when all factors have been taken into consideration.

There are numerous aspects under which a transaction should be analyzed. The relative importance of each factor depends upon the specifics of the situation. Some of these aspects are:

Asset/Liability Matching. If a corporation is considering a swap in order to match its assets and liabilities, then the justification for the transaction is obvious. All other factors become relatively less important.

Value. To the extent that a corporation is *managing* rather than *matching* its assets and liabilities, or to the extent that its assets (or liabilities) are not financial as in the case of an industrial corporation, any expectation of value that the transaction can achieve gains importance. Therefore, in such a situation, a swap transaction is evaluated by determining if the swap creates value, e.g., by reducing the borrowing cost for the corporation.

A swap can provide value in different ways:

- True arbitrage: A corporation might be able to execute a swap to reduce its borrowing cost by arbitraging the imbalances in different market segments. The corporation itself is exposed to no significant market risk. The only tradeoff might be the added credit risk of the swap counterparty. Notwithstanding the high level of efficiency of the financial markets, such arbitrage situations are found frequently.
- Liquidity: A swap, in combination with other transactions (e.g., fixed-rate bond issue), might provide other types of value to the corporation such as increased liquidity.
- Risk arbitrage: Often a corporation has a market view that might make a particular swap transaction attractive. The corporation takes the risk that its view regarding the course of rates might be incorrect. If any loss resulting from an incorrect view of the market is acceptable and the view is based on concrete examination of the market situation, then we consider such a transaction a value-creating arbitrage, not pure speculation.
- Diversification: A swap transaction can also diversify a corporation's debt portfolio into different maturities and currencies. Diversification, in and of itself, is value, whether or not some immediate savings, measured in basis points, are achieved.

Credit Risk. Unlike a straight borrowing, a swap transaction exposes the corporation to the credit risk of the counterparty. Therefore, any value realized by the transaction should be in examined in relation to this additional risk.

Market View. The transaction should be consistent with any market view in terms of short- and long-term trends in interest and perhaps currency-exchange rates. Note here that it is not incorrect or imprudent to have a market view. On the other hand, liability and asset managers should be in constant touch with the market and draw continually corrected and updated views of the market. Market view does not necessarily mean that the manager believes the rates will reach a particular level over a particular time period. The view could be more broad, e.g., rates are trending down, rates are volatile or stable, etc.

Maximum Market Risk. In cases where the corporation is taking a certain market risk in return for a certain expected benefit, the probability as well as the magnitude of maximum amount of loss must be considered carefully. Often, the impact of this maximum risk is so great that no amount of expected benefit justifies the transaction.

Suitability. In an efficient and liquid market, outside of the true arbitrage situations mentioned above, it is rare that a corporation can expect to reduce its interest expenses without a corresponding exposure to some type of risk. Often the risk-reward tradeoff is such that the corporation can easily justify a transaction based on the expected and maximum risk levels compared to the reduction in interest expense. However, there is another overriding factor that should be considered and that can veto an otherwise justifiable transaction. That factor is suitability. That is, the transaction should be analyzed to see if the risk, however small, is a suitable one for the corporation. An unsuitable risk should be avoided no matter how great the reward in terms of reduced interest cost.

Situation *(Unsuitable Transaction).* SCC is a specialty chemicals company which supplies chemicals to other domestic manufacturing companies via long-term supply contracts. It has little foreign currency exposure, direct or indirect. SCC needs 10-year-term funds. A transaction has been proposed to SCC which has a play on the relationship between Swiss francs and German marks. Compelling analysis has shown that the recent divergence between the two currencies is unsustainable, and they should get in line soon. Assuming that this realignment happens, SCC could save over 50 basis points per annum using the proposed transaction.

SCC rejected the transaction as it includes risks, in particular currency risks, in which the company has no experience or prior exposure. Notwithstanding the compelling analysis and the very attractive savings under the assumptions, the risks are unsuitable for SCC.

In addition to evaluating the impact of a transaction on the corporation, a prudent manager should also comparatively evaluate the impact of *inaction*. Errors of omission can be as costly as errors of commission. Often, corporations are reluctant to enter into a swap transaction because it might imply a market view. The concern is that such an implication might term the transaction a speculative one, at best a tainted attribute in most situations. However, we should bear in mind that inaction itself implies a market view, and is therefore speculative by the same process of implication.[1]

---

1 Unfortunately, in many situations, entering into a transaction that results in a small loss is less desirable than not entering into one that could have resulted in a large gain. Thus, in the eyes of many managers, errors of commission are costly, errors of omission have no cost.

Many analytical techniques are available to examine a transaction systematically under these different aspects. Some of the more useful techniques include the following.

Historical Analysis

A quick and easy way to test a hypothesis or review a transaction is to subject it to historical analysis. The basic test is whether the transaction, if it had been executed sometime in the past, would have been beneficial to the corporation. We are implicitly making the assumption that we can draw conclusions about the future using data from the past. Even assuming that such conclusions can be drawn, the problem is that many different, often diametrically opposite, conclusions can result from the same data. For example, consider the recent dramatic fall in U.S. dollar interest rates. It is possible to infer from the recent historical data that the trend will continue and that the rates will fall further. On the other hand, it is also plausible that rates will return to normal and will go back to their historical average level. Thus, it is not clear if history will repeat—or reverse—itself. Nonetheless, historical analysis is useful and may point to any glaring shortcomings of a proposed transaction.

Even in historical analysis, it is preferable, where possible, to have a theoretical model in mind as otherwise incorrect conclusions might result. For example, when rates fall, spreads between Treasuries and corporate bonds increase. This might not mean that corporate bonds are cheap, just that the value of the call option found in many corporate bonds has increased. This makes the bonds *less expensive,* not necessarily *cheap.*

In the swap area, consider Exhibit 5–1, which shows the historical swap spreads for the last several years. Clearly, the spreads are very low compared to levels in the recent

EXHIBIT 5–1 Historical U.S.$ 5-Year Interest-Rate Swap Spread

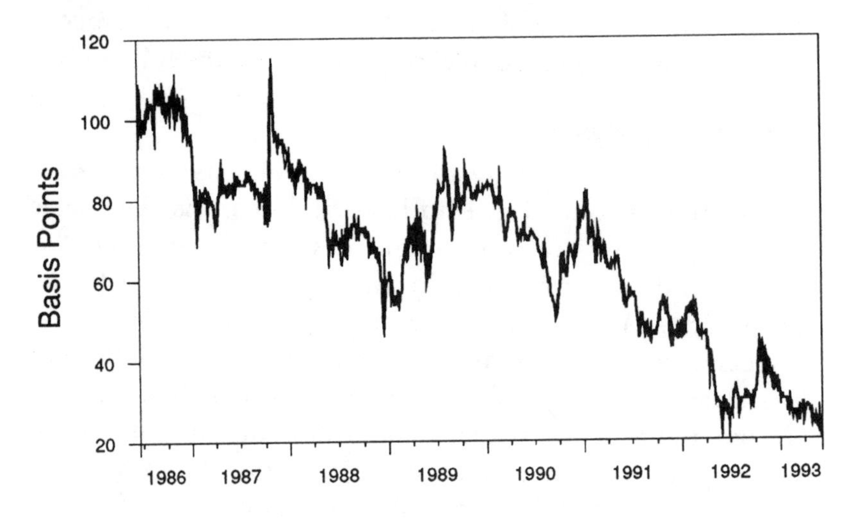

past. However, before jumping to the conclusion that the spreads are attractive, let us consider the empirical observation that usually the swap spreads are high when Treasury rates are low and low when Treasury rates are high. Therefore, it is more useful to analyze the swap spreads in relation to levels of yields on Treasuries. Exhibit 5–2 shows the 5-year Treasury yields over time. We observe that the yields are also at historically low levels. Exhibit 5–3 plots a scatter diagram of swap spreads in relation to Treasury levels. A linear regression fit of the points is also shown. To compute this regression fit, the outlying points close to the origin have been excluded.

Exhibit 5–3 shows that in general the swap spreads widen when Treasury rates drop. The relationship can be loosely described as linear. However, recently, interest rates have dropped and the swap spreads have tightened as well. Such a deviation from traditional behavior points

EXHIBIT 5–2 Historical U.S.$ 5-Year Treasury Yields

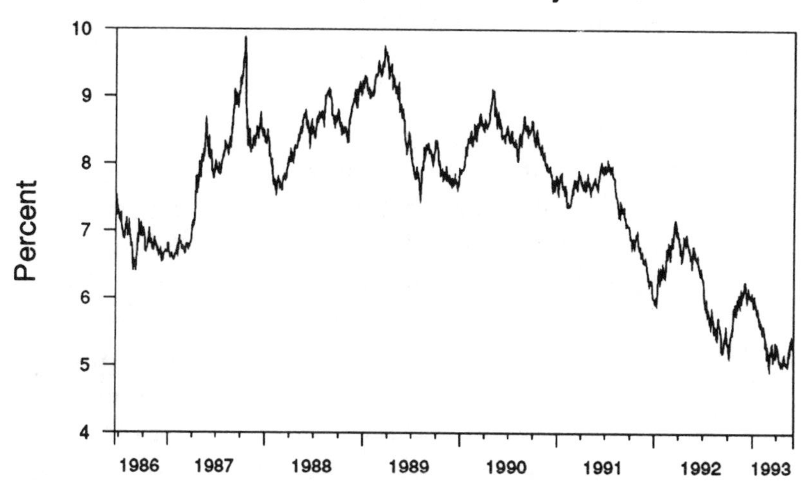

EXHIBIT 5–3 Scatter Diagram of Treasury Yields versus Swap Spreads, with Linear Regression Fit

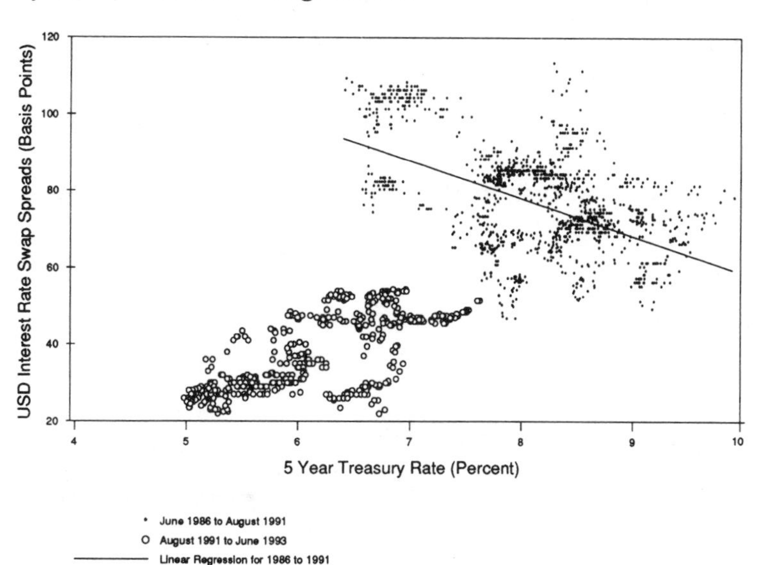

to possible value capture opportunities in the swap market, e.g., by entering into a swap paying a fixed rate and receiving floating.

Breakeven Analysis

A corporation enters into a transaction with the hope that the market will move in a way advantageous to the corporation so that it can realize some benefits. Breakeven analysis considers the possibility that the market might move in a way disadvantageous to the corporation. The analysis determines the limits within which market moves will still be beneficial to the corporation. Moves beyond the breakeven point result in losses for the corporation.

Breakeven analysis is simple because it usually requires no historical data and can be useful in obtaining a feel for the tradeoffs present in any transaction. However, simple-minded breakeven analysis can result in correct, but trivial, results.

> ***Situation*** *(Breakeven Analysis).* JAF is a Japanese automotive corporation considering swapping its fixed-rate debt into floating with the view that short-term rates will re-

EXHIBIT 5–4 Breakeven Analysis: Converting to Floating Rate

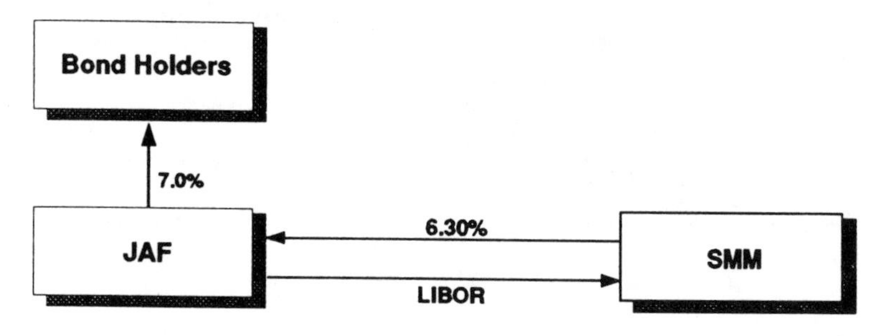

main stable at prevailing low levels. The maturity of its debt is 5 years. Coupon is 7 percent. With the 5-year Treasury rate at 5.95 percent and a swap spread of 35 basis points, the swap rate is 6.30 percent on an actual/360 day basis. That means that the nest cost to JAF after swapping is LIBOR + 70 basis points.

In analyzing this swap transaction, JAF is examining the risk that floating rates might rise and stay at a high level. The breakeven rate clearly is 6.30 percent. That is, if LIBOR rises to 6.30 percent and stays at that level, then JAF would be indifferent to whether JAF executes this swap or not. If LIBOR rises and stays at a higher level, JAF will lose. If LIBOR remains below 6.30 percent, then the swap transaction is advantageous to JAF.

Thus, a simple-minded analysis results in the trivial answer that the breakeven level is the swap rate. A more interesting analysis would use the corporation's view that rates will remain stable at low levels.

Situation *(Breakeven Analysis—Continued).* JAF is comfortable in assuming that short-term rates, represented by 3-month LIBOR, will remain at prevailing low levels at 3.25 percent for the near future, perhaps as long as two years. Using this assumption, breakeven analysis will determine the level to which 3-month LIBOR should rise and stay after the end of the second year. Breakeven will be determined by equating the present values of the two swap legs, discounting at the 5-year swap rate of 6.30 percent.

Under the breakeven scenario, the cash flow paid by JAF under the swap will resemble a step-up rate swap. For the first two years, the rate will be 3.25 percent. For the remaining three years, the rate will be the breakeven rate.

The breakeven rate, determined by an iterative trial-and-error process, is 8.674 percent. Thus, short-term rates have to rise by more than 550 basis points before JAF begins to suffer any disadvantage from the swap transaction.

TABLE 5–1 Breakeven Analysis

Period	Fixed Leg Cash Flow	Present Value	Floating Leg Cash Flow	Present Value
1	3.150	3.054	1.625	1.575
2	3.150	2.961	1.625	1.527
3	3.150	2.870	1.625	1.481
4	3.150	2.782	1.625	1.435
5	3.150	2.698	4.337	3.714
6	3.150	2.615	4.337	3.600
7	3.150	2.535	4.337	3.490
8	3.150	2.458	4.337	3.384
9	3.150	2.383	4.337	3.280
10	3.150	2.310	4.337	3.180
Present Value:		**26.666**		**26.667**

In this analysis, we have used the present value as a standard for determining the breakeven rate. Alternatively, we could use an internal rate of return standard by including the notional principal flows and treating each leg as a full liability with principal and interest payments. In most cases, the two methods should yield similar results.

Scenario Analysis

Breakeven analysis basically divides the possible market moves into two halves, one advantageous and the other disadvantageous. Scenario analysis takes this one step further by allowing for several possible market moves. The analysis thus becomes more comprehensive and perhaps more realistic. The scenario approach also can point to some of the important aspects of the transaction that we discussed earlier such as the maximum potential loss (and the corresponding scenario) from the transaction.

Again as in the case of breakeven analysis, we can easily eliminate trivial results and ensure that the analysis produces interesting conclusions. Also, the scenarios can be more complex than the simple hypothesis of rates reaching a level and staying there. Usually, however, the complexity of each scenario is kept to a manageable extent using linearity and other assumptions.

> ***Situation*** *(Scenario Analysis).* MLD is a corporation considering fixing their floating-rate debt via a swap. Under the swap, MLD will pay a fixed rate of 6.30 percent and receive 6-month LIBOR for a period of 5 years. In order to analyze this transaction, they would like to determine the present value of the payments under different scenarios. In order to simplify the analysis, they assume that short-term rates will rise (or fall) linearly until the maturity of the swap.

Table 5–2 shows three possible scenarios, with rates at maturity of 5 percent, 7 percent, and 9 percent. Assuming that short-term rates rise linearly from present levels to these maturity levels, the present values for each scenario is also shown.[2] By computing the present value similarly for other likely scenarios, MLD can determine if the swap transaction is attractive.

---

2 The present values have been computed by using a fixed discount rate of 6.30% for every cash flow in each scenario. More complex methods, which use higher (lower) discount rates for high (low) interest-rate scenarios are available.

TABLE 5–2 Scenario Analysis

	Fixed Leg		Terminal Rate 5% Floating Leg		Terminal Rate 7% Floating Leg		Terminal Rate 9% Floating Leg	
Period	Cash Flow	Present Value	Cash Flow	Present Value	Cash Flow	Present Value	Cash Flow	Present Value
1	3.150	3.054	1.625	1.575	1.625	1.575	1.625	1.575
2	3.150	2.961	1.722	1.619	1.833	1.723	1.944	1.827
3	3.150	2.870	1.819	1.658	2.042	1.860	2.264	2.063
4	3.150	2.782	1.917	1.693	2.250	1.987	2.583	2.282
5	3.150	2.698	2.014	1.725	2.458	2.105	2.903	2.486
6	3.150	2.615	2.111	1.753	2.667	2.214	3.222	2.675
7	3.150	2.535	2.208	1.777	2.875	2.314	3.542	2.851
8	3.150	2.458	2.306	1.799	3.083	2.406	3.861	3.013
9	3.150	2.383	2.403	1.818	3.292	2.490	4.181	3.162
10	3.150	2.310	2.500	1.833	3.500	2.567	4.500	3.300
Net Present Value:		26.666		17.249		21.242		25.234
Mean NPV of Floating Legs:		21.242						
Standard Deviation of NPV of Floating Legs:		3.260						

Note that scenario analysis can also provide statistical information[3] that is absent from breakeven analysis. For example, by assigning specific probabilities to each scenario, or by assuming that each scenario is equally likely, we can determine a mean or average present value. The dispersion of present values can be estimated by computing their standard deviation.

Monte Carlo Simulation

The function of asset or liability portfolio management is to assume and manage interest-rate risk in a judicious manner in order to maximize the goals of the institution. Specifically, it does not necessarily attempt to create an optimal bet on an interest-rate forecast. Therefore, in general, we have to examine a broad range of possible outcomes

---

3 Table 5–2 considers only three scenarios. For the statistical information to be meaningful, we need more scenarios.

rather than a best guess in evaluating a transaction. Scenario analysis is one way to carry out this examination. Monte Carlo[4] simulation takes scenario analysis to its final step and can assist in the portfolio management process by providing valuable insight into the behavior of the assets and/or liabilities, in various market situations. Simulation can deal with more complex market conditions and assumptions than can analytical methods. The more complex the transaction, the more useful simulation is relative to breakeven or simple scenario analysis.

In Monte Carlo simulation, each scenario can be made more complex. For example, instead of assuming a rate level at maturity with a linear path from prevailing rates, we can assume a more realistic statistical distribution at each payment period. The complexity of each scenario also implies that the number of scenarios can be very large. In addition, many scenarios might be describing very similar market moves. Therefore, the individual scenario loses its importance whereas the statistical summaries gain significance.

Simulation, in order to be useful, should avoid totally random interest-rate scenarios. Such simple-minded simulations are not very useful since we can never optimize or manage the risk under *all* possible scenarios without putting excessive constraints on the allowable assets and liabilities. It is not unreasonable to assume that interest rates move in a less-than-totally-random, more structured, way.

---

4 This methodology has been attributed to Karl Pearson, a statistician. He went to Monte Carlo in 1892 for two weeks and his observations of gambling there motivated him to publish a work on probability theory in 1900.

Yield curve models[5] provide a way to simulate rate moves in an organized, reasonable way. These models not only generate many possible scenarios, but also provide the appropriate probability to use along with each scenario. This helps us focus on the most probable scenarios without wasting our efforts on remote possibilities. These models also make possible the use of a variety of asset and/or liability combinations and broaden the asset and liability base.

One convenient way to implement a simulation model is to use a *binomial tree* similar to the one used in the valuation of options. The tree has *nodes* or branching points that represent a state of the market at a given point in time. Starting at today's market rate at the root, the tree branches out into two at each level from each node, one branch in which rates rise and another in which rates fall. The level of rates at each node depends upon the parameters of the assumptions made to develop the tree.[6] Thus, the tree shows possible future rate levels under the assumptions of the model.

---

5 Yield curve models, also known as term structure models, provide a systematic way to assume the random movement of the interest rates along the yield curve. They constrain the range of movement of the rates and the corresponding probabilities such that they are (i) internally consistent, that is, there is no riskless profitable arbitrage, and (ii) externally consistent, that is, the values of certain securities implied from the model agree with the market values. For an introduction to internally and externally consistent yield curve models, see Ravi E. Dattatreya and Frank J. Fabozzi, *Active Total Return Management of Fixed-Income Portfolios,* (Chicago: Probus, 1989).

6 Please see Ravi E. Dattatreya and Frank Fabozzi, *Active Total Return Management of Fixed-Income Portfolios* (Chicago: Probus, 1989), for a discussion of how to develop the binomial tree and use it for Monte Carlo simulation.

Monte Carlo simulation can provide insight into the *price* as well as *value* of a financial instrument.[7] The price is obtained by superimposing an objective methodology, such as a yield curve model, on the simulation. The value to the user can be determined by modifying the simulation in accordance with any views that the user might have regarding market movements.

Even without an elaborate yield curve model, we can constrain the movement of interest rates in a simulation by observing that:

- The further into the future we look, the less accurate our knowledge of rates becomes. Therefore, the dispersion of rates should increase with the passage of time.
- Nominal interest rates are bounded from below, i.e., they are nonnegative.
- Interest appears to be positively correlated. That is, a high (low) interest-rate level in one period tends to be followed by a high (low) level of rates in the next period.

One simple way to incorporate these factors is to estimate the mean of the distribution of rates in each period to the maturity of the swap transaction under review and then allow rates to deviate from this estimated mean by using ever-increasing standard deviations. We might get clues from the forward rate computations to determine mean rates remembering that they do not necessarily rep-

---

7 One of the earliest applications of simulation to valuation can be found in "Options: A Monte Carlo Approach," *Journal of Finance* (1977), by P.P. Boyle, professor of finance at the University of Waterloo.

resent either our expectations or the market's expectations of rate moves.

Situation *(Monte Carlo Simulation).* SSD is a corporation that is considering fixing its floating liabilities. In order to evaluate a swap transaction in this connection, SSD is conducting a simulation study of its floating-rate debt before the swap. SSD has decided that the forward rates as computed by the rates are overestimates of the mean rates in the future and has determined appropriate corrections. SSD has also computed the historical volatility of interest rates and has decided to use a variance of rates that is linearly increasing in time.[8] That is, the variance is 10 percent for the first year, 20 percent for the second year and so on. Scenarios, actually interest-rate paths, are simulated under these parameters. Some typical paths along with the mean and the customary standard deviation boundaries are shown in Exhibit 5–4.

Now, for each path or scenario we can compute the present value cost or, alternatively, the total cost as an annual rate. The results from a large number of such simulations is summarized and shown in Exhibit 5–5. The exhibit depicts the distribution of probable interest costs. Also shown are the mean cost and standard deviation.

Once the simulation study is done, the decision to evaluate the results in comparison to available alternatives still remains. More often than not, the decision is not black and white, but is rather a subjective one. There will always be tradeoffs, such as lower mean cost for the floating-rate option along with higher variance. We should remember also that the results from the study themselves are dependent upon certain of our initial assumptions.

---

8 Standard deviation, therefore, varies as the squareroot of time. That is, it doubles every four years.

EXHIBIT 5–5 Simulated Path of Three-Month LIBOR

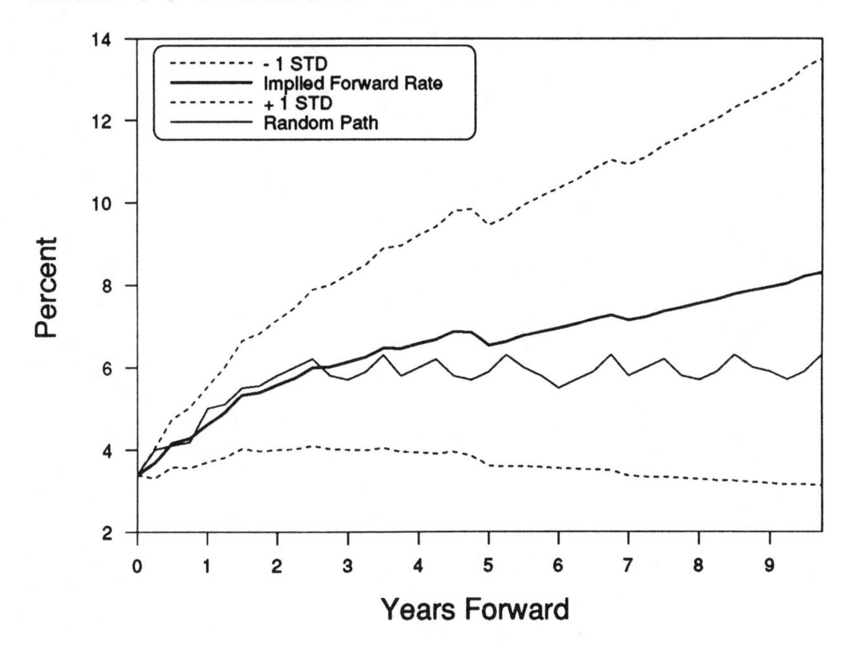

6

Pricing and Risk Characteristics

Participants in the Swap Market

As in all financial markets, different participants in the swap business serve different functions.

An *end user* is the ultimate consumer of swaps. End users usually have some assets or liabilities that they wish to hedge using swaps. There are also those who enter into swap transactions seeking trading profits. In addition to outright swap positions, a popular trade is to match a short-term swap against a position in Eurodollar futures.

A *market maker*, as the name implies, provides liquidity by making two-way markets in swaps. In general, market makers are the major source of swaps for end users. That is, end users execute swaps mostly with market makers rather than with other end users.[1] Market makers usually hedge their swap positions with more liquid instruments, such as Treasuries and futures, until an offsetting position can be executed in the swap market itself. They also ac-

1 Among the reasons for this are that end users do not have access to or knowledge of other end users with matching swap needs, and they do not have the resources necessary to measure, monitor, and manage the resulting credit risk.

tively seek offsetting swaps to reduce the size of their hedge positions and limit any risk not easily hedgeable with liquid market instruments.

An *intermediary* stands between two swap parties, shielding each from the other's credit risk. The major risk to the intermediary itself is the credit exposure to the two parties. The intermediary earns a fee as compensation for the credit risk. Intermediation is used when one party cannot take the credit risk of the other party or when other considerations, e.g., those related to tax and regulatory issues, apply.

These three types of players are principals in swap transactions, that is, they actually are the counterparties. On the other hand, *brokers* or *agents* do not enter into swaps themselves. For a fee, they find and bring together parties that can execute swap transactions. The cost to the end user is increased by the amount of the brokerage fee. Among brokers are many investment banks that do not have their own swap operations and brokers who provide information on available swaps through data screens.

Swap Pricing Basics

The maturity of the dollar–interest-rate swap market is indicated by the widely available bid and offer quotations in maturities from 1 to 10 years. Swap rates are quoted as a spread over the bond yield of the on-the-run (i.e., the most liquid) Treasury,[2] of appropriate maturity. Sometimes, the spread is added to a rate interpolated from two on-the-run

---

2 Usually, simultaneous execution of offsetting swaps by a swap dealer is uncommon. Therefore, it is likely that one or both parties to a swap will execute a Treasury trade to hedge the swap position. Swaps of maturities of up to 5 years are usually hedged in the Eurodollar futures market. In general, the fixed-rate payer will base the rate on the offered price and the receiver will base it on the bid side. Some end users control the bid-offered difference by actually selling or purchasing the appropriate Treasury from the dealer.

Treasuries whose maturities straddle that of the swap. For short maturities (up to 4 years), swap rates are often quoted using the money-market practice, that is, as an absolute level on an annual (actual 360-day) basis.[3]

> **Example.** On July 16, 1993, the 2-year swap rate was quoted at 4.12 percent on an actual/360 basis. The 5-year swap rate was quoted at 24 basis points over the 5-year Treasury note, which in turn was quoted at a yield of 4.987%.

A swap is an exchange of two streams of cash flows. Therefore, a swap can be priced by determining the value of each stream of cash flows. The price of the swap is simply the difference between the values of the two cash flows. The value of each stream of cash flows is the net present value (NPV), that is, the sum of the discounted present values of each cash flow in the stream. If the cash flows are in different currencies, the NPVs are converted to one currency at the prevailing exchange rate before the difference is taken to price the swap.

For new swaps, this price has to be zero. In other words, if we are willing to exchange one stream of cash flows (one leg of the swap) for another, then the values of the two legs or streams of cash flows should be equal. In this context, pricing a swap means determining one or more parameters of the swap to determine how to make the values of the two streams equal. A common parameter that is computed in pricing a swap is the fixed rate on the fixed leg of a swap. That is, to price a new interest-rate swap is to determine the *fixed rate* applied to the leg of the swap. To price existing swaps, we compute the *market value* of the swap, which is the difference between the NPVs of the two legs.

---

3 The reason for using money-market convention is that short-dated swaps are priced from the Eurodollar futures.

The swap may be arbitrarily complex, and the market data that is used to determine the net present value of the legs may be large in number and may be obtained from different sources, yet the fundamental principal in pricing the swap remains the same: if two streams of cash flows are exchanged, then their values must be equal. If they are not, then one party to the swap must compensate the other for the difference. This compensating payment is the price of the swap.

It helps to visualize the situation as a balance scale,[4] one side of which carries the NPV of one leg, and the other side carrying the NPV of the other leg. If the scale is not balanced or level, if the NPVs of the two legs are not equal, we have to add an adjustment weight to the lighter side. This adjustment, an upfront payment from one party to another, is the value of the swap. The balance-scale analogy also illustrates another fact in swap pricing: the value of the swap to one party is equal and opposite to the value to the other parties. That is, if one party has a gain (one side of the balance goes up, swap value becomes positive) in the swap, the other party has a loss (the other side of the balance goes down, swap value becomes negative) of an exactly equal amount.

Other common financial evaluation techniques, such as the internal rate of return (IRR), are of little practical use in swap pricing. IRRs for different cash flows are not comparable in any way.[5] NPV, on the other hand, is in current

---

4 The balance-scale analogy is due to R.A. Beckstrom.

5 See discussion of this fact in the context of bond trading in Ravi E. Dattatreya and Frank Fabozzi, *Active Total Return Management of Fixed Income Portfolios* (Chicago: Probus, 1989).

dollars and has the attractive property of additivity and comparability.[6]

Conceptually, then, the value of a swap can be easily computed by discounting the cash flows from each leg of the swap. There are a few complications that need to be addressed before we can apply the discounting rules.

First, we need an appropriate *discount function,* that is, a set of discount rates corresponding to the timing of each cash flow. The discounting function is popularly known as the *zero curve* or the *zero-coupon curve,* since the rates correspond to yields on zero-coupon bonds as compared to the *par curve,* which represents the yield on full-coupon bonds.[7] Often, it is represented in the form of *discount factors.* The discount factor for a given date is the present value of a $1 cash flow occurring on that date and is a number between 0 and 1.[8] In practice, discount factors and zero rates are generated using a variety of market data such as cash LIBOR deposit rates, the swap rates for plain-vanilla structures, Eurodollar futures prices, and current Treasury yields. The goal in using all this data is to derive a

---

6 Many weak measures—such as IRR, yield, option-adjusted spread (OAS)—somehow tend to get entrenched in capital market analyses. However, NPV is a more robust measure and will eventually prevail. Practitioners in the swap and other derivative markets, more than any other group, have contributed to the development of the correct line of thinking on the matter.

7 The curve representing rates for plain-vanilla or standard at-market swaps is also called the par curve. Note that rates from the par curve are not suitable for discounting. They represent a blend of various discount rates corresponding to each of the cash flows in a par bond. Compare this situation with the discussion of risk points in chapter 5, where we show that the risk of a par bond is a combination of the risks in zero-coupon bonds corresponding to the coupon and principal cash flows.

8 As opposed to discount rates, discount factors have the attractive property that they do not have any attached conventions such as compounding frequency or day-count method.

curve that represents the rates that can be used for pricing swaps.[9] We discuss the derivation of zero rates and discount factors in more detail in the next section.

Second, unlike bonds or other investments, the swap has 2-way cash flows. This problem can be handled simply either by computing the values algebraically (i.e., by including the sign) or by splitting the incoming and outgoing cash flows and valuing them separately.

Third, the cash flows on the floating side are unknown, except perhaps for the first payment, which is set at the outset. The solution to this problem is to replace each of the unknown floating-rate flows by rates that can be locked in through hedging transactions in the capital markets. These rates are called *forward rates* and are discussed in detail in the next section. Forward rates are computed from the discount function or derived from the prices of Eurodollar futures.

Note that the zero curve of the discount function is being used to serve two functions:

1. To determine the implied forward rates, which in turn fix, for valuation purposes, the future floating-rate cash flows
2. To determine the appropriate discounting rate to use for cash flows occurring at various times on the fixed side as well as the floating side of the swap

Normally, the zero curve derived represents LIBOR, given that the par curve is driven by swap rates and Eurodollar futures prices. However, if the floating-rate index used is not LIBOR, we need two zero curves: one to gener-

---

9 Also, additional care is taken to ensure that the swap rates obtained are consistent with all liquid markets such as FRA (forward rate agreement) or Eurodollar futures. Otherwise, an arbitrage condition may exist between these markets and the swap market.

ate forward rates corresponding to the actual index and another (based on LIBOR) to discount all cash flows.[10]

Thus, known forward rates are used to represent unknown future floating-rate cash flows. As far as swap valuation is concerned, we are indifferent to the distinction between the unknown floating-rate cash flows or the known cash flows represented by forward rates.[11] Once the floating side has been so "fixed," its present value is computed by discounting each flow to the present.[12] The swap rate can then be determined by finding that fixed rate which will produce the same discounted present value as the floating side. Since the values of the two sides are equal, the swap is therefore said to have zero (net) value. The rate so derived is called the *midpoint* or the *breakeven rate*. Bid-

---

10 For example, in a T-bill-for-fixed swap, a Treasury curve is used to derive assumed cash flows corresponding to future T-bill rates, and the standard swap curve is used to derive the discount factors to present value the cash flows.

Discounting "at LIBOR" has become a standard in the swap market and assumes the willingness and ability to lend and borrow at LIBOR. However, if the swap structure implies significant net lending or borrowing, e.g., as in a zero-coupon swap, then appropriate spreads are added before discounting.

11 Note, however, that there is no assumption, implicit or explicit, that the interest rate in the future will actually be equal to the forward rate. We are willing to substitute known forward rates for unknown future rates for valuation purposes because we can, if we so desire, effectively lock in or fix the future cash flow at a level implied by the forward rates by using appropriate hedging techniques.

12 Appropriate day-count conventions are used in computing the interest payments as well as in discounting. Payments on the fixed side are usually quoted on a 30/360-day basis. Floating payments are generally computed on an actual/360 basis. In addition, if there is any compounding involved, the correct forward rates based on the compounding calendar have to be used to compute the cash flows. Compounding usually is required when the reset frequency is greater than the payment frequency, e.g., LIBOR set monthly, paid semiannually.

offered spreads are used to appropriately modify the swap rates derived as needed.

If market rates, and therefore zero-coupon rates and forward rates, have moved since the initial pricing of a swap, then the value of the fixed side of the swap will diverge from the value of the floating side. Even though the cash flows on the fixed side are fixed, its value will change because of the change in the zero-coupon rates that are used for discounting. On the floating-rate side, the change in value results from changes in both the representative cash flows and the discounting rates. In this situation, the swap is said to be *off-market*. That is, the present values of the floating side and the fixed side will not be equal due to changes in the forward rates.

The value of an off-market swap is not zero: Its positive or negative value with respect to a counterparty depends upon whether the receive or the pay side of the cash flow has greater value. The swap value is determined by

1. Fixing the floating side using the currently prevailing forward rates
2. Computing the present values of each side by discounting using the current discount function
3. Finding the difference between the two present values

Again, the value of the swap as derived is the midpoint or breakeven value. The actual price to the end user is obtained by modifying the breakeven value by the usual bid-offered spread.

The confidence and comfort in this simple and logical procedure has enabled swap dealers to price virtually arbitrary sets of cash flows. This has increased the availability of swap structures while providing greater liquidity, larger notional amounts, and narrower bid/offered spreads. In practice, however, several factors enter into the pricing of swaps. Among them are

1. ***Prevailing market conditions,*** for example, the term structure of interest rates such as the par curve or the Eurodollar futures prices. Market data represent the most visible and objective information in the pricing of swaps
2. ***Structure of the swap,*** for example, its maturity, floating index, and size. The structure of a swap is important because it influences the liquidity of the swap as well as the nature and number of the hedge instruments required. The structure also determines the level of credit risk in the transaction, as when significant lending or borrowing is implied, which in turn can modify the discounting procedure.
3. ***The current position of the dealer.*** Normally, each dealer strives to balance the net swap positions, i.e., to make equal the total receive-fixed position in each maturity to the total pay-fixed position. If this balance is achieved, then the amount of liquid market securities used to hedge any net position is minimized. This in turn reduces the basis risk between the hedge and the swap position.
4. ***Ready availability of offsetting swaps.*** If transactions outside the swap market are required to hedge and manage a swap position, then the dealer has to price the resulting basis risk into the swap. If offsetting swaps are readily available, then basis risk is minimized, improving the price to the end user.
5. ***Credit quality of the counterparty.*** In general, the swap market does not appear to price credit risk. It is not uncommon to quote the same rate for an AAA-rated counter party and an A-rated party. Nonetheless, certain weak credits, such as construction projects, have

to pay a higher rate. If intermediaries are used for credit-risk sharing or protection, then the fee paid to the intermediary increases the swap cost.

6. ***Nature and level of competition.*** However, the savings, if any, resulting from increasing the number of dealers bidding, are not significant. Many times, depending upon the depth of the market, it is possible that increasing the number of bidders might actually move the market *adversely*.
7. ***Client relationship.*** Often, a transaction is awarded because of qualitative aspects of a relationship between the corporate end user and the dealer. In return, the dealer offers detailed analyses of the problem at hand, market information, innovative ideas, new techniques, and efficient solutions.
8. ***Regulatory constraints*** such as, capital requirements and the required minimum return on capital. Under current rules, the capital required for a corporate counterparty is higher than that for a bank, and higher for currency swaps.
9. ***The quantity and type of hedge instruments,*** including swaps, required. Since the dealer is subject to the bid-offered spread on the hedge instruments, the larger the hedge used, the larger is the cost of hedging. The cost, of course, is reflected in the swap price.

The market maker considers all these factors and others (such as desire for market share) in a quantitative as well as in a qualitative manner to determine the final swap price to the end user.

Exhibit 6-1 summarizes the pricing procedure: The par curve is generated using available market data. The zero curve is derived either from the par curve or in a more straightforward manner from Eurodollar futures. The NPV of the fixed leg is computed using these discount factors.

EXHIBIT 6–1 Summary of Interest-Rate Swap Pricing Procedure

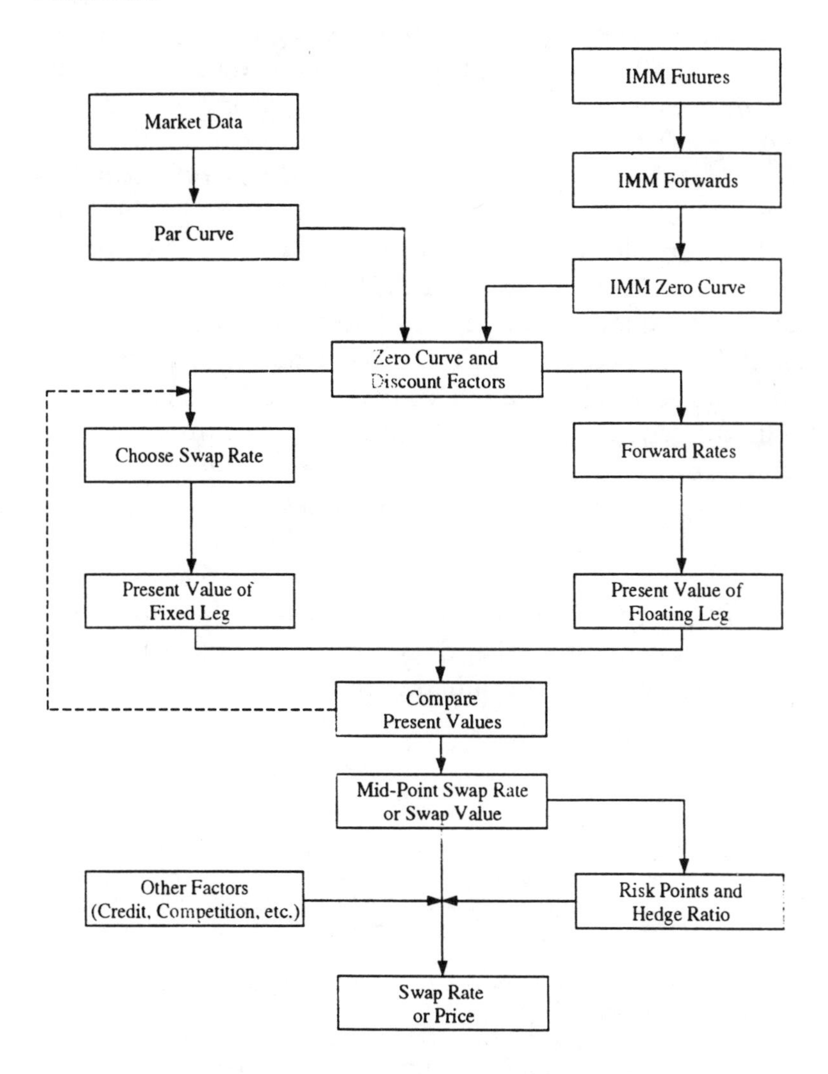

On the floating side, assumed cash flows are first obtained from forward rates derived from the zero curve and then discounted. The NPV of the floating leg is then compared with the NPV of the fixed leg in order to determine either the midpoint swap rate for new swaps or the midpoint swap price for existing swaps. The present value of the fixed leg is recomputed at a different fixed rate, if necessary, to obtain equality of the present values of the fixed and floating legs (dotted line in the exhibit). The various risk points are also computed. Finally, various other qualitative and quantitative factors (credit, required return on capital, competition, etc.) are used along with the risk points to determine the rate or price to the end user.

In this chapter, we illustrate the pricing methodology with a few examples.[13] Some simplification is necessary to facilitate exposition. In some examples, swaps are priced using only Eurodollar futures prices; in others only rates for standard swaps (Treasury rates plus swap spreads) are used for pricing. More comprehensive models would use a combination of all market data. Pricing of a currency swap and its variants are also illustrated.

---

13 The pricing examples are presented in the familiar spreadsheet format with lettered columns and numbered rows. The formulas describing the relationships between the rows and columns are also shown in the spreadsheet format. These devices are used to help the reader implement these pricing models.

Also, where possible, many of the numbers are shown up to several decimal places. The implied accuracy is purely illusory, given that data with less accuracy (e.g., Eurodollar futures prices to two decimal places) have been used to generate them. The additional decimal places are provided to help verify the reader's implementation of these models.

Forward Rates

Forward rates play such an important role in swap pricing that it is useful to understand their properties more fully, what exactly they represent and what they do not.

A forward rate for a given period in the future is one that can be locked in using other available market transactions. We can derive forward rates from either direct or indirect sources.

We can often observe forward rates in the market via *direct sources.* These include forward-rate agreements (FRAs) and financial futures, in particular futures on Eurodeposits. In the U.S. dollar market, Eurodollar futures based on 3-month LIBOR are available out to 5 years and trade in the world's largest futures market. Liquidity is excellent out to three years, a significant amount of trading activity arising out of swap hedging transactions. In other currencies, Euroyen is liquid to 18 months and Euromarks to 12 months. Futures prices are an excellent representation[14] of forward 3-month LIBOR rates. No complicated assumptions or computations are necessary to determine the forwards.

When futures and FRAs are not available, we look to *indirect sources,* and compute forward rates from other market data. These data include cash LIBOR rates, swap rates, Treasury rates, and swap spreads. Indirect sources are used in the long end of the U.S. dollar market (5 years and longer). In most other currencies, the only way to determine forwards is via indirect sources.

---

14 A small adjustment is necessary in the price of the future to estimate forward rates. This adjustment corrects for the effect of the variation margin requirements of futures. This effect is discussed under "Pricing an IMM Swap," in this chapter.

Determination of forwards from indirect sources takes a 3-step process. First, the par curve—rates corresponding to standard swaps—are generated from the market data. This can take the form of prevailing Treasury rates plus the prevailing spreads for standard swaps in the market. These swap rates are represented on the par curve.

The second step is to determine the zero curve, or, equivalently, the discount factors, from the par curve. Discount factors can be derived sequentially from the par curve one after another. This process is called *bootstrapping*. This procedure builds the zero curve in a step-by-step or inductive manner. For each maturity, it uses the fact that the price of a bond is the sum of the present values of all the cash flows (coupon and principal) from the bond. It is best illustrated using algebraic notation.

Suppose we have already determined the first n semiannual discount factors, $f_1, f_2, \ldots, f_n$. Then the discount factor for the next period, $f(n+1)$ is determined using the following relationship:

$$1 = c \times f_1 + c \times f_2 + \ldots + c \times f_n + (1 + c) \times f_{(n+1)}$$

where the left-hand side, 1, represents the price of par, c is the semiannual coupon payment (one-half of the par rate) and $(1 + c)$ represents the final payment with principal and interest for a par bond maturing at the end of the $(n + 1)th$ period. Each of the factors of the form $(c \times f_1)$ represents the present value of a cash flow. The relationship simply says that the sum of the present values of all cash flows is equal to the price of the bond. The required discount factor, $f_{(n+1)}$, is therefore given by

$$f_{(n+1)} = \frac{[1 - (c \times f_1 + c \times f_2 + \ldots + c \times f_n)]}{(1 + c)}$$

Or,

$$f_{(n+1)} = \frac{[1 - c \times (f_1 + f_2 + \ldots f_n)]}{(1 + c)}$$

Thus, given the par curve, if we know the first discount factor, we can compute all other discount factors sequentially. The first discount factor is easy to determine, since the 6-month par rate is also a 6-month zero rate, since a 6-month (semiannual) bond has just one cash flow.

From the discount factors, it is easy to compute the zero rates. The *n*th zero rate, z_n, is related to the *nth* discount factor, f_n, via the relationship:

$$f_n \times \left(1 + \frac{z_n}{2}\right)^n = 1$$

assuming semiannual compounding.

In computing forwards from the zero curve, an arbitrage argument is used. To illustrate this procedure, assume that the 6-month rate is 3.50 percent and the 12-month rate is 3.60 percent. Assume all illustrative rates are semiannually compounded.

Now, an investor with a 12-month horizon can consider the following options.

1. Invest for 12 months at 3.60 percent.
2. Invest for 6 months at 3.50 percent. At the end of 6 months, reinvest the principal and interest earned for an additional 6 months at the then-prevailing 6-month rate.

Of course, in the second option, the total return to the investor over the 12-month horizon is unknown at the outset, since the reinvestment rate for the second 6 months is unknown. If a forward rate contract is available, the investor can use it to hedge the uncertainty in total return. Let *f* be the forward rate. Then, each dollar invested over the 12-month holding period in the second option will return:

$$\left(1 + \frac{0.035}{2}\right) \times \left(1 + \frac{f}{2}\right)$$

The combination of the forward rate contract along with the 6-month investment removes the market risk, i.e., the reinvestment risk, in the investment over the 12-month horizon. Therefore, the return from this combination should be equal to the return on a straight 12-month investment, or,

$$\left(1 + \frac{0.036}{2}\right)^2$$

If one of the returns, say the straight 12-month investment, is greater than the other, then investors will reject the 6-month investment and prefer the 12-month investment. This behavior will bring the rates into balance so as to make the two returns equal. The equality of the two returns has only one unknown, f, which can derived as:

$$f = 2 \times \left(\frac{(1 + \frac{0.036}{2})^2}{(1 + \frac{0.035}{2})} - 1 \right)$$

of, $f = 3.70$ percent. In other words, if a rate of 3.70 percent can be locked in for the second half-year, the investor will have no preference between the two investment options.

Notice that the forward rate is greater than the spot (current) rates. In the first option, the investment is earning 3.60 percent for the first half-year, whereas in the second option interest is accruing at only 3.50 percent. Therefore, a much higher accrual rate is required in the second half of the investment period to make up for the shortfall in the first half.

In fact, longer the duration of shortfall, the higher the forward rate that will be required. For example, if the 30-month rate is 3.60 percent and the 24-month rate is 3.50 percent, the forward 6-month rate two years from now will be 4.00 percent. If the 66-month rate is 3.60 percent and 60-month rate is 3.50 percent, the forward 6-month rate five years from now will be 4.60 percent.

Steepness in the zero-coupon curve also strongly influences forward rates. In the 5-year case, if the rates for 60 and 66 months are 3.50 and 3.70 percent, respectively, that is, if the slope of the zero curve increases by 10 basis points, the forward rate jumps to 5.71 percent.

Similarly, if the zero curve is negatively sloped, that is, if longer rates are lower than shorter rates, forward rates will be lower. For example, if the 60-month and 66-month rates are 3.60 and 3.50 percent, respectively, the 6-month forward rate five years from now will be just 2.50 percent.

Exhibit 6-2 shows the relative shapes and levels of the full-coupon curve (or the par curve), the zero-coupon curve, and the 6-month forward rates starting from an up-

EXHIBIT 6–2 Upward Sloping Par Curve

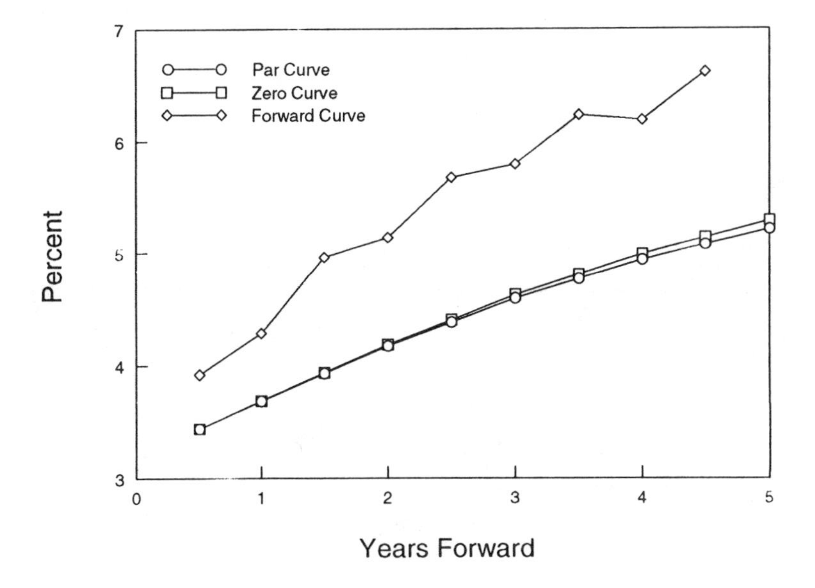

ward-sloping par curve. Note that the zero curve is completely above the par curve and the forward-rate curve is completely above the zero curve. Similarly, in Exhibit 6-3 we have a downward-sloping par curve. Downward-sloping curves normally occur when the general level of rates is relatively high. The corresponding zero curve is entirely below the par curve and the forward-rate curve is entirely below the zero curve. Finally, in Exhibit 6-4, we have a humped par curve, which often occurs in the U.S. dollar market. With a humped par curve, the zero curve and the forward curve may cross the par curve from above.

Now that we know what forward rates are, it is also important to understand what they are not. In particular, forward rates do not represent the actual rate that is going to prevail in the future.

EXHIBIT 6–3 Downward Sloping Par Curve

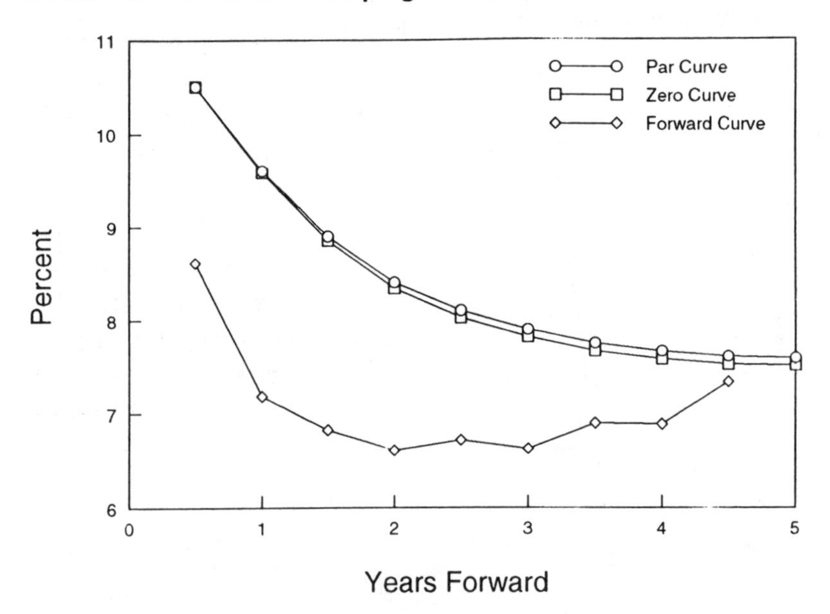

EXHIBIT 6–4 Humped Par Curve

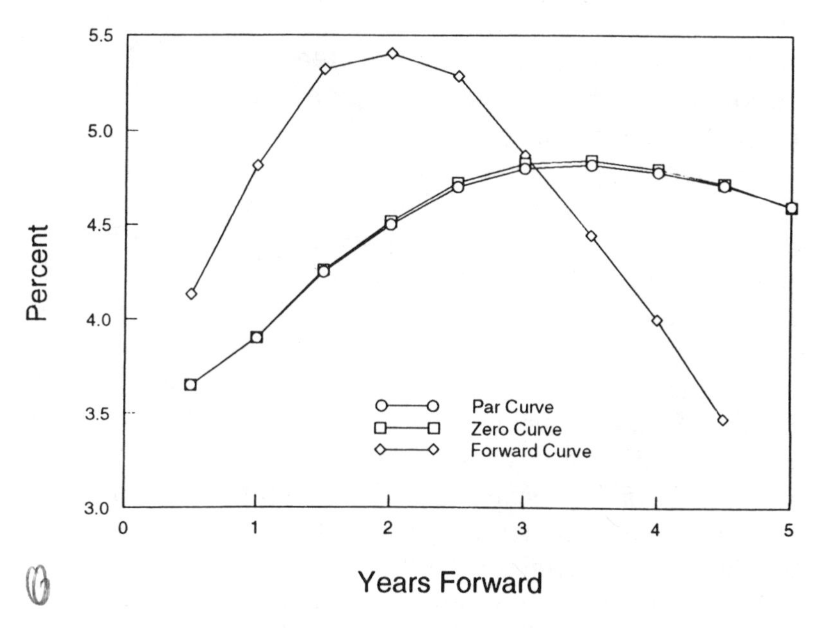

Forward rates also do not represent the market's belief of what the actual rates in the future are going to be.[15] In fact, the market explicitly recognizes the reality that future interest rates vary randomly and can be different from the forward rates in pricing cap[16] and other option-related products.

It is possible to assume that forward rates represent the market's estimation of the mean (or expected value) of the distribution of rates that will prevail in the future. This assumption causes no major theoretical problems except that it implies that market participants act purely based

---

15 The confusion in this context is perhaps due to terminology. A more descriptive term for forward rates might be *hedgeable rates*. These are rates that can be locked in now for a specified period in the future.

16 Caps and other related products are discussed in chapter 7.

upon expected values, i.e., that they are risk neutral.[17] In other words, the implication is that the investor in the example above would have no preference between the first option of a 12-month investment guaranteed to return 3.60 percent and the second option of investing in a 6-month investment at 3.50 percent and an uncertain reinvestment for another 6 months at the then-prevailing rates, assuming that the mean of the possible prevailing rates is 3.70 percent, the forward rate. This assumption makes no adjustment for the inherent risk or uncertainty in the second option as compared to the first.

More completely, in finance theory, we commonly allow for the mean of possible rates to be different from forward rates. This difference is known by various terms, such as *risk premium, liquidity premium,* etc. The premiums can be positive or negative and represent the cost the market assigns for accepting the uncertainty in estimating future rates.

Even empirically, forward rates appear to provide little information about the future. Exhibit 6-5 shows the error, that is, the difference between 6-month forward rates computed from the Treasury yield curve and the actual 6-month rate in the future for the same period over the 17-year interval from 1974 to 1991. Weekly samples of the forward rates were derived from levels at the 6-month and 1-year points from the Treasury yield curve. As can be seen, the distribution of the error is symmetric around zero, similar to the familiar normal distribution. The error

---

17 If all market participants were risk neutral, there would be no preference for one position over another and there would be no need for hedging if prices are fair.

Technically, under risk neutrality, it can be shown that *futures prices,* not forwards, represent expected rates. Forward and futures prices differ, due to the effect of variation margin. See the discussion on convexity of futures elsewhere in this chapter.

EXHIBIT 6–5 Forward Rate as a Predictor of Actual Rates—6M T- Bill Rate Distribution of Error (1974-1993)

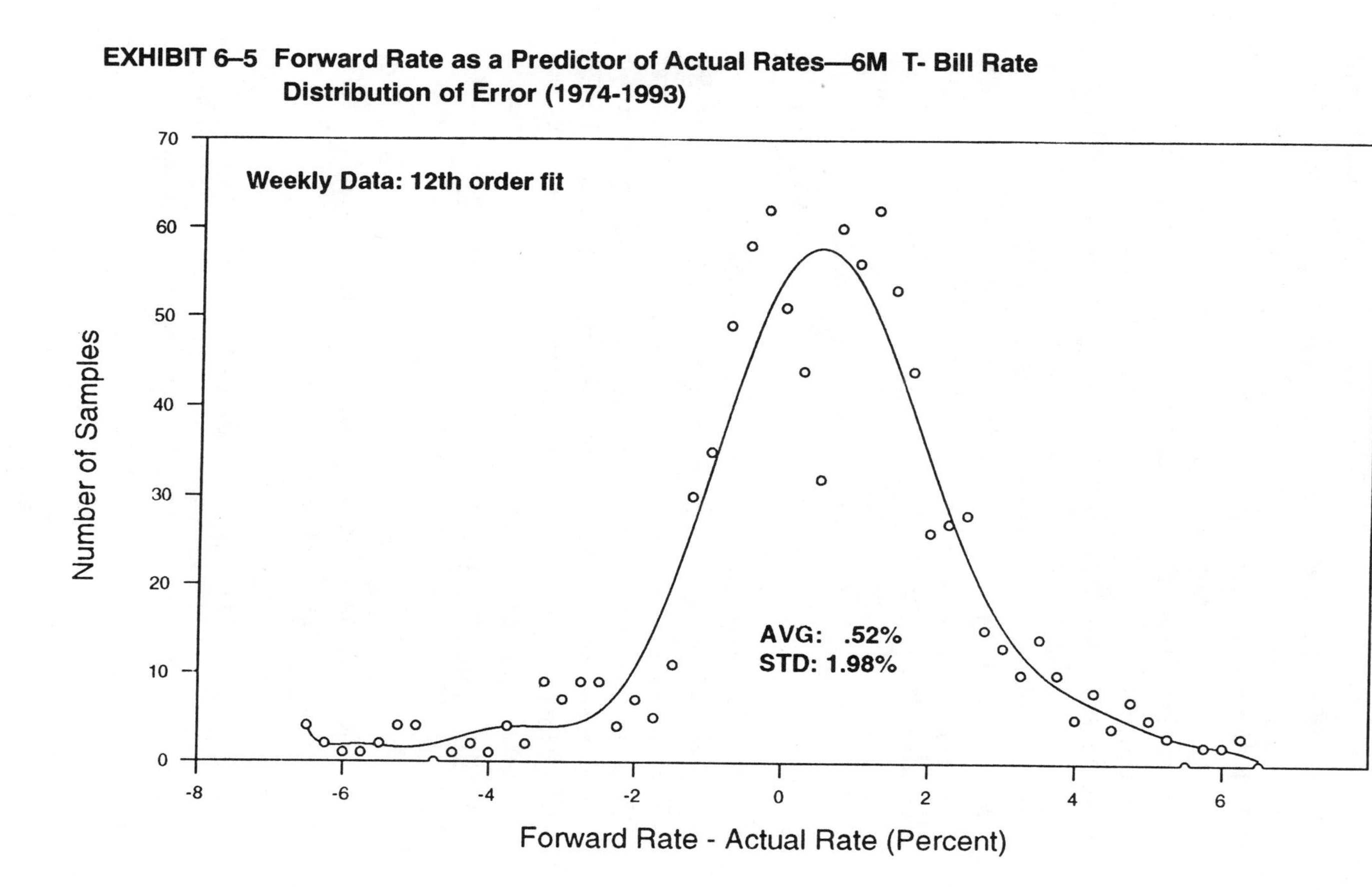

distribution has a mean of 52 basis points. However, the magnitude of error has been as large as 600 basis points. The standard deviation is 198 basis points. In other words, forward rates are unbiased predictors of future rates, but with too large an error. The correlation between forward rates and future rates is a low 53 percent.

These results imply that forward rates are a poor indicator of future rate levels. In fact, the current or spot-rate level is as good a predictor (correlation 57 percent) as the forward rate.

During the recent past, the failure of forward rates to predict future rates has been more dramatic. Over the period from January 1991 to August 1993, the curve has been steeply positively sloped resulting in high forward rates relative to spot rates. However, spot rates have been tending downward over the entire period. Exhibit 6-6 shows the distribution of error of the difference between actual and forward rates computed weekly from the LIBOR yield curve. The mean of the error distribution is 64 basis points with a standard deviation of 45 basis points.

The market's expectation of rates, then, differs from the forward rates. However, unlike forward rates, expected rates are not visible either directly or indirectly in the open market parameters. Fortunately, it turns out that there is no need to know the market's expectation of rates. Our actions are not driven by either the market's actual or its assumed expectations, but by our own. The prudent procedure to follow is

- For pricing purposes, use forward rates as if they will prevail, since, if need be, we can actually lock in those rates using appropriate hedges[18]

---

18 Of course, we cannot replace unknown floating rates by forward rates in all situations. For example, in pricing caps, we are specifically pricing the volatility of rates, i.e., how future rates can differ from forward rates.

EXHIBIT 6–6 Forward Rate as a Predictor of Actual Rates—3M LIBOR Rate Distribution of Error (1991-1993)

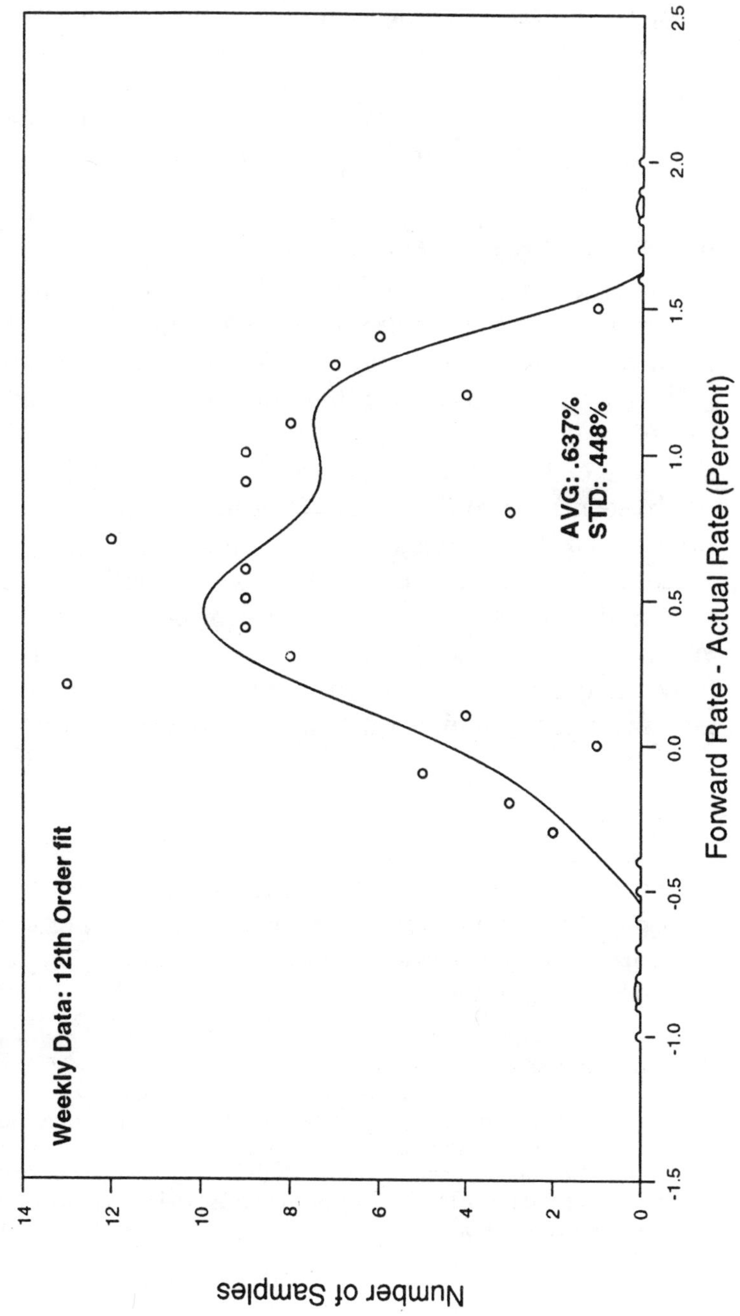
Weekly Data: 12th Order fit
AVG: .637%
STD: .448%
Number of Samples
0
2
4
6
8
10
12
14
-1.5
-1.0
-0.5
0.0
0.5
1.0
1.5
2.0
2.5
Forward Rate - Actual Rate (Percent)

- Use our own projection of rate movements to select transactions for execution

Thus, the markets (forward rates) determine *pricing*, our own views determine *preference*.[19]

Interest-Rate Risk Characteristics

The risk characteristics[20] of a swap are quite interesting. The popular risk measure, *duration*,[21] can be roughly defined as the change in value for a unit change in interest rates. Duration is additive; therefore, we can determine the price sensitivity of a swap as the algebraic sum of the sensitivities of the floating and the fixed sides. We have already seen how to determine the duration of a fixed cash flow such as that corresponding to the fixed side of a swap.

Floating-rate bonds usually have very small interest-rate sensitivity, i.e., low duration. We can see this intuitively. When rates increase, the size of the floating-rate coupon flow increases, increasing the value of the coupon flow. However, at the higher interest rates, the present value of

---

19 Our preferences, of course, are modified by other goals and constraints, e.g., suitability and risk tolerance, before execution. See chapter 5 for more detailed analysis.

20 See chapter 4. For a more detailed discussion of popular interest-rate risk measures, their computation, usage, and limitations, see Ravi E. Dattatreya and Frank J. Fabozzi, *Active Total Return Management of Fixed Income Portfolios* (Chicago: Probus, 1989).

21 Duration is traditionally defined as the percentage change in value for a unit change in rates. Since at-market swaps have zero value, the percentage change is undefined. Therefore, it is more useful to deal with *dollar duration*, which is the actual dollar change in value for a unit change in rates. In this discussion, we use the term *duration* to mean dollar duration.

the principal payment at maturity falls. Thus, the present values of the coupon flow and the principal payment move in opposite directions as rates move. It turns out that they change in the opposite direction but in almost equal magnitudes. This leads to the low price sensitivity of floating-rate bonds.

It is tempting to jump to the conclusion that the floating side of the swap is also of small duration like a floating-rate note. However, the floating side of a swap does not have a small duration. In fact, it has a large, negative duration.[22] This fact can be easily demonstrated. A little reflection reveals that the floating side resembles the coupon stream from a floating-rate bond. In other words, we can synthesize a floating-rate bond by combining the floating side with a zero-coupon bond representing the principal payment. Viewing this another way, the floating side is equivalent to a portfolio of a long position in a floating-rate bond and a short position in the zero-coupon bond representing the principal payment.

Floating side of swap + Zero–coupon bond = Floating–rate bond

Floating side of swap = Floating–rate bond – Zero–coupon bond

The equality holds not only for value, but also for change in value, i.e., for interest-rate risk or duration. Therefore, the duration of the floating side should be equal to the duration of this portfolio. The long position in the floating-rate bond has a very low duration. Therefore, the portfolio duration is roughly equal to that of the short posi-

---

22 The floating side of a swap has been marketed under the name VIRA, Variable Interest Rate Asset. The VIRA is an asset with the negative-duration property of a fixed-rate liability.

tion in the zero-coupon bond. Thus, the floating side of a swap behaves like a short position in a zero-coupon bond. That is, it has negative duration in the sense that, unlike most fixed-income instruments, its value increases if rates increase and decreases if rates fall.

From the point of view of the fixed-rate receiver in a swap transaction, the fixed receipts have the same duration as the coupon stream on a fixed-coupon bond. The floating payments have the negative of the duration of a zero-coupon bond.[23] Combining these two durations algebraically, i.e., changing the sign of the duration of the payment side, we conclude that the duration of a swap is equal to the sum of the duration of the coupon stream on a fixed-coupon bond and the duration of a zero-coupon bond representing the principal. That is, the duration of a swap is equal to the duration of a bond of equal maturity with a coupon equal to the fixed rate.[24]

We can arrive at the same conclusion in a different way. From the risk point of view, a swap position is essentially similar to the leveraged holding of a bond. For example, we can synthesize the cash flows of a receive-fixed swap by borrowing cash at a floating rate and investing in a bond. The floating interest payments represent the floating leg and the fixed coupon receipts from the bond represent the fixed leg. The principal payment on the bond offsets the return of principal on the borrowing. Thus, the interest-rate sensitivity of the swap should be equal to that of the

---

23 Floating *receipts* have negative duration. Floating *payments* have the negative of negative duration, that is, positive duration, equal to that of a zero-coupon bond.

24 This is the concept behind the so-called "par FRN" method of pricing swaps in which the floating side is reduced to a floating-rate note priced at par (par FRN) by adding a principal flow. Then the fixed-rate side (along with the same principal flow) should also have par value, and this fact is used to determine the fixed rate.

leveraged position. In other words, swap duration is equal to bond duration.

There is another way to determine the risk characteristics of a swap. Since the swap is valued based on market rates such as Treasury yields, it is possible to determine the change in the value of the swap as a result of a small change in one of the market rates, say the 5-year Treasury yield. This number, called the *risk point*,[25] represents the interest-rate sensitivity of the swap *relative* to the particular Treasury yield. To completely represent a swap's risk profile, we have to compute the risk point of the swap relative to each market rate used in its valuation. The risk-point vector is not as compact a summary measure as traditional duration, but it is more comprehensive and is very useful in many hedging situations.

In the following sections, we present numerical examples of pricing as well as the determination of the risk points for swaps.

Pricing an International Money-Market (IMM) Swap

The short end of the U.S. dollar interest-rate swap is pegged to the Eurodollar futures market. The futures contract is a cash-settled contract based on the Eurodollar deposit rate, which in turn represents 3-month LIBOR. The contracts are priced at 100, a rate that in some way is based on and reflects the market's estimation of where the 3-month LIBOR will be on the settlement date. Eurodollar futures are traded in quarterly cycles with expiration (or settlement) in March, June, September, and December.

---

25 See chapter 4. See also Ravi E. Dattatreya, "A Practical Approach to Asset/Liability Management," in Atsuo Konishi and Frank Fabozzi, eds., *Asset/Liability Management* (Chicago: Probus, 1990).

These dates are called IMM dates. Twenty contracts, that is, contracts out to five years, are on trade at any one time. The size and liquidity of the contracts is excellent for earlier contracts up to three years and acceptable for the fourth year. A significant amount of activity in Eurodollar futures is contributed by the swap market.

Eurodollar futures prices are used to determine discount rates and forward rates corresponding to swap cash flows. However, in most cases, swap cash flows occur at times different from IMM dates. In these cases, as well as when LIBOR rates other than for a 3-month maturity are required, interpolation is used.

In order to illustrate how Eurodollar futures prices can be used to price swaps, we will first look at a simple swap, called an *IMM swap*, with payment dates coinciding with the IMM dates. As shown in Table 6-1, the IMM swap has

TABLE 6–1 The IMM Swap—Swap Parameters

Type	Short-Dated Swap
Trade Date **Effective Date**	June 29, 1993 July 1, 1993
Notional Amount **Maturity**	$100,000,000 2 Years
Receive Side	Fixed Actual/360 Day Count Basis Quarterly Payments
Pay Side	Floating 3-Month LIBOR Actual/360 Day Count Basis Quarterly Payment and Reset
Swap Rate	4.1124% (From Table 2D)

quarterly payments on the IMM dates, the floating side is set to the 3-month LIBOR, and the day-count convention is actual/360 for both the fixed and floating sides.

Table 6-2 shows the market data used to price the IMM swap. In column A we find the dates of the cash flows, including the effective date of July 8, 1993. The first period, from the effective date to the first IMM date (September 15, 1993), is not a full quarter and is called a *stub period*. Column B shows the number of days in each of the 12 periods. The stub period has only 69 days. The interest rate for the stub period, 3.20 percent, called the *stub rate*, is obtained from the cash LIBOR market by interpolation.

Consider the first future, priced at 96.65. Eurodollar futures are unlike forward-rate contracts in that the former require posting of variation margin. Because of this, futures prices do not exactly represent forward rates. The effective forward rates depend on the futures price and the cost of posting variation margin. The cost, however, is not fixed, is unknown at the outset, and depends upon the volatility of rates and the correlation between futures price and financing cost.

For example, suppose that interest earned or paid on margin is negatively correlated with futures price. Then, as margin interest rates rise, futures price tends to fall. Thus, a short seller of Eurodollar futures will receive margin flow that can be invested at the higher interest rate. Similarly, if margin interest rates fall, futures price tends to rise. Again, the short seller has the advantage because the margin that needs to be posted can be financed at a lower rate. Thus the short seller enjoys the advantage of earning higher interest rates when margin balances are positive and financing at lower rates when margin balances are negative. This property is called *convexity*. Conversely, a buyer of Eurodollar

TABLE 6–2 The IMM Swap—Market Data

	IMM Date	Day Count	Futures Price	Convexity Adjustment (bp)	Forward Rate (%)	Discount Factor
	(A)	(B)	(C)	(D)	(E)	(F)
1	07/08/93				3.20	
2	09/15/93	69	96.65	0.0	3.35	0.99390406
3	12/15/93	91	96.31	0.0	3.69	0.98555829
4	03/16/94	91	96.24	0.0	3.76	0.97645045
5	06/15/94	91	95.95	0.0	4.05	0.96725721
6	09/21/94	98	95.66	(1.0)	4.33	0.95670949
7	12/21/94	91	95.24	(1.0)	4.75	0.94635141
8	03/15/95	84	95.13	(1.0)	4.86	0.93597766
9	06/21/95	98	94.89	(1.0)	5.10	0.92375636
10	09/20/95	91	94.69	(1.0)	5.30	0.91199917
11	12/20/95	91	94.39	(1.0)	5.60	0.89994244
12	03/20/96	91	94.35	(1.0)	5.64	0.88738107
13	06/19/96	91	94.20	(1.0)	5.79	0.87490780

futures is at a disadvantage in this context whether rates rise or fall.

In pricing swaps, it is common to assume a negative correlation between Eurodollar futures prices and margin interest rates. A dealer receiving fixed and paying floating on a swap will sell Eurodollar futures to hedge the swap position. As a short seller, the dealer has the advantage due to the convexity of futures. This is reflected in the ability to offer a slightly lower fixed rate to the end user. That is, the convexity advantage is passed on to the end user.

The effect of convexity is higher

- If volatility of interest rates is higher
- For the back contracts than for the front contracts
- If a larger number of futures contracts are needed to hedge a given swap position

Column D in Table 6-2 shows an adjustment to the futures price for each futures contract. In practice, this adjustment is driven by supply and demand.

The forward rates can be obtained by subtracting the adjustment amount from the futures price and taking the difference between 100 and the adjusted futures price. For the September 94 contract, the futures price is 95.66, the adjustment is -1 b.p. and the adjusted futures price is 95.67, that is, 95.66-(-1 b.p.). Therefore, the forward rate is 4.33% (100-95.67). The forward rates are shown in column E of Table 6-2.

The last set of numbers, the discount factors corresponding to each of the cash-flow dates, can be determined in a recursive manner. Starting with a discount factor of 1.00, each successive factor is equal to:

$$\frac{\textit{Previous discount factor}}{(1 + \textit{Previous forward rate} \times \textit{Number of days} / 360)}$$

This formula is a result of the fact that the zero-coupon or the spot rate for a given date can be obtained by compounding the forward rates for the intervening periods.

Table 6-3 completes the procedure for pricing the IMM swap. Column G presents the assumed cash flows on the floating side. These flows are obtained by multiplying the notional amount by the forward rate and the number of days in the period and dividing by 360. Column H, showing the present values of the floating leg cash flows, is simply the product of the assumed cash flow for a given date and the discount factor for that date.

Finally, columns I and J show the cash flows and present values for the fixed leg of the swap. Since we have not yet determined the appropriate fixed rate for the swap, we first use our best guess of the rate. The fixed leg cash flows, column I, are obtained by multiplying the fixed rate by the notional amount and the number of days in the period and dividing by 360. The present values, column J, are the product of the cash flows and the discount factors.

The total present values of the floating leg and the fixed leg are then compared. If they are equal, then we have found the correct swap rate. If the PV of the fixed leg is greater, then the swap rate has to be decreased; if the PV is smaller, the swap rate has to be increased. This type of trial-and-error procedure is continued until equality of the total present values is obtained and the swap rate is determined. For the swap under consideration, the equality is obtained at a rate of 4.4613 percent. The corresponding total present values are $12,509,220.

If the dealer is paying fixed, then the swap rate so obtained is adjusted downward; if the dealer is receiving fixed, then the swap rate is adjusted upward. Such an adjustment reflects dealers' costs and return-on-capital re-

TABLE 6–3 The IMM Swap—Cash Flows and Pricing of the Swap

	IMM Date	Day Count	Forward Rate (%)	Discount Factor	Floating Leg Cash Flow ($)	Floating Leg Present Value ($)	Fixed Leg Cash Flow ($)	Fixed Leg Present Value ($)
	(A)	(B)	(E)	(F)	(G)	(H)	(I)	(J)
1	07/08/93		3.20					
2	09/15/93	69	3.35	0.99390406	613,333.33	609,594.49	855,078.51	849,866.00
3	12/15/93	91	3.69	0.98555829	846,805.56	834,576.24	1,127,712.24	1,111,426.15
4	03/16/94	91	3.76	0.97645045	932,750.00	910,784.16	1,127,712.24	1,101,155.13
5	06/15/94	91	4.05	0.96725721	950,444.44	919,324.24	1,127,712.24	1,090,787.80
6	09/21/94	98	4.33	0.95670949	1,102,500.00	1,054,772.21	1,214,459.34	1,161,884.77
7	12/21/94	91	4.75	0.94635141	1,094,527.78	1,035,807.90	1,127,712.24	1,067,212.07
8	03/15/95	84	4.86	0.93597766	1,108,333.33	1,037,375.23	1,040,965.15	974,320.12
9	06/21/95	98	5.10	0.92375636	1,323,000.00	1,222,129.66	1,214,459.34	1,121,864.54
10	09/20/95	91	5.30	0.91199917	1,289,166.67	1,175,718.93	1,127,712.24	1,028,472.63
11	12/20/95	91	5.60	0.89994244	1,339,722.22	1,205,672.89	1,127,712.24	1,014,876.11
12	03/20/96	91	5.64	0.88738107	1,415,555.56	1,256,137.20	1,127,712.24	1,000,710.49
13	06/19/96	91	5.79	0.87490780	1,425,666.67	1,247,326.89	1,127,712.24	986,644.24
Swap Rate: 4.46127920%					13,441,805.56	12,509,220.04	13,346,660.28	12,509,220.04

quirements and is largely a function of supply-and-demand pressures.

Note that the total of all assuming floating, undiscounted, cash flows is slightly greater than the total of fixed cash flows. This is the case when the yield curve is positively sloped and the current floating payments are smaller than the fixed payments. In the later periods, the floating payer "pays back" the excess receipts in the earlier periods. The effect of the time value of money makes the floating payments slightly larger in sum.

Table 6-4 shows the formulas used in this example in a spreadsheet format.

In addition to the price of the swap, i.e., the swap rate, we can determine certain other interesting parameters. Since the swap is priced or valued entirely on the prices of the Eurodollar futures, it is possible to determine the *risk points* relative to each of the futures contracts for the swap. Recall that the risk point for a swap relative to a pricing (or hedging) instrument is the change in the value of the swap resulting from a small change in the price of the pricing instrument. To determine the risk points relative to the first contract, we first change the price of the September 93 futures contract by one basis point (or tick) from 96.65 to 96.64, while keeping all other futures prices as well as the fixed rate unchanged. As a result of this, the forward rate for September 93 and all discount factors will change. The total present value of each leg will change as well. Therefore, the price of the swap is no longer zero. As seen in Table 6-5, the PV of the floating leg will increase by $2,192.94 to $12,511,412.98, and that of the fixed leg will decrease by $292.24 to $12,508,927.80. The change on the floating side is larger because the change in the futures price changes not only the discount factors but also the (assumed) cash flows. The change on the fixed leg is nega-

TABLE 6–4 The IMM Swap—Formulas

1.	**Day Count**	B5	A5-A4
2.	**Forward Rate**	E5	(100-(C5-D5/100))/100
3.	**Discount Factor**	F5	F4/(1+E4*B5/360)
4.	**Floating Leg Cash Flow**	G5	E4*B5/360*Notional Amount
5.	**Present Value Floating Leg**	H5	G5*F5
6.	**Fixed Leg Cash Flow**	I5	Swap rate*Notional Amount*B5/360
7.	**Present Value Fixed Leg**	J5	H5*F5

TABLE 6–5 The IMM Swap—Risk Points and Hedge Ratio

	IMM Date	New NPV of Floating Leg ($)	Change in NPV of Floating Leg ($)	New NPV of Fixed Leg ($)	Change in NPV of Fixed Leg ($)	Risk Factor ($)	Number of Futures Contracts
	(A)	(B)	(C)	(D)	(E)	(F)	(G)
1	07/08/93	12,508,981.74	(238.30)	12,508,981.74	(238.30)	0.00	*
2	09/15/93	12,511,412.98	2,192.94	12,508,927.80	(292.24)	2,485.18	-99
3	12/15/93	12,511,411.12	2,191.08	12,508,955.88	(264.16)	2,455.23	-98
4	03/16/94	12,511,410.73	2,190.69	12,508,983.50	(236.54)	2,427.23	-97
5	06/15/94	12,511,575.69	2,355.65	12,508,995.06	(224.98)	2,580.64	-103
6	09/21/94	12,511,407.61	2,187.57	12,509,040.16	(179.88)	2,367.45	-95
7	12/21/94	12,511,239.06	2,019.02	12,509,078.65	(141.39)	2,160.41	-86
8	03/15/95	12,511,570.57	2,350.53	12,509,081.61	(138.43)	2,488.96	-100
9	06/21/95	12,511,403.41	2,183.37	12,509,119.45	(100.59)	2,283.95	-91
10	09/20/95	12,511,402.32	2,182.28	12,509,145.15	(74.88)	2,257.16	-90
11	12/20/95	12,511,400.69	2,180.65	12,509,170.51	(49.53)	2,230.18	-89
12	03/20/96	12,511,400.47	2,180.43	12,509,195.45	(24.59)	2,205.02	-88
13	06/19/96	12,509,220.04	0.00	12,509,220.04	0.00	0.00	0
Original NPV of Floating/Fixed Leg: $12,509,220.04							-1038

tive, as expected: if rates rise, the PV of a fixed stream of cash flows decreases. The value of the swap changes by $2,485.18. This is the risk point for the swap relative to the September 93 contract. The risk points relative to the other futures contracts are determined similarly and are shown in Table 6-5.

The risk point relative to a given contract can be used to determine the hedge ratio or number of contracts to be sold or bought to hedge the swap. Since each basis point of change in the price of a Eurodollar futures contract represents a change in value of $25, the hedge ratio is obtained by dividing the risk point by 25. For example, 99 September 93 contracts (2485.18/25) will be required to hedge the swap against changes in that contract's price. The fact that we would actually sell the contracts for hedging is shown in column G by using negative numbers. The contract sizes for other futures contracts are similarly obtained. In fact, a swap dealer offering this swap will hedge the risk in the swap position by means of series of Eurodollar contracts determined using this procedure. Observe that the risk corresponding to the June 96 future is zero. The swap will mature by then.

There is one other risk: that due to the change in the rate (3.20 percent) corresponding to the stub period (Table 6-2, column E, row 1). The risk is zero for swaps priced at midpoint but nonzero if the offered (or bid) spread is included. This risk is not easily hedged, as there is no Eurodollar future corresponding to this rate. Dealers usually look to the 1-month LIBOR futures to partially hedge this risk.

Pricing a Short-Dated Swap

We will now consider a 2-year, $100 million swap whose payment dates do not coincide with IMM dates, as shown in Table 6-6. The floating side pays 3-month LIBOR quar-

TABLE 6–6 The Short-Dated Swap—Swap Parameters

Type	IMM Swap
Trade Date **Effective Date**	July 6, 1993 July 8, 1993
Notional Amount **Maturity**	$100,000,000 3 Years
Receive Side	Fixed Actual/360 Day Count Basis Quarterly Payments on IMM Dates
Pay Side	Floating 3-Month LIBOR Actual/360 Day Count Basis Quarterly Payment and Reset on IMM Dates
Swap Rate	4.4613% (From Table 1C)

terly starting on the spot date of July 1, 1993, on an actual/360 day-count basis. The fixed side will also pay quarterly on an actual/360 day-count basis. The only complexity here is that the prices of the futures contracts provide information about the forward rates on IMM dates, not on the cash-flow dates. We therefore have to use some form of interpolation to estimate forward and zero rates corresponding to cash-flow dates. The convention in the swap market is to interpolate market interest rates just enough to generate a sufficient number of zero rates and then interpolate the zero rates further as needed.

The 2-year swap, being short-dated, is priced off the Eurodollar futures. Table 6-7 shows the input market data as well as some computed information. Column A shows the IMM dates. Column B shows the number of days in

TABLE 6–7 The Short-Dated Swap—Computing the IMM Zero Rates

	IMM Date	IMM Day Count	Cum. IMM Day Count	Futures Price	Convexity Adjustment (bp)	IMM Forward Rate (%)	IMM Discount Factor	IMM Zero Rate (%)
	(A)	(B)	(C)	(D)	(E)	(F)	(G)	(H)
1	07/01/93					3.28	1.00000000	
2	09/15/93	76	76	96.58	0.0	3.42	0.99312317	3.28000000
3	12/15/93	91	167	96.21	0.0	3.79	0.98461121	3.36919177
4	03/16/94	91	258	96.12	0.0	3.88	0.97526787	3.53850937
5	06/15/94	91	349	95.83	0.0	4.17	0.96579556	3.65320712
6	09/21/94	98	447	95.56	(1.0)	4.43	0.95495523	3.79888660
7	12/21/94	91	538	95.15	(1.0)	4.84	0.94438001	3.94098096
8	03/15/95	84	622	95.06	(1.0)	4.93	0.93383391	4.10088813
9	06/21/95	98	720	94.83	(1.0)	5.16	0.92146731	4.26128463
10	09/20/95	91	811	94.64	(1.0)	5.35	0.90960305	4.41147165

each IMM period. In column C we have the cumulative days from the effective date. The information in this column is used for interpolating the zero rates. Columns D and E show the futures prices and the corresponding convexity adjustments as before. The resulting forward rates for IMM dates are shown in column F. Also shown here (column F, row 1) is the cash LIBOR rate, 3.28 percent, for the period starting from the effective date to the first futures date. The discount factors (column G) and the zero rates for the IMM dates (column H) are computed as in the previous section. The IMM zero rates will be interpolated to generate rates for other dates as required.

In Table 6-8, column I shows the actual cash-flow dates for the swap under consideration. The IMM dates (column A) and corresponding zero rates (column H) are repeated for the reader's convenience. Columns J and K show the number of days in each actual period and the number of cumulative days from the start date. Using this data, we can interpolate the IMM zero rates to get the zero rates for the cash-flow dates (column L). From this we compute the implied forward (i.e., 3-month LIBOR) rates (column M) and the discount factors (column N) as before.

The interpolated 3-month LIBOR rate is 3.29 percent. We will use this rate for discounting.[26] However, the first cash flow is based on the cash 3-month LIBOR rate of 3.3125 percent.

Finally, in Table 6-9, we have the computation of the swap rate. Once the forward rates and discount factors for the cash-flow dates have been determined via interpolation, swap pricing is straightforward as in the previous

---

26 We use this interpolated rate rather than the cash rate so as to have the same consistent discounting methodology at all maturities.

TABLE 6–8 The Short-Dated Swap—Computing the Interpolated Rates

	IMM Date	IMM Day Count	Cum. IMM Day Count	IMM Zero Rate (%)	Cash Flow Date	Day Count	Cum. Day Count	Interpolated Zero Rate (%)	Implied Discount Factor	Implied Forward Rate (%)
	(A)	(B)	(C)	(H)	(I)	(J)	(K)	(L)	(M)	(N)
1	07/01/93				07/01/93				1.00000000	3.29568207
2	09/15/93	76	76	3.28000000	10/01/93	92	92	3.29568207	0.99164804	3.48176485
3	12/15/93	91	167	3.36919177	01/03/94	94	186	3.40454380	0.98271392	3.81730845
4	03/16/94	91	258	3.53850937	04/01/94	88	274	3.55867601	0.97362880	3.92687691
5	06/15/94	91	349	3.65320712	07/01/94	91	365	3.67699152	0.96405928	4.20686402
6	09/21/94	98	447	3.79888660	10/03/94	94	459	3.81762432	0.95358455	4.48304302
7	12/21/94	91	538	3.94098096	01/02/95	91	550	3.96382484	0.94289948	4.85436763
8	03/15/95	84	622	4.10088813	04/03/95	91	641	4.13198541	0.93146964	4.96277709
9	06/21/95	98	720	4.26128463	07/01/95	89	730	4.27778870	0.92017987	
10	09/20/95	91	811	4.41147165	10/02/95	93	823	4.41298580		

TABLE 6–9 The Short-Dated Swap—Cash Flows and Pricing of the Swap

	Cash Flow Date	Day Count	Implied Discount Factor	Implied Forward Rate (%)	Floating Leg Cash Flow ($)	Floating Leg Present Value ($)	Fixed Leg Cash Flow ($)	Fixed Leg Present Value ($)
	(I)	(J)	(M)	(N)	(O)	(P)	(Q)	(R)
1	07/01/93		1.00000000	3.29568207				
2	10/01/93	92	0.99164804	3.48176485	846,527.78	839,457.62	1,050,951.88	1,042,174.38
3	01/03/94	94	0.98271392	3.81730845	909,127.49	893,412.24	1,073,798.66	1,055,236.89
4	04/01/94	88	0.97362880	3.92687691	933,119.84	908,512.35	1,005,258.32	978,748.45
5	07/01/94	91	0.96405928	4.20686402	992,627.22	956,951.49	1,039,528.49	1,002,167.09
6	10/03/94	94	0.95358455	4.48304302	1,098,458.94	1,047,473.47	1,073,798.66	1,023,957.81
7	01/02/95	91	0.94289948	4.85436763	1,133,213.65	1,068,506.57	1,039,528.49	980,170.88
8	04/03/95	91	0.93146964	4.96277709	1,227,076.26	1,142,984.28	1,039,528.49	968,289.23
9	07/01/95	89	0.92017987		1,226,908.78	1,128,976.77	1,016,681.71	935,530.05
	Swap Rate: 4.11242040%				8,367,059.96	7,986,274.78	8,339,074.71	7,986,274.78

section. In Table 6-9, the cash-flow dates (column I), the forward rates (column M), and the discount factors (column N) have been brought forward from Table 6-8. The assumed cash flow on the floating side and the corresponding present values are shown in columns O and P. The cash flows for the fixed leg and the corresponding present values are shown in columns Q and R, respectively. The fixed cash flows use a fixed rate of 4.1124 percent. This rate was determined by an iterative process so as to make the total present value of the fixed leg equal to that of the floating leg. Therefore, the at-market swap rate is 4.1124 percent.

As in the case of the IMM swap, it is possible to determine the risk points for this swap as well as the number of futures contracts required to hedge the swap position, as in Table 6-10. We determine the risk points by sequentially changing the price of each contract by a basis point and recomputing the resulting total present values of the fixed leg and the floating leg and the net change in the value of the swap. The number of contracts is obtained by dividing the risk point by $25.

If the cash rate (3.28 percent) to the first futures date changes, then the value of the swap will change slightly. This risk is about $190 per basis point, representing eight futures contracts.

Formulas for computing the columns in Tables 6-7 to 6-9 are shown in Table 6-11 in spreadsheet format.

Pricing a Generic Swap—Bootstrapping

LIBOR-based swaps can be conveniently priced using Eurodollar futures, since they directly represent forward rates.[27] From the forward rates we can obtain the necessary zero rates and discount factors. This convenience is not

---

27 With the convexity adjustment, as discussed earlier.

TABLE 6–10 The Short-Dated Swap—Risk Points and Hedge Ratio

	IMM Date	New NPV of Floating Leg ($)	Change in NPV of Floating Leg ($)	New NPV of Fixed Leg ($)	Change in NPV of Fixed Leg ($)	Risk Factor ($)	Number of Futures Contracts
	(A)	(B)	(C)	(D)	(E)	(F)	(G)
1	07/01/93	7,985,913.23	(361.55)	7,986,103.95	(26.39)	(190.72)	8
2	09/15/93	7,988,339.25	2,064.47	7,986,096.60	(178.18)	2,242.65	-90
3	12/15/93	7,988,581.60	2,306.82	7,986,122.55	(152.23)	2,459.05	-98
4	03/16/94	7,988,581.08	2,306.30	7,986,148.00	(126.78)	2,433.08	-97
5	06/15/94	7,988,754.69	2,479.91	7,986,165.68	(109.10)	2,589.01	-104
6	09/21/94	7,988,577.91	2,303.13	7,986,199.61	(75.16)	2,378.30	-95
7	12/21/94	7,988,400.55	2,125.77	7,986,227.87	(46.91)	2,172.68	-87
8	03/15/95	7,988,749.63	2,474.85	7,986,245.08	(29.70)	2,504.55	-100
9	06/21/95	7,986,504.53	229.75	7,986,272.44	(2.34)	232.09	-9
10	09/20/95	7,986,274.78	0.00	7,986,274.78	(0.00)	0.00	0
Original NPV of Fixed/Floating Leg: $7,986,274.78							-680

TABLE 6–11 The Short-Dated Swap—Formulas

1.	**Day Count**	B5	A5-A4
2.	**Cumulative Day Count**	C5	@sum(B5..B2)
3.	**IMM Forward Rate**	F5	(100-(D5-E5/100))/100
4.	**IMM Discount Factor**	G5	G4/(1+F4*B5/360)
5.	**IMM Zero Rate**	H5	(1/G5-1)*(360/C5)
6.	**Day Count**	J5	I5-I4
7.	**Cumulative Day Count**	K5	@ sum (J5..J2)
8.	**Interpolated Zero Rates**	L5	H5+((H6-H5)*(K5-C5)/B6
9.	**Implied Discount Factor**	M5	1/(1+I5*K5/360)
10.	**Implied Forward Rate**	N5	(M5/M6-1)*360/K6
11.	**Floating Leg Cash Flow**	O5	N4*K5/360*Notional Amount
12.	**Fixed Leg Cash Flow**	P5	Swap Rate*Notional Amount*K5/360
13.	**Floating Leg Present Value**	Q5	O5*M5
14.	**Fixed Leg Present Value**	R5	P5*M5

available when other market data, such as swap rates and Treasury rates and spreads, have to be used for computation. However, it is possible to derive zero rates from this data by means of a process called bootstrapping, as discussed earlier.

Consider the swap described in Table 6-12. This is a 5-year, $100 million swap with semiannual payments. The floating side is based on 6-month LIBOR and actual/360 day count. The fixed side is bond-basis, i.e., semiannual 30/360 day count.

Table 6-13 shows the market data used to price the generic swap. Column A shows the number of years (semiannual periods) from the start date. Column D shows the

TABLE 6–12 The Generic Swap—Swap Parameters

Type	Generic Swap
Trade Date **Effective Date**	July 17, 1993 July 19, 1993
Notional Amount **Maturity**	$100,000,000 5 Years
Receive Side	Fixed 30/360 Day Count Basis Semi-Annual Payments
Pay Side	Floating Cash Curve Actual/360 Day count Basis Semi-Annual Payments
Swap Rate	5.2108% (On-Market: From Table 3C) 7.0000% (Off-Market: From Table 3E)

TABLE 6–13 The Generic Swap—Bootstrapping

	Year	Date	Day Count	UST-Yield (%)	Swap Sprea (bp)	Swap Rate (%)	Discount Factor	Cumulative Sum	Zero Rate (%)	Forward Rate (%)
	(A)	(B)	(C)	(D)	(E)	(F)	(G)	(H)	(I)	(J)
1	0.0	07/21/93					1.00000000			3.43750000
2	0.5	01/21/94	184			3.4375	0.98273391	0.98273391	3.43750000	3.87358688
3	1.0	07/21/94	181			3.6875	0.96396027	1.94669418	3.68750000	4.21905780
4	1.5	01/23/95	186			3.9171	0.94339569	2.89008987	3.92260300	5.00109405
5	2.0	07/21/95	179	3.9706	20.17	4.1723	0.92050589	3.81059576	4.18477378	5.13872359
6	2.5	01/22/96	185			4.3836	0.89682318	4.70741894	4.40364249	5.67287826
7	3.0	07/22/96	182	4.2749	32.00	4.5949	0.87181978	5.57923872	4.62508648	5.79023504
8	3.5	01/21/97	183			4.7652	0.84689260	6.42613132	4.80484810	6.23309510
9	4.0	07/21/97	181	4.6254	31.00	4.9354	0.82115863	7.24728995	4.98713862	6.18930218
10	4.5	01/21/98	184			5.0731	0.79597847	8.04326842	5.13556397	6.61176520
11	5.0	07/21/98	181	4.9758	23.50	5.2108	0.77036948		5.28635750	

yields of representative on-the-run Treasury instruments on a semiannual bond-equivalent basis. Column E shows the spreads over Treasuries for standard swaps.[28] The sum of the Treasury yields and the swap spreads gives the swap rates (column F). Any missing data in this column (e.g., 2.5 years) is interpolated.

For the bootstrapping process, column F is assumed to represent the yield of semiannual coupon bonds priced at par except for the half-year and 1-year points, which represent LIBOR or money-market equivalent rates. Now, the 0.5 year yield, 3.4375 percent, is a zero-coupon rate, since a half-year bond has just one cash flow. Therefore, the discount factor using actual/360 convention is

$$\frac{1}{1 + 3.4375 \times \frac{182}{360}}$$

or 0.983. The discount factor at the 1-year point is computed similarly, using the actual/360 convention.

The other discount factors can be determined through a process of induction as discussed earlier. Suppose the first n discount factors, $f_1, f_2, f_3, \ldots, f_n$, have been computed. Then the next factor $f\,(n + 1)$ is related to the others as follows:

$$f\,(n+1) = \frac{[1 - c \times (f1 + f2 + \ldots fn)]}{(1 + c)}$$

Column H contains the cumulative sums of the discount factors. The factors in column G are computed using column H sequentially. From the discount factors, we can compute the zero rates (column I), if needed.

---

28 For this purpose, we define a standard swap as semiannual pay, spot-start, 30/360 on the fixed side and actual/360 on the floating side, 6-month LIBOR, and level notional amount.

The forward rates are derived from the discount factors as follows. If f_1 and f_2 are the discount factors for 6 months and 1 year, the forward rate R is related to f_1 and f_2 by the following equation:

$$\frac{1}{f2} = \frac{1}{f1} \times (1 + R \times \frac{d}{360})$$

where d is the number of days in the period. In this equation, the left side, $(1/f_2)$, is the future value of a $1 investment at the end of 1 year. The right side is the value of $1 invested for 6 months and reinvested for another 6 months at the forward rate of R. The equation simply means that an investor would have no preference between a 1-year investment on one hand and a 6-month investment reinvested at the forward rate for another 6 months. The forward rate, then is

$$R = (\left(\frac{f1}{f2}\right) - 1) \times \frac{360}{d}$$

Forward rates for other periods (column J) are similarly derived.

Once the forward rates and discount functions have been obtained, the pricing of the swap becomes straightforward. In Table 6-14, columns K and M show the assumed floating cash flows and the fixed-rate cash flows. Columns L and N show the present values of these cash flows. The rate for the fixed leg has been selected (by an iterative procedure) so as to make the total present value of the fixed and floating legs equal. This fixed rate is 5.2108 percent.

We observe that the computed swap rate is exactly equal to the market rate for 5-year swaps from Table 6-13. Clearly, we expect this to be the case since the swap rate was derived from the market data. If the swap differed from the standard swap in any way, e.g., if it has quarterly payments, the swap rate would differ from the standard swap rate.

TABLE 6–14 The Generic Swap—Cash Flows and Pricing of the On-Market Version

	Year	Date	Day Count	Discount Factor	Forward Rate (%)	Floating Leg Cash Flow ($)	Floating Leg Present Value ($)	Fixed Leg Cash Flow ($)	Fixed Leg Present Value ($)
	(A)	(B)	(C)	(G)	(J)	(K)	(M)	(L)	(N)
1	0.0	07/21/93		1.00000000	3.43750000				
2	0.5	01/21/94	184	0.98273391	3.87358688	1,756,944.44	1,726,608.89	2,605,400.00	2,560,414.93
3	1.0	07/21/94	181	0.96396027	4.21905780	1,947,553.40	1,877,364.10	2,605,400.00	2,511,502.09
4	1.5	01/23/95	186	0.94339569	5.00109405	2,179,846.53	2,056,457.83	2,605,400.00	2,457,923.14
5	2.0	07/21/95	179	0.92050589	5.13872359	2,486,655.10	2,288,980.65	2,605,400.00	2,398,286.03
6	2.5	01/22/96	185	0.89682318	5.67287826	2,640,732.96	2,368,270.53	2,605,400.00	2,336,583.11
7	3.0	07/22/96	182	0.87181978	5.79023504	2,867,955.12	2,500,340.00	2,605,400.00	2,271,439.25
8	3.5	01/21/97	183	0.84689260	6.23309510	2,943,369.48	2,492,717.84	2,605,400.00	2,206,493.98
9	4.0	07/21/97	181	0.82115863	6.18930218	3,133,861.70	2,573,397.57	2,605,400.00	2,139,446.68
10	4.5	01/21/98	184	0.79597847	6.61176520	3,163,421.11	2,518,015.11	2,605,400.00	2,073,842.32
11	5.0	07/21/98	181	0.77036948		3,324,248.61	2,560,899.67	2,605,400.00	2,007,120.64
Swap Rate: 5.2108%						26,444,588.46	22,963,052.18	26,054,000.00	22,963,052.18

As before, we can also determine the risk points for this swap relative to the Treasury securities (Table 6-15). To do this, we change the yield on any given Treasury by 1 basis point, and the risk point is the resulting change in the value of the swap. Interestingly, the risk point for this swap is zero for all maturities except at 6 months[30] and 5 years. This results from the fact that the standard 5-year swap rate depends upon the 5-year Treasury yield (plus the spread) and does not depend upon any other rate. Note, however, that the total present values of the fixed and the floating legs do change when the yields on the other Treasuries change. However, the change in one leg is exactly matched by the change in the other leg. Thus, the value of the swap stays at zero.

To determine the hedge ratio, we need the dollar duration, or the price value of a basis point (PVBP) for each hedge security (Treasury), per million. The amount (in millions) of each Treasury for hedging is obtained by dividing the risk point by the PVBP. As expected, the par amount of 5-year Treasuries required to hedge the swap is very close to the notional amount of the swap.[31]

The formulas for Tables 6-13 and 6-14 are presented in Table 6-16 in spreadsheet format.

---

30 The risk at the first cash flow is zero when Eurodollar futures are used (as in IMM swaps) and nonzero when the cash curve is used for pricing and hedging. The reason for this is subtle. Briefly, the difference arises from the fact that when futures are used, we assume that a change in the cash rate does not change the first forward rate (rate for the second period), as the latter depends solely upon the futures price, not the cash rate. When the cash curve is used, a change in the rate for the first period automatically changes the forward rate for the second period. The forward rate depends upon the cash rate for the first period.

31 The par amount of Treasuries is slightly larger, since the actual maturity of the Treasury is slightly shorter than 5 years.

TABLE 6–15 The Generic Swap—Risk Points and Hedge Ratio of the On-Market Version

	Year	New NPV of Floating Leg ($)	Change in NPV of Floating Leg ($)	New NPV of Fixed Leg ($)	Change in NPV of Fixed Leg ($)	Risk Factor ($)	PVBP ($/$mm)	Hedge Ratio ($mm)
	(A)	(B)	(C)	(D)	(E)	(F)	(G)	(H)
1	0.5	22,957,922.49	(5,129.69)	22,962,945.10	(107.08)	(5,022.61)	49.16	102.18
2	1.0	22,962,691.96	(360.22)	22,962,691.96	(360.22)	0.00	97.29	0.00
3	2.0	22,962,211.33	(840.85)	22,962,211.33	(840.85)	0.00	185.81	0.00
4	3.0	22,961,763.58	(1,288.60)	22,961,763.58	(1,288.60)	0.00	263.05	0.00
5	4.0	22,961,299.34	(1,752.84)	22,961,299.34	(1,752.84)	0.00	150.41	0.00
6	5.0	23,005,500.40	42,448.22	22,961,435.31	(1,616.87)	44,065.09	435.25	(101.24)

Original NPV of Fixed/Floating Leg: $22,963,052.18

TABLE 6–16 The Generic Swap—Formulas

1.	**Day Count**	C5	B5-B4
2.	**Discount Factor**	G5	(1-F5/2*H4)/(1+F5/2)
3.	**Cumulative Sum**	H5	@sum(G5..G2)
4.	**Zero Rate**	I5	2*((1/G5)^(0.5/A5)-1)
5.	**Forward Rate**	J5	(G5/G6-1)*360/C6
6.	**Floating Leg Cash Flow**	K5	J4*C5/360*Notional Amount
7.	**Floating Leg Present Value**	L5	K5*G5
8.	**Fixed Leg Cash Flow**	M5	Swap Rate*Notional Amount/2
9.	**Fixed Leg Present Value**	R5	M5*G5

Pricing a Swap Termination

A swap normally matures with the last scheduled payment. Mechanisms are in place to make available a level of liquidity, however, and a swap can be terminated before its maturity date by mutual agreement between the counterparties. Usually, a swap terminated before its maturity is off-market, that is, it has some residual value. Therefore, an appropriate payment from one party to the other is necessary at termination. To determine this adjustment, the swap is revalued at the market conditions prevailing at the time of termination.

There are three ways to eliminate a swap position.

1. A swap can be terminated by a *buyout*: an up-front payment that reflects the adjustment for the prevailing market conditions is made.
2. In a *reversal*, a new swap transaction that exactly offsets the original is executed. This new swap is obviously off-market and requires an up-front payment from one party to another. As an alternative, the up-front payment can be effectively amortized over the remaining life of the swap by using the current market fixed payment rate on the new swap.
3. Another way is by *assignment*, in which the swap is assumed by a third party on behalf of one of the counterparties. This technique is used when one of the parties in the original swap does not want a complete termination. The party that is willing to terminate or assign will receive from or pay to the third party a fee reflecting the value of the swap. The party that assigns out the swap is free from all obligations on the original swap. The rights and responsibilities are completely transferred to the third party.

Let us price an off-market swap with the given data. Table 6-17 shows the pricing for a swap with a coupon of 7.0 percent. Since the fixed rate is much higher than the market rate, the present value of the fixed side is much larger than that of the floating side. The value of the swap, $7,884,680, is the difference between the two present values. If this swap is terminated, the fixed receiver receives a lump-sum payment.

More interesting is the risk profile of the off-market swap, shown in Table 6-18. The off-market swap can be considered a combination of a strip of cash flows (annuity) of 1.79 percent (7.00 percent swap coupon less the 5.21 percent at-market swap rate) and an on-market swap at 5.21 percent. The on-market swap has all its risk at the 5-year point, but the annuity has risk at all points. The risk of the swap is the sum of the risks of the two components. The hedge ratios are shown as well.

Pricing a Currency Swap

The pricing procedure for a currency swap is similar to that for pricing an interest-rate swap and is based on the same fundamental principle of equating the present values of the two legs of the swap. For each currency leg, appropriate market data is used to determine discount factors and forward rates as needed. If a floating leg is present, assumed floating cash flows are generated from the forward rates. Recall that in a currency swap, in addition to the cash flows corresponding to interest rates, notional flows are also included twice: at the *initial exchange* on the start date and at the *final exchange* on the maturity date. For each leg, the total present value of the cash flows (assumed or actual) is computed and brought into a single currency using spot exchange rates. The value of the swap is the difference between the two present values.

TABLE 6–17 The Generic Swap—Cash Flows and Pricing of the Off-Market Version

	Year	Date	Day Count	Discount Factor	Forward Rate (%)	Floating Leg Cash Flow ($)	Floating Leg Present Value ($)	Fixed Leg Cash Flow ($)	Fixed Leg Present Value ($)
	(A)	(B)	(C)	(G)	(J)	(K)	(M)	(L)	(N)
1	0.0	07/21/93		1.00000000	3.43750000				
2	0.5	01/21/94	184	0.98273391	3.87358688	1,756,944.44	1,726,608.89	3,500,000.00	3,439,568.69
3	1.0	07/21/94	181	0.96396027	4.21905780	1,947,553.40	1,877,364.10	3,500,000.00	3,373,860.95
4	1.5	01/23/95	186	0.94339569	5.00109405	2,179,846.53	2,056,457.83	3,500,000.00	3,301,884.92
5	2.0	07/21/95	179	0.92050589	5.13872359	2,486,655.10	2,288,980.65	3,500,000.00	3,221,770.60
6	2.5	01/22/96	185	0.89682318	5.67287826	2,640,732.96	2,368,270.53	3,500,000.00	3,138,881.13
7	3.0	07/22/96	182	0.87181978	5.79023504	2,867,955.12	2,500,340.00	3,500,000.00	3,051,369.23
8	3.5	01/21/97	183	0.84689260	6.23309510	2,943,369.48	2,492,717.84	3,500,000.00	2,964,124.11
9	4.0	07/21/97	181	0.82115863	6.18930218	3,133,861.70	2,573,397.57	3,500,000.00	2,874,055.19
10	4.5	01/21/98	184	0.79597847	6.61176520	3,163,421.11	2,518,015.11	3,500,000.00	2,785,924.66
11	5.0	07/21/98	181	0.77036948		3,324,248.61	2,560,899.67	3,500,000.00	2,696,293.17
Swap Rate: 7.0000%				Profit: $7,884,680.46		26,444,588.46	22,963,052.18	35,000,000.00	30,847,732.65

EXHIBIT 6–18 The Generic Swap—Risk Points and Hedge Ratio for the Off-Market Version

	Year	New NPV of Floating Leg ($)	Change in NPV of Fixed Leg ($)	New NPV of Fixed Leg ($)	Change in NPV of Fixed Leg ($)	Risk Factor ($)	PVBP ($/$mm)	Hedge Ratio ($mm)
	(A)	(B)	(C)	(D)	(E)	(F)	(G)	(H)
1	0.5	22,957,922.49	(5,129.69)	30,847,588.80	(143.85)	(4,985.84)	49.155	101.43
2	1.0	22,962,691.96	(360.22)	30,847,248.74	(483.91)	123.69	97.294	(1.27)
3	2.0	22,962,211.33	(840.85)	30,846,603.08	(1,129.57)	288.72	185.81	(1.55)
4	3.0	22,961,763.58	(1,288.60)	30,846,001.59	(1,731.06)	442.46	263.05	(1.68)
5	4.0	22,961,299.34	(1,752.84)	30,845,377.95	(2,354.70)	601.86	150.41	(4.00)
6	5.0	23,005,500.40	42,448.22	30,845,560.60	(2,172.05)	44,620.26	435.25	(102.52)
Original NPV of Floating Leg: $22,963,052.18					Original NPV of Fixed Leg: $30,847,732.65			

If the at-market swap rate is required, one of the parameters of the swap is varied until the swap value is zero, i.e., until the present values of the two legs are equal. A currency swap can have many variable parameters such as the fixed rate on one or two legs, the exchange rate used, or the spread over the floating index in a float/float swap. Traditionally, the exchange rate is set to the spot rate for spot-start swaps and to the forward rate for forward-start swaps. The appropriate fixed rate (or spread over index) is then determined so as to make the value of the swap zero.

As a pricing example, consider the swap described in Table 6–19. This is a $100mm, 2-year USD/DEM swap. The DEM side is fixed and semi-annual on a 30/360 basis. The

TABLE 6–19 The Cross-Currency Swap—Swap Parameters

Type	Currency Swap and Variants
Trade Date **Effective Date**	July 19, 1993 July 21, 1993
Notional Amount **Maturity** **Spot Fx Rate**	$100,000,000 2 Years DM 1.727 = $1
Receive Side	DEM Fixed 30/360 Day Count Basis Semi-Annual Payments
Pay Side	USD Floating 3-Month LIBOR Actual/360 Day Count Basis Quarterly Payments
Swap Rate	6.1200% (From Table 4E) 6.5000% (From Table 4H) 4.2801% (From Table 4K)

USD side is floating, quarterly and based on 3-month LIBOR with the usual actual/360 day basis. The spot exchange rate is 1.7270 DEM per USD.

In Tables 6-20 and 6-21, we show the step-by-step derivation of the IMM discount factors and IMM zero rates from the Eurodollar futures data, and then the interpolated zero rates, discount factors, and forward rates. These steps are exactly the same as in the short-dated swap example above.

Table 6-22 uses this information to generate the assumed floating-rate cash flows on the USD side, along with the initial and final notional flows (column O). Column P shows the present values of each cash flow and their sum. The sum does not include the value of the initial notional flow.

Observe that the total present value of the floating USD leg is very close to the notional amount. This is not just a coincidence, but results from the fact that the cash flows on the USD leg correspond to the flows from a LIBOR-flat floating-rate note priced at par.[31] Note that if the value of the initial notional flow is included in the sum, the total PV will be zero for this leg.

To price the DEM leg, it helps to first break up the swap into more common or basic or standard swaps. In the USD/DEM market, USD LIBOR/DEM LIBOR swap is more standard. Exhibit 6-7 shows the USD/DEM swap split into two swaps, a DEM fixed-to-floating interest-rate

---

31 We expect the price of the floating-rate note to be at par because it earns LIBOR and the discount factors represent LIBOR. The small difference is due to the fact that the cash flow (3.20 percent) at the 3-month point is based on 3-month LIBOR, whereas the corresponding discounting factor is based on an interpolated rate (3.28 percent), and the two are slightly different.

TABLE 6–20 The Cross-Currency Swap—Computing the IMM Zero Rates

	IMM Date	IMM Day Count	Cum. IMM Day Count	Futures Price	Convexity Adjustment (bp)	IMM Forward Rates (%)	IMM Discount Factor	IMM Zero Rate (%)
	(A)	(B)	(C)	(D)	(E)	(F)	(G)	(H)
1	07/21/93					3.17	1.00000000	
2	09/15/93	56	56	96.64	0.0	3.36	0.99509309	3.17000000
3	12/15/93	91	147	96.28	0.0	3.72	0.98671261	3.29787576
4	03/16/94	91	238	96.20	0.0	3.80	0.97752065	3.47843007
5	06/15/94	91	329	95.93	0.0	4.07	0.96822036	3.59154551
6	09/21/94	98	427	95.64	(1.0)	4.35	0.95761057	3.73201440
7	12/21/94	91	518	95.22	(1.0)	4.77	0.94719536	3.87440691
8	03/15/95	84	602	95.13	(1.0)	4.86	0.93676912	4.03647850
9	06/21/95	98	700	94.92	(1.0)	5.07	0.92453749	4.19769775
10	09/20/95	91	791	94.76	(1.0)	5.23	0.91283870	4.34565907

TABLE 6–21 The Cross-Currency Swap—Computing the Interpolated Rates

	IMM Date	IMM Day Count	Cum. IMM Day Count	IMM Zero Rate (%)	Cash Flow Date	Day Count	Cum. Day Count	Interpolated Zero Rate (%)	Implied Discount Factor	Implied Forward Rate (%)
	(A)	(B)	(C)	(H)	(I)	(J)	(K)	(L)	(M)	(N)
1	07/21/93				07/21/93				1.00000000	3.22058821
2	09/15/93	56	56	3.17000000	10/21/93	92	92	3.22058821	0.99183679	3.49323698
3	12/15/93	91	147	3.29787576	01/21/94	92	184	3.37128795	0.98306085	3.76877211
4	03/16/94	91	238	3.47843007	04/21/94	90	274	3.52317904	0.97388498	3.89979239
5	06/15/94	91	329	3.59154551	07/21/94	91	365	3.64314633	0.96437832	4.16396475
6	09/21/94	98	427	3.73201440	10/21/94	92	457	3.77895699	0.95422419	4.49599552
7	12/21/94	91	518	3.87440691	01/23/95	94	551	3.93807789	0.94315201	4.80497161
8	03/15/95	84	602	4.03647850	04/21/95	88	639	4.09734699	0.93220284	4.93476328
9	06/21/95	98	700	4.19769775	07/21/95	91	730	4.24647621	0.92071782	
10	09/20/95	91	791	4.34565907	10/23/95	94	824	4.34976086		

TABLE 6–22 The Cross-Currency Swap—Cash Flows and Pricing of the USD Leg

	Cash Flow Date	Day Count	Cum. Day Count	Implied Discount Factor	Implied Forward Rate (%)	USD Floating Leg Cash Flow ($)	USD Floating Leg Present Value ($)
	(I)	(J)	(K)	(M)	(N)	(O)	(P)
1	07/21/93			1.00000000	3.22058821	(100,000,000.00)	(100,000,000.00)
2	10/21/93	92	92	0.99183679	3.49323698	830,555.56	823,775.56
3	01/21/94	92	184	0.98306085	3.76877211	892,716.12	877,594.27
4	04/21/94	90	274	0.97388498	3.89979239	942,193.03	917,587.63
5	07/21/94	91	365	0.96437832	4.16396475	985,780.86	950,665.68
6	10/21/94	92	457	0.95422419	4.49599552	1,064,124.33	1,015,413.17
7	01/23/95	94	551	0.94315201	4.80497161	1,173,954.38	1,107,217.44
8	04/21/95	88	639	0.93220284	4.93476328	1,174,548.62	1,094,917.55
9	07/21/95	91	730	0.92071782		101,247,398.49	93,220,283.68
10	10/23/95	94	824				
						108,311,271.38	100,007,454.99

EXHIBIT 6–7 A Typical Cross-Currency Swap

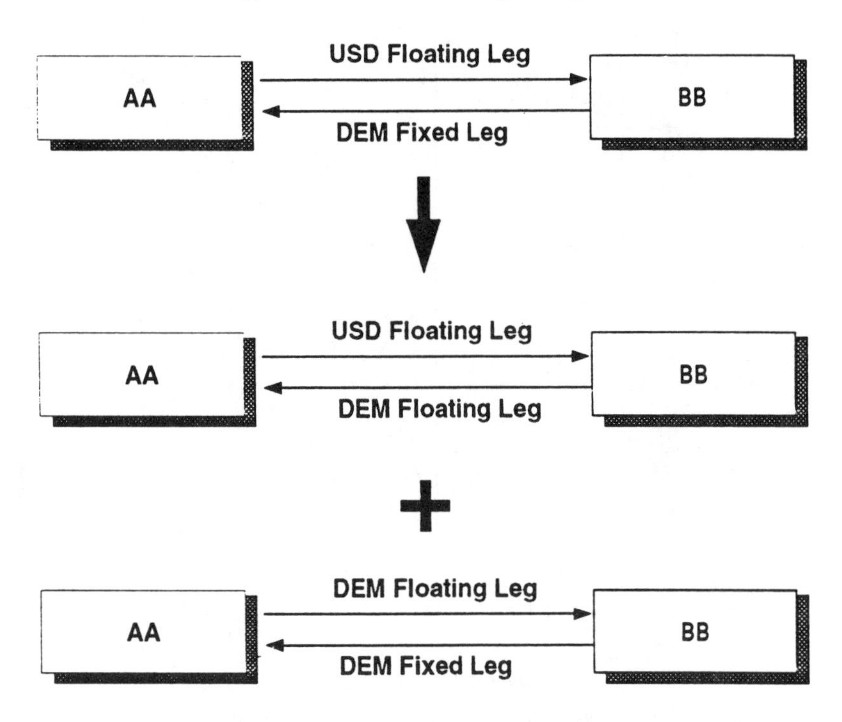

swap and a USD/DEM LIBOR swap (basis swap). Thus, to price the currency swap, we will need the prevailing prices for standard DEM interest-rate swaps and DEM/USD basis swaps. The spread paid over (or under) DEM LIBOR in this swap against USD LIBOR flat is known as the *basis cost*. Effectively, the basis cost modifies the DEM interest-rate swap rates to generate rates for standard USD LIBOR/DEM fixed swaps.

Table 6-23 shows the market data and computations for the DEM leg. Column T shows the market rates in DEM.

TABLE 6–23 The Cross-Currency Swap—Cash Flows and Pricing of the DEM Leg

	Year	Date	Day Count	Swap Rate (%)	Basis Cost (bp)	Net Swap Rate (%)	Discount Factor	DEM Leg Cash Flow (DM)	DEM Leg Present Value (DM)
	(Q)	(R)	(S)	(T)	(U)	(V)	(W)	(X)	(Y)
1	0.0	07/21/93					1.00000000	(172,700,000.00)	(172,700,000.00)
2	0.5	01/21/94	184	6.8249	4.00	6.8649	0.96610212	5,213,444.22	5,036,719.50
3	1.0	07/21/94	181	6.3327	4.00	6.3727	0.93930926	5,213,444.22	4,897,036.42
4	1.5	01/23/95	186				0.91373410	5,213,444.22	4,763,701.77
5	2.0	07/21/95	179	6.0800	4.00	6.1200	0.88815895	177,913,444.22	158,015,417.07
Swap Rate: 6.03757292%									172,712,874.76

The 6-month and 1-year points are LIBOR. The 2-year point is the annual-pay DEM interest-rate swap rate. The rate corresponding to 1.5 years is obtained by first determining the discount factors for 1 and 2 years and then interpolating[32] them to obtain the 1.5 year discount factor. The 1.5 year rate can then be inferred. Column U shows the basis cost for each maturity. Column V shows the sum of the interest-rate swap rate and the basis cost. Thus, column V represents the swap rates for USD/DEM currency swaps.

For the DEM leg, we use the bootstrapping method to generate the discount factors (column W) form the currency-swap rates in column V. There is no need to compute the forward rates, because the DEM side is fixed. Column X shows the fixed cash flows, including the notional flows on the start date and the maturity date. Column Y shows the present values of these cash flows and their sum. This sum does not include the value of the initial notional flow.

At a fixed rate for the DEM leg of 6.038 percent (as shown in Table 6-23), the total present value of the DEM flows equals DEM 172.0 million, or $100 million at an exchange rate of 1.7270 DEM/USD. This rate was determined by trial and error. Observe that the total PV is close to the notional amount in DEM. Again, this is not a coincidence. If the cash flows on the USD leg represent a par bond (a floating-rate note), the cash flows on the DEM leg should also represent a par bond (a fixed-rate note). Second, note that the swap rate, 6.037 percent, is close to the input mar-

---

32 We interpolate discount factors rather than rates since the former are independent of day-count and compounding-frequency conventions. For example, in the DEM case the 1-year rate is annual actual/360 whereas the 2-year rate is annual 30/360. A direct interpolation between these rates would not be correct.

ket rate (6.120 percent) for a 2-year standard interest-rate swap (column V). The difference is due to the fact that the swap is semiannual, whereas the standard swaps are annual-pay.

As in the interest-rate swaps, we can easily use the pricing data to generate the risk points for the currency swap, as shown in Tables 6-24 and 6-25. As expected, the DEM risk is concentrated entirely at the 2-year point. On the other hand, the risk on the USD side is essentially zero at all maturities. This is a result of the fact that the USD cash flows resemble that from a floating-rate note, which in turn has little interest-rate risk. The only risk on the USD side under the modeling conditions is in the first payment, the rate for which has already been set.

TABLE 6–24 The Cross-Currency Swap—Risk Profile for USD Leg

	IMM Date	New NPV of USD Floating Leg ($)	Risk Factor ($)	Number of Futures Contracts
	(A)	(B)	(C)	(D)
1	07/21/93	100,005,537.69	(1,917.30)	-77
2	09/15/93	100,006,831.14	(623.84)	-25
3	12/15/93	100,007,454.99	0.00	0
4	03/16/94	100,007,454.99	0.00	0
5	06/15/94	100,007,454.99	0.00	0
6	09/21/94	100,007,454.99	0.00	0
7	12/21/94	100,007,454.99	0.00	0
8	03/15/95	100,007,454.99	0.00	0
9	06/21/95	100,007,454.99	0.00	0
10	09/20/95	100,007,454.99	0.00	0
Original NPV of USD Leg: $100,007,454.99				

TABLE 6–25 The Cross-Currency Swap—Risk Profile for DEM Leg

	Year	Date	New NPV of DEM Leg (DM)	Risk Factor (DM)	PVBP (DM/mmDM)	Hedge Ratio (mmDM)
	(A)	(B)	(C)	(D)	(E)	(F)
1	0.5	07/21/94	172,712,626.07	(248.69)	48.34	5.15
2	1.0	01/23/95	172,713,106.48	231.72	93.91	(2.47)
3	2.0	07/21/95	172,681,790.73	(31,084.04)	185.66	167.42
Original NPV of DEM Leg: DM172,712,874.76						

Table 6-26 shows how the value of this swap would change if the coupon were at 6.50 percent instead of at the breakeven rate of 6.037 percent. Also shown is the effect of a change in the USD/DEM exchange rate from 1.72 to 1.7. In general, a change in the exchange rate has a much stronger effect on the value of the swap than does a change in interest rates.

It is interesting to look at a variation of the standard currency swap known as a *coupon-only currency swap*. The cash flows are similar to the standard swap except that the initial and final notional flows have been eliminated, as in Tables 6-27 and 6-28. Tables 6-29 and 6-30 show the risk profiles for the coupon swap. It is insightful to compare the rates and risk measures for the coupon swap and the standard swap.

Swap Spreads

Basically, swap spreads can be viewed as a measure of credit risk. The LIBOR rate represents on the aggregate an A- to AA-rated financial institutional (i.e., bank) credit. Therefore, intuitively, we can say that the swap spread should be related to the spread over Treasuries commanded by institutions of this credit quality on their intermediate-term borrowings.

TABLE 6–26 The Cross-Currency Swap—Effects of Changes in the Swap and Exchange Rates

Swap Rate (%)	Market Rate (%)	Fx Rate	DEM Leg ($)	Value ($)
6.0376	6.0376	1.727	100,007,454.99	0.00
6.5000	6.0376	1.727	100,864,633.97	857,178.98
6.0376	6.0376	1.700	101,595,808.69	1,588,353.70

TABLE 6–27 The Cross-Currency Swap—USD Leg of the Coupon-Only Swap

	Cash Flow Date	Day Count	Implied Discount Factor	Implied Forward Rate (%)	USD Floating Leg Cash Flow ($)	USD Floating Leg Present Value ($)
	(I)	(J)	(M)	(N)	(O)	(P)
1	07/21/93		1.00000000	3.22058821		
2	10/21/93	92	0.99183679	3.49323698	830,555.56	823,775.56
3	01/21/94	92	0.98306085	3.76877211	892,716.12	877,594.27
4	04/21/94	90	0.97388498	3.89979239	942,193.03	917,587.63
5	07/21/94	91	0.96437832	4.16396475	985,780.86	950,665.68
6	10/21/94	92	0.95422419	4.49599552	1,064,124.33	1,015,413.17
7	01/23/95	94	0.94315201	4.80497161	1,173,954.38	1,107,217.44
8	04/21/95	88	0.93220284	4.93476328	1,174,548.62	1,094,917.55
9	07/21/95	91	0.92071782		1,247,398.49	1,148,502.02
10	10/23/95	94				
					8,311,271.38	7,935,673.32

TABLE 6–28 The Cross-Currency Swap—DEM Leg of the Coupon-Only Swap

	Year	Date	Day Count	Swap Rate (%)	Basis cost (bp)	Net Swap Rate (%)	Discount Factor	DEM Leg Cash Flow (DM)	DEM Leg Present Value (DM)
	(Q)	(R)	(S)	(T)	(U)	(V)	(W)	(X)	(Y)
1	0.0	07/21/93					1.00000000		
2	0.5	01/21/94	184	6.8249	4.00	6.8649	0.96610212	3,696,731.17	3,571,419.81
3	1.0	07/21/94	181	6.3327	4.00	6.3727	0.93930926	3,696,731.17	3,472,373.82
4	1.5	01/23/95	186				0.91373410	3,696,731.17	3,377,829.34
5	2.0	07/21/95	179	6.0800	4.00	6.1200	0.88815895	3,696,731.17	3,283,284.86
Swap Rate: 4.28110153%									13,704,907.83

TABLE 6–29 The Cross-Currency Swap—Risk Profile for the USD Leg of the Coupon-Only Swap

	IMM Date	New NPV of USD Floating Leg ($)	Risk Factor ($)	Number of Futures Contracts
	(A)	(B)	(C)	(D)
1	07/21/93	7,935,185.53	(487.79)	-20
2	09/15/93	7,937,364.21	1,690.89	68
3	12/15/93	7,937,985.97	2,312.65	93
4	03/16/94	7,937,985.51	2,312.18	92
5	06/15/94	7,938,159.73	2,486.41	99
6	09/21/94	7,937,982.33	2,309.00	92
7	12/21/94	7,937,804.43	2,131.11	85
8	03/15/95	7,938,154.46	2,481.13	99
9	06/21/95	7,936,378.49	705.16	28
10	09/20/95	7,935,673.32	0.00	0
Original NPV of USD Leg: $7,935,673.32				636

TABLE 6–30 The Cross-Currency Swap—Risk Profile for the DEM Leg of the Coupon-Only Swap

	Year	Date	New NPV of DEM Leg (DM)	Risk Factor (DM)	PVBP (DM/mmDM)	Hedge Ratio (mmDM)
1	0.5	07/21/94	13,704,731.49	(176.34)	48.34	3.65
2	1.0	01/23/95	13,704,411.84	(495.99)	93.91	5.28
3	2.0	07/21/95	13,703,953.01	(954.82)	185.66	5.14
Original NPV of DEM Leg: DM 172,712,874.76						

Typically, fixed-rate bond markets have tended to require a wider credit quality spread between higher- and lower-rated parties than in the floating-rate markets. Although the higher-rated issuer borrows more cheaply than does the other in either market, the former enjoys a greater advantage in bond markets. Conversely, the lower-rated issuer faces less of a quality differential in the floating-rate market. If each borrower raises funds in the market in which it has a relative advantage, the resulting interest-rate payments can be swapped to achieve cheaper funding for both. Note, however, that the weaker credit rolling over short-term funding is still exposed to funding risk.

To date, the driving force in the swap market has been the perceived advantage enjoyed by both high-rated and low-rated credits. Thus, swap spreads have followed closely the yield levels of investment grade corporates over Treasuries in the public debt markets in the United States and in Europe. They basically have remained in the range of approximately 30 basis points straddled by AA and A spreads. This relationship can be explained in the context of the credit arbitrage mentioned above. The fixed rate available through the swap market must be lower than that in the bond market for the fixed payer—usually the lower-rated party. Thus, the A-rated bond yield spread over Treasuries less the spread over LIBOR for floating-rate funding forms an upper bound for swap spreads.[33]

---

33 This result can be derived from the relationship

$$T + B > T + S + M$$

where T is the Treasury yield, B is the spread over Treasuries for the bond, S is the swap spread, and M is the spread over LIBOR for floating-rate funding by the weaker credit. T + B is the rate on a bond issue. T + S is the swap rate. T + S + M is the effective fixed rate obtained via the swap market. This relationship reduces to

$$B - M > S$$

Similarly, the synthetic floating rate obtained through a swap must be lower than that of a straight floating borrowing for the higher-rated party. Thus, the lower bound for swap spreads is the spread *over* Treasuries paid by AA-rated issuers plus the spread *under* LIBOR commanded by them for floating-rate borrowing.[34] Due to various market factors, these upper and lower bounds are not strict.

Swap spreads in the short maturities are strongly tied to the Eurodollar futures market. A borrower wishing to fix the exposure on short-term liability indexed to LIBOR could either enter into a swap or sell a series of Eurodollar contracts matching payments on the underlying liability. Either technique provides an acceptable hedge into a fixed rate. If LIBOR rises, the corresponding higher financing costs are offset either by matching swap payments or by gains realized on the futures contracts. Note that even in the shorter end, the spreads are related to perceived corporate credit through the Eurodollar futures, which are tied to LIBOR.

Historically, higher swap spreads (and corporate spreads) have been associated with lower absolute Treasury levels, and lower spreads with higher levels. To the extent that lower Treasury levels reflect "flight to quality," the corresponding higher swap spreads can be explained by the corporate credit represented by the swap market.

The recent several months, however, have provided a significant exception to conventional wisdom. The Treas-

---

34 This result can be derived from the following relationship:

$$(T + S) - (T + B) > M$$

Here, T+B is the rate paid on the bond issues, T+S is the rate received on the swap. The difference, (T + S) - (T + B), should be greater than M, the spread under LIBOR for floating-rate financing by the higher-rated credit. This relationship reduces to:

$$S > B + M$$

ury rates have fallen to very low historical levels, and, at the same time, the swap spreads have tightened to very low historical levels. (See Exhibit 5-1.) Several explanations are available for this phenomenon:

1. With the lower rates and continued expectation of either stable or further fall in short-term rates, there is very little fixing going on in the swap market. The corresponding lack of fixed-rate payers puts a downward pressure on spreads.
2. The yield curve is steeply sloped. Therefore, those fixing rates via the swap market pay a much higher rate relative to short-term rates. This negative carry inhibits fixing.
3. There has been a credit crunch, and the spread over LIBOR that bank borrowers pay has risen sharply.
4. Lower credits are unwilling to take the rollover risk. Therefore, they are funding in fixed-rate directly rather than through the swap market.

Nonetheless, for many borrowers, this environment provides an excellent opportunity to fix at very attractive, historically low, rates.

Types of Risks in Swaps

Swaps are unlike most other financial instruments in that they involve two-way payments and, correspondingly, two-way exposure to risk. That is, each party is exposed to the other in terms of *credit risk*. Usually, some type of offset is agreed upon such that if one party defaults, the other party is not obligated to continue to make the payments. It is useful to review the types of exposure in the swap markets. Credit risk in a swap, which has gained significant importance recently, is analyzed in more detail in the next section.

Interest-rate risk or *market risk* is well understood but is clearly the leading concern of swap players. We have seen above that the interest-rate sensitivity or duration of a swap is similar to that of a bond. Therefore, when interest rates move, the value of the swap moves as well. To the extent that the swap is being used to match the gap between assets and liabilities, the variation in the value of the swap in response to market changes is not a concern. Swap dealers with unmatched swaps in their inventory are exposed to market risk and hedge appropriately.

Another type of risk is *mismatch risk*. Normally, mismatch refers to the position of a swap dealer who has two offsetting swaps that hedge each other but are not exactly matched. They may differ in the timing and frequency of payments, maturity, floating-rate index used, etc. End users of swaps are also exposed to mismatch in certain circumstances.

Consider a situation in which an industrial corporation, IC, seeking fixed-rate funding, uses the commercial-paper market to raise funds and swaps into fixed. In this case, the corporation might be exposed to several mismatches. The floating payments on the CP/fixed swap are set to the A1/P1 commercial-paper composite index. The actual rate paid on IC's commercial paper may be different from the index. In addition, the maturity and timing of the commercial paper actually issued may differ from the payment frequency and timing of the swap's cash flows. The mechanism by which the index is set may be different from the way the borrowing rate is determined.

In general, however, as far as the end user is concerned, the credit risk of the counterparty is the main concern. Since the swap market does not seem to differentiate finely between high- and low-quality credits, it is in the best interests of the end user to always deal with the highest-rated counterparty available at the desired rate. However, other considerations, such as diversification or offsetting exposures to the same counterparty, will determine the final decision.

Credit Risk in Swaps

Credit risk is an integral part of a swap transaction. However, in a generic interest-rate swap, credit risk is small compared to that in an outright loan of the notional amount. There are two reasons for this property. First, in interest-rate swaps, only the interest payments are involved, not the principal amount. Since the principal amount represents a larger proportion of the value of a shorter maturity loan, the shorter the maturity of the swap, the smaller is its credit risk relative to an outright loan. Second, there is usually an offset arrangement such that in the event of default by one party, the other is no longer required to continue to make payments on the swap.[36]

However, in some special swap structures, the credit risk can be significant, e.g., zero-coupon swaps, where one party makes all payments before the other makes any. In such cases, it is best to examine the credit risk of the swap as if it were a loan or a combination of a loan and a swap. The swap spread used to price such transactions should also reflect this fact.

Currency swaps also have significant credit exposure, much greater than do interest-rate swaps. Some major reasons are:

---

36 Note, however, that in general the effective termination of a swap due to a default can suddenly increase the interest-rate risk in a hedged position.

1. Currency swaps include, in addition to coupon flows, principal cashflows at maturity. In contrast, interest-rate swaps include just the coupon flows.
2. Currency exchange rates are, in general, more volatile than interest rates.
3. The effect of the change in value of a swap due to change in currency-exchange rate is much greater than that due to change in interest rates.

The wider bid-offered spread in the currency-swap market partly reflects the increased credit exposure.

Measuring credit exposure accurately on swap transactions can be a difficult and complex exercise. However, it is important to allocate sufficient thought and resource in order to manage swap positions both from the point of view of a dealer and from that of an end user. For example, if a corporation raises funds via a fixed-rate bond issue, it is not exposed to any credit risk. If, on the other hand, it raises funds via a floating-rate borrowing and swaps into fixed, then it will be exposed to the credit risk of the swap counterparty. In the latter case, the corporation should determine if taking on the credit risk is prudent relative to other existing risks, determine if any savings in interest cost provide an adequate return for the additional risk taken, and finally consider whether some loss reserves against swap counterparty default are necessary. Thus, there are three primary reasons for estimating credit exposure accurately:

1. To determine the maximum likely future exposure to a specific counterparty or industry for monitoring overall credit risk
2. To determine the relative economic return on a transaction compared to an on-balance-sheet asset or liability

3. To determine the risk-asset size for capital adequacy and capital allocation purposes (where necessary)

The risk-capital requirements for swap transactions also provide a measure of the credit risk. The Bank for International Settlements (BIS) has proposed two procedures that compute the credit-risk equivalents as a function of maturity of volatility of rates. These procedures resulted from Monte Carlo simulation of the movements in interest and currency exchange rates.

BIS requires that minimum capital standards be set for internationally active banks. The Basel Committee on Banking Regulations and Supervisory Practices issued a report called the Basel Accord of 1988 governing the maintenance of capital and the calculation of risk-asset values. The Basel Accord is an agreement between the central banks and supervisory authorities of the G11 countries: Belgium, Canada, France, Germany, Italy, Japan, Netherlands, Sweden, Switzerland, the United Kingdom, and the United States. The Basel Accord describes two methods for deriving risk capital for off-balance-sheet transactions such as swaps.

The BIS Current-Exposure Method

This procedure computes the credit-risk equivalent or the risk-asset in three steps:

1. The replacement cost for the transaction, that is, the mark-to-market value, is computed. Only positive values are used.
2. An add-on factor that reflects the future exposure over the remaining life of the contract is computed as follows:

	Maturity less than 1 year (%)	Maturity 1 year and longer (%)
Interest-rate swap	0.0	0.5
Currency swap	1.0	5.0

Note that as the contract moves toward maturity, the add-on factor will decrease. Also, currency swaps will have larger add-on factors, reflecting the higher volatility of currency swaps. Swaps that have a negative mark-to-market value will just have a risk amount equal to the add-on factor.

3. Once the exposure has been computed, the risk asset is obtained by using a risk weighting depending upon the counterparty, as follows (the minimum capital required is 8 percent of the risk asset):

Counterparty	Risk weighting (%)
OECD central governments and central banks	0
Domestic public-sector entities	10
OECD banks Nondomestic public-sector entities Non-OECD banks for less than 1 year Multilateral development Banks	20
Others	50

The 0 percent risk weighting is also available to transactions that are collateralized by appropriate government obligations.

Example. Consider a $25 million interest-rate swap with an OECD bank with 5 more years remaining to maturity and a current market value of $100,000. This swap will generate a risk asset of $45,000 ($100,000 + $25mm × 0.5%) × (risk weighting of 20%).

The BIS Original-Exposure Method

This is a more conservative approach, as it is computed at the inception of a swap and is not updated as markets move. It therefore has a cautious bias and results typically in a larger risk asset. The risk asset is determined by applying to the notional principal amount a conversion factor computed using the following rules:

Maturity	Interest-rate swap (%)	Currency swap (%)
Less than 1 year	0.5	2.0
Less than 2 years	1.0	5.0
Each additional year	1.0	3.0

The exposure is then multiplied by the risk weighting depending upon the counterparty to arrive at the risk asset.

Example. Consider the same swap as above, the 5-year maturity implies a conversion factor of 4 percent. Therefore, the risk asset is $200,000 ($25mm × 4% × 20%).

One of the motivations in developing the BIS procedures was to have a simple rule of thumb that can apply to as many practically occurring situations as possible and that does not require complex computations. There are, unfortunately, some serious deficiencies in the application of this procedure. First, the BIS approach does not handle transactions that are not "plain vanilla." A large proportion of the so-called "structured transactions" may not fit into this mold, and a mechanical application of the BIS formulas may result in misleading or meaningless exposure calculations. Second, this approach is inherently unable to account for netting of exposures in the case of two or more offsetting transactions between the same two counterparties.[36]

The Option Approach

One way to view credit exposure is to equate it to the cost of replacing a defaulting counterparty. Thus one way to protect ourselves from exposure to a counterparty is to purchase an option to enter into an identical contract from a creditworthy counterparty. That is, if the original counterparty defaults, we exercise the option and put the new (creditworthy) counterparty in place of the original counterparty. A second way to obtain protection from credit exposure is to obtain a guarantee from the creditworthy counterparty. There is really no practical difference between the alternatives of obtaining a guarantee or an option. Analytically, the option approach provides us with some clear benefits over BIS methodology:

- Since option mathematics looks at the actual cash flows that might occur and not just notional amounts, transactions that are more complex than plain vanilla can be easily evaluated.
- Again, since cash flows are analyzed, portfolios can be evaluated as easily as single transactions. This naturally provides for netting.
- Option pricing techniques can incorporate the current value of a transaction, unlike the original exposure method.

Standard option-pricing techniques such as the binomial tree approach can be applied. In trying to under-

---

36 Recently, the BIS has made new proposals which consider netting in both risk management and capital adequacy issues.

stand such a complex issue as credit exposure, it is best to analyze a variety of scenarios rather than reduce it to a single number. Such an analysis will depict the actual exposure associated with a swap better than any simple formulaic answer.

Simulation methods, such as those used in the BIS formulation, in combination with the advanced option pricing methodology, are useful as well in developing more complete credit-risk models. In the context of credit-risk estimation, we have to examine a broad range of possible outcomes of the market environment rather than a best guess. Monte Carlo simulation of different scenarios can assist in the risk-estimation process by providing useful insight into the behavior of the swap transactions in various market situations. Simulation can also deal with more complex market conditions and assumptions than can analytical methods.

However, simple-minded simulations using totally random interest-rate moves are not very useful, since we can never cover the losses under all possible scenarios without putting excessive constraints on the allowable transactions. It is not unreasonable to assume that interest and currency-exchange rates move in a less random, more structured way. For example, yield-curve models provide a way to simulate rate moves in an organized, reasonable way. These models not only generate many possible scenarios but also provide the appropriate probability to use with each scenario. This helps us focus on the most probable scenarios without wasting our efforts on remote possibilities. These models also indicate the possible use of a variety of hedging vehicles, e.g., purchase of a low-cost, out-of-the-money option, notwithstanding the fact that credit risk cannot efficiently be hedged with traditional market instruments.

Simulation can easily provide a feel for the three important factors in determining credit risk:

1. The maximum exposure within a particular confidence band at each time in the life of a transaction
2. The date when the exposure is maximum (This is important, since the longer the elapsed time, the greater the risk that the credit quality of a counterparty has deteriorated.)
3. The maximum maturity below a given level of exposure (If an exposure threshold has been established for a counterparty, this parameter indicates at what point a credit-control operation, e.g., mark-to-market payment, will be necessary.)

These factors can be quickly grasped if the exposure is graphically represented. Imagine a standard interest-rate swap with a notional amount of $100 million and a term of 10 years between two parties, AA and BB. AA receives floating and pays a fixed rate. Exhibit 6-8 shows the value of this interest-rate swap under various interest-rate scenarios. The values are from the point of view of AA. That is, if rates rise, the swap has a positive value to AA; if rates fall, the swap value is negative. Each line in the exhibit represents one possible realization of interest-rate levels. In each case, the value of the swap starts out at zero. As time passes, the variability of the value of the swap increases due to the volatility of interest rates. Balancing this variability is the fact that the swap has a smaller number of years to mature. The latter effect dominates beyond the fifth year and the value of the swap as well as its variability falls rapidly to zero under all interest-rate scenarios as we approach the tenth year. At the maturity of the swap, the only variability of value of the swap is due to the single last exchange.

EXHIBIT 6–8 Value of Standard Interest Rate Swap—Various Scenarios

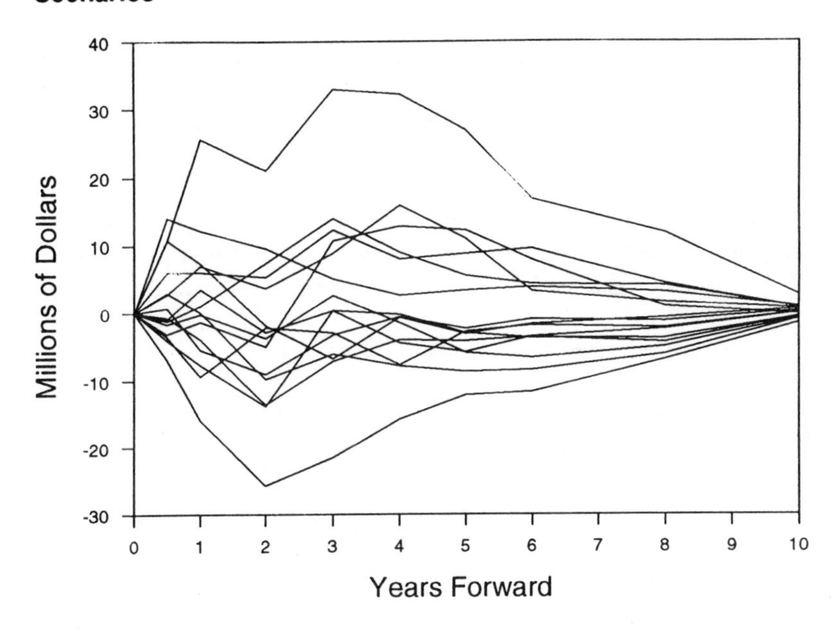

Exhibit 6-9 summarizes a statistical representation of a large number of interest-rate scenarios. In particular, the exhibit shows the maximum, minimum, and average values of the swap at different times. Also shown are the one-standard-deviation confidence bands on either side of the average line. In a positively sloped yield-curve environment, on average, the value of the swap increases slowly, reaches a maximum, and then declines to zero. We can explain it in two ways. One way is to observe that in a positively sloped yield-curve environment, the interest-rate paths are selected so that rates have a tendency to increase on average. As rates increase, the value of the swap to the fixed-rate payer, AA, increases. At later years, as the swap matures, the value of the remaining part of the swap begins to fall.

EXHIBIT 6–9 Statistical Summary of Swap Exposure

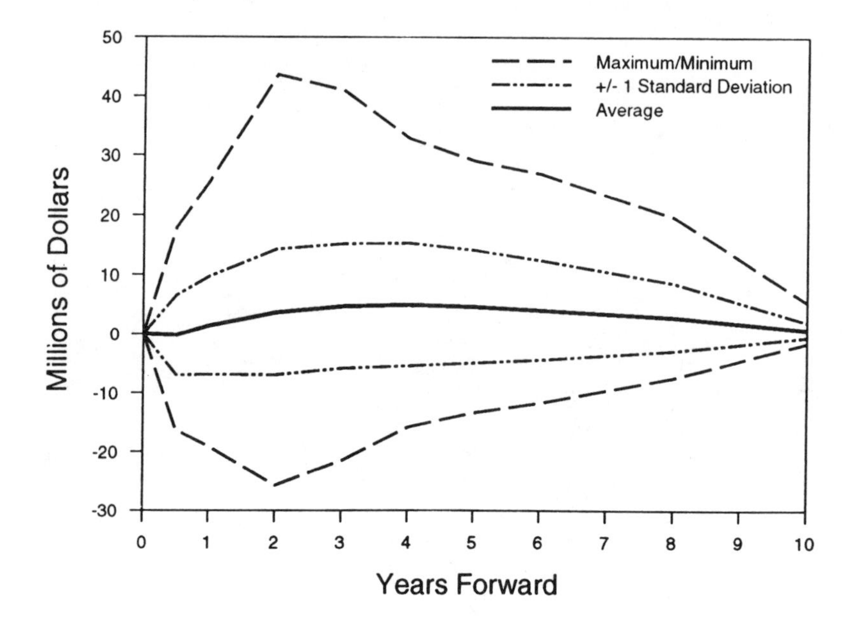

Another way to analyze the situation is that in a positively sloped yield-curve environment, LIBOR is less than the fixed rate on the swap. The modeling assumption is that LIBOR will rise and exceed the fixed rate in later years. Therefore, AA is a net payer on the swap during the initial years but expects to be a net receiver on average in the later years. The two effects offset exactly at the beginning of the swap. As AA makes the net payments initially, the value begins to build in the swap. At later years, when LIBOR exceeds the fixed rate, AA will begin to receive net payments and the swap value amortizes down.

Exhibit 6-10 shows the statistical summary considering only those cases where the value is positive to AA. This selection has been made because when the value is positive, AA is exposed to credit risk from BB. If the value of the swap is negative to AA, then it is BB that is exposed to the credit risk from AA.

Currency swaps behave in an entirely different manner. Imagine a simple currency swap between AA and BB in which AA receives fixed yen and pays fixed dollars. The notional amount is $100 million and the tenure is 10 years.

Because of the large exchange of principal payments at maturity, the variability of value of this exchange is large and dominates the total value of the swap. Therefore, the paths diverge in the later years, unlike the case of an interest-rate swap. Exhibit 6-11 shows the statistical repre-

EXHIBIT 6–10 AA's Exposure to BB

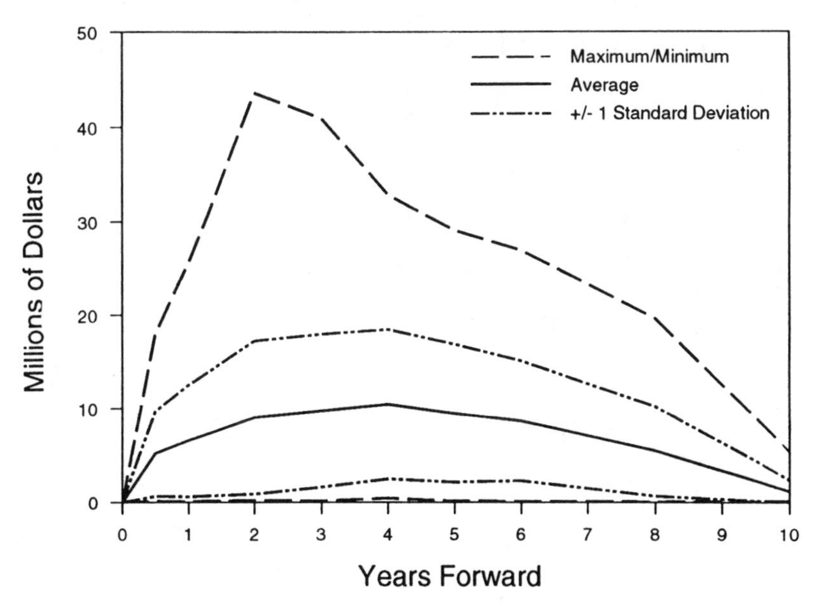

sentation of a large number of paths and Exhibit 6-12 shows the statistical summary for only those cases where the value is positive to AA. Exhibit 6-12 depicts the credit exposure of AA to BB.

The graphical representations form a starting point from which the credit exposure analysis should begin. We could apply statistical techniques (e.g., means or moments) to these time-exposure graphs to estimate capital allocation and the required economic return.

The exposure that is estimated by this procedure should, of course, be modified by our opinion of the credit quality of the counterparty in determining the capital requirements and return targets. A given level of exposure to an AAA-rated party does not have the same level of actual credit risk as the same level of exposure to an A-rated party. One way of modifying the raw exposure is to weight it by the probability that default would occur.

EXHIBIT 6–11 Statistical Summary of Currency Swap Exposure

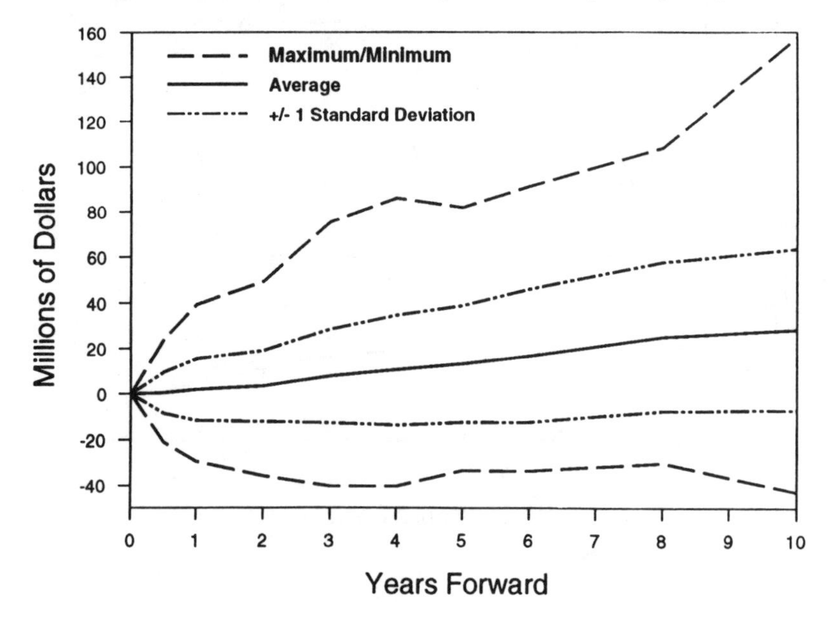

EXHIBIT 6–12 Statistical Summary—AA's Exposure to BB

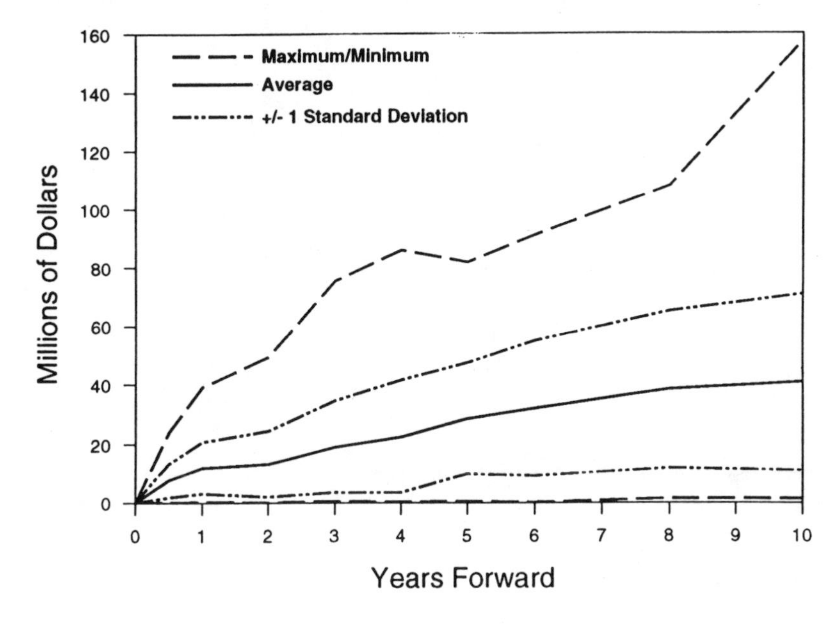

About the Authors

Ravi E. Dattatreya is a Senior Vice President at Sumitomo Bank Capital Markets, Inc., with coverage responsibility for major corporations and institutional investors. He received his master's degree from the University of Wisconsin at Madison and his doctorate in Operations Research from the University of California at Berkeley. He later joined Goldman, Sachs & Co., where he worked on the development of the now commonly accepted parametric approach to fixed income securities. Before joining Sumitomo Bank Capital Markets, Dr. Dattatreya was director of the Financial Strategies Group at Prudential Securities. he has co-authored *Active Total Return Management of Fixed Income Portfolios* (with Frank Fabozzi, Probus, 1989). He is an editor or co-editor of several books, including *The Handbook of Derivative Instruments* (with Atsuo Konishi, Probus, 1991) and *Fixed Income Analytics* (Probus, 1991). He is also the series editor for the *Institutional Investor Monograph Series in Finance.* Dr. Dattatreya is a member of the editorial advisory board of *The Journal of Portfolio Management.*

Raj E. S. Venkatesh is currently responsible for analytics in interest rate, commodity, emerging markets and hybrid derivatives at J.P. Morgan Guaranty Trust Company. He received his masters degree from Brown University and his doctorate degree in engineering from New Mexico Institute of Mining and Technology.

Prior to joining J.P. Morgan, Dr. Venkatesh worked at Chase Manhattan Bank, where he worked on modeling exotic options. Prior to that, he was in fixed income research at Dean Witter Reynolds, Inc., where he developed optimal refunding and sinking fund strategies for corporate bond issuers.

Dr. Venkatesh has taught at the University of Alaska, the University of Oklahoma and the Sun Jung University in Seoul, Korea. His current interests are in option pricing models and the development of new derivative products. He has published several articles.

Vijaya E. Venkatesh is Assistant Treasurer, Credit Lyonnais, New York. Her current responsibilities in the Treasury Products Group include analysis and mortgage and asset-backed securities. She is also working in the area of currency exposure management.

Prior to joining Credit Lyonnais, Ms. Venkatesh worked at the Security Pacific Bank in their Financial Strategies Group. At Security Pacific, she worked in the portfolio analysis, securitization, prepayment analysis and modeling of mortgage-backed securities. Later, as a member of the interest rate swap team, she developed analytical tools in this area.

Prior to joining the finance industry, Ms. Venkatesh worked as a research engineer at Conoco, Inc. She has published several articles. She is also an accomplished singer in the Classical Karnatic style and has completed advanced study in the Sanskrit language.